PERSONALITY IN ADULTHOOD

PERSONALITY
IN ADULTHOOD

Robert R. McCrae

Laboratory of Personality and Cognition
Gerontology Research Center, NIA/NIH

Paul T. Costa, Jr.

Laboratory of Personality and Cognition
Gerontology Research Center, NIA/NIH
and
Georgetown University School of Medicine

THE GUILFORD PRESS
New York   London

© 1990 The Guilford Press
A Division of Guilford Publications, Inc.
72 Spring Street, New York, NY 10012

Printed in the United States of America

This book is printed on acid-free paper.

Last digit is print number: 9 8 7 6 5 4 3 2

Library of Congress Cataloging-in-Publication Data

McCrae, Robert R.
    Personality in adulthood/ Robert R. McCrae, Paul T. Costa.
        p. cm.
    Rev. ed. of: Emerging lives, enduring dispositions. 1984.
    Includes bibliographical references.
    ISBN 0-89862-429-0 (hard)   ISBN 0-89862-528-9 (pbk.)
        1. Personality. 2. Maturation (Psychology) 3. Adulthood-
    -Psychological aspects. I. Costa, Paul T. II. McCrae, Robert R.
    Emerging lives, enduring dispositions. III. Title.
BF637.C5M36 1990
155.6—dc20   89-78494
                                                                    CIP

This book was written by Robert R. McCrae and Paul T. Costa, Jr., in their private capacities. No official support or endorsement by the National Institute on Aging is intended or should be inferred.

PREFACE

During the 1970s several major longitudinal studies of personality were completed and published, providing for the first time a solid scientific basis for evaluating theories of personality and aging. To almost everyone's surprise, all these studies pointed to an extraordinary degree of stability: personality apparently changes little after age 30 in most people. After several years of testing our interpretation of the data and working out some of its implications for personality psychology and for an understanding of adult life, we published a small book on the topic (McCrae & Costa, 1984) organized around a three-dimensional model of personality traits.

Since that time several additional longitudinal studies have been reported. They have extended and deepened our knowledge of age and personality, but they have not materially altered the conclusions we reached. In this respect, the current volume is a modest update of the earlier work.

In another respect, however, this book is dramatically different from its predecessor, reflecting a major advance in trait psychology. The three-dimensional model we employed in 1984 was only one of many competing models of personality structure, none clearly superior to the others, and none with any real claim to comprehensiveness. In the past five years, personality psychologists from a variety of different perspectives have converged on a five-factor model of personality (adding Agreeableness and Conscientiousness to our original dimensions of Neu-

roticism, Extraversion, and Openness to Experience) that is truly comprehensive: it accommodates virtually all the traits identified in common
speech and in scientific theories of personality. By studying these five
factors across the life span, we can provide a virtually complete account
of what happens to personality as men and women age.

Traditionally, theories of age and personality were concerned with
predicting the changes that personality would undergo as a result of aging
and the physical, social, and historical changes that accompanied it. But
to the extent that personality is stable, this concern is misguided. Instead,
we need to reverse the question and ask how enduring dispositions affect
the processes of aging and shape the individual's life course. This newer
approach is being adopted by an increasing number of researchers, and
a review of recent work provides a much fuller picture of emerging lives
than we were able to paint even a few years ago.

ROBERT R. McCRAE
PAUL T. COSTA, JR.

CONTENTS

The longitudinal studies of personality on which this book is chiefly based have resulted from the collaborative efforts of a number of distinguished researchers and thousands of dedicated volunteers. We have benefited most directly from the generosity and commitment of the men and women participants in the Baltimore Longitudinal Study of Aging (BLSA). This book is dedicated to all of them.

·1·

FACTS AND THEORIES
OF ADULT DEVELOPMENT

Suppose for a moment that people consulted life-span developmental psychologists as they do fortune tellers—to get a glimpse of their own future. What would we tell them to expect as they grow older? Are there predictable crises ahead? Are they likely to continue to mature and grow, or is it all downhill from here? Will their basic natures and temperaments remain essentially as they are, or will internal unfolding or changing circumstances (such as wars, illness, or technological innovations) reshape existing personalities? Do married couples grow apart with the years, or do they come to resemble each other in personality as they sometimes seem to do in appearance?

If asked to make these kinds of predictions for individuals, we would hedge—and properly so. We would point out that the scientific study of adulthood is very young, and little is known with certainty. Only in the past two decades have a substantial number of investigators been active in the field, and these have succeeded mainly in framing useful questions, not in providing definitive answers to them. We would also emphasize that science is concerned with generalizations, not specifics. Epidemiologists, for example, can tell us the life expectancy of the average man or the average woman, and some of the factors (such as smoking and exercise) that influence longevity, but they certainly cannot predict the age of death for any particular individual. Too many people smoke and drink and live to 90 and too many athletes die young to allow anything more than statements of probability.

But individuals inevitably apply these statements to themselves. When Gail Sheehy published *Passages* (1976), tens of thousands of people read the book, not because of a disinterested curiosity about human development, nor because they admired her prose style (engaging as it was). People read *Passages* because they wanted to make sense of their own past, present, or future lives. In short, the topic of this book is likely to be of personal as well as academic interest to most readers, and our approach must take that fact into consideration. We will argue for a particular position fully aware that many people find it unappealing. We will therefore try to anticipate objections, and in general, we will adopt an approach that Maddi (1976) characterizes as "partisan zealotry" rather than "benevolent ecclecticism" in order to "provide the reader with a vivid account" (p. 2) of our views. We believe that we can accomplish that goal without sacrificing scientific objectivity, and we hope our presentation will stimulate lively discussion and further research.

Some readers are likely to have a strong background in personality psychology but less knowledge of gerontology, some the reverse. We will try to accommodate both groups by reviewing some fundamentals in each discipline. Although our conclusions are driven by data and our research has been squarely in the tradition of quantitative empiricism, we will not burden the reader with much technical detail about the studies we discuss—the cited literature can be consulted for that. We will, however, spend considerable time on the logic of research: how scientific questions should be formulated and how particular measures, samples, or analyses can be used to answer them. Because aging is a relatively new field and personality psychology a contentious one, there are a large number of issues to address. We will consider the problems of distinguishing aging from generational and time-of-measurement effects, the validity of self-report methods of assessment, the adequacy of a trait theory of personality, and the advantages and dangers of interviews as a source of data on personality. At each step we will try to weigh the evidence carefully, taking into account both strengths and limitations. We can state our point of view in a few paragraphs, but a critical examination of it will require the whole book.

When the first edition of this book was written (McCrae & Costa, 1984), personality psychology had just emerged from a decade of self-searching with renewed confidence that the basic principles of trait psychology were scientifically justified. There was, however, little agreement on the traits themselves or their organization into basic trait dimensions. But in the past 5 years a consensus has emerged among many personality psychologists on the value of a five-factor model (Borkenau, 1988; Digman & Inouye, 1986; Hogan, 1983; Goldberg, 1982). Each factor defines a broad domain of related traits; the factors and some representative traits are listed in Table 1. These factors—Neuroticism, Extraversion, Openness, Agreeableness, and Conscientiousness—recur throughout this book; they are the basic dispositions that, as we will see, endure through adulthood and help to shape emerging lives.

The Pendulum of Opinion on Personality Stability

When psychologists first asked themselves what happens to personality across the life span, they found a great deal to say about infancy, childhood, and adolescence. Most assumed, however, that adulthood was the endpoint of personality development. William James (1890), in

TABLE 1. *The Five-Factor Model of Personality*

Neuroticism	*Agreeableness*
Calm—Worrying	Ruthless—Soft-hearted
Even-tempered—Temperamental	Suspicious—Trusting
Self-satisfied—Self-pitying	Stingy—Generous
Comfortable—Self-conscious	Antagonistic—Acquiescent
Unemotional—emotional	Critical—Lenient
Hardy—Vulnerable	Irritable—Good-natured
Extraversion	*Conscientiousness*
Reserved—Affectionate	Negligent—Conscientious
Loner—Joiner	Lazy—Hardworking
Quiet—Talkative	Disorganized—Well-organized
Passive—Active	Late—Punctual
Sober—Fun-loving	Aimless—Ambitious
Unfeeling—Passionate	Quitting—Persevering
Openness to experience	
Down-to-earth—Imaginative	
Uncreative—Creative	
Conventional—Original	
Prefer routine—Prefer variety	
Uncurious—Curious	
Conservative—Liberal	

Adapted from Costa & McCrae(1986c).

a now famous dictum, claimed that by age 30 character was "set like plaster." Freud wrote volumes on the first few years of life, but almost nothing on the later years; certainly they held no major role in his theory of personality. The parallel to other forms of development seemed obvious: By age 20 the vast majority of men and women have reached their full height, and, although they may settle a bit over the years, the tall remain tall, the short, short. The same seems to be true for certain kinds of intelligence. Why should we expect anything different in the case of emotionality or warmth or modesty?

It was therefore a feat of great intellectual daring to propose that psychological development might continue throughout life, and one of history's boldest thinkers, C. G. Jung, was among the earliest to take this step. His chapter on "The Stages of Life" in *Modern Man in Search of a Soul* (Jung, 1933) foreshadowed many of the central ideas in gerontological thinking, including the curve of life (Bühler, 1935), the rise of the repressed (Levinson, Darrow, Klein, Levinson, & McKee, 1978), the feminization of men and masculinization of women (Gutmann, 1970), disengagement theory (Cumming & Henry, 1961), and the midlife crisis.

A more elaborated and systematic position was offered by Erikson (1950), who postulated stages of psychosocial development to parallel Freud's stages of psychosexual development, and then extended them beyond adolescence and across the remaining years of life.

The next few decades saw the beginnings of empirical research on personality and aging, some of it guided by the theories of Erikson or Jung, much of it in search of new theoretical perspectives (Block, 1971; Butler, 1963; Lowenthal, Thurner, & Chiriboga, 1975; Maas & Kuypers, 1974; Neugarten, 1964; Reichard, Livson, & Peterson, 1962). In the late 1970s, a new generation of theories of adult development emerged (Gould, 1978; Levinson et al., 1978; Vaillant, 1977), Sheehy's *Passages* became a major bestseller, and the popular press began to feature stories on crises in adulthood, particularly the midlife crisis.

During the 1970s there was also a proliferation of undergraduate and graduate programs in human development and gerontology. Most of these programs were explicitly interdisciplinary, examining the sociology, biology, and economy of aging as well as its psychology. Stage theories of adult development had a powerful appeal as a way of integrating such diverse material: Predictable changes in personality might prepare the individual for the transitions and changes of adult life.

All these intellectual developments were consistent with the *Zeitgeist*.

The 1950s had focused on children, the 1960s on youth. As the baby boomers passed 30, their lives still seemed to form the center of the culture's interest. Personal growth and development were promised by humanistic psychology, and theories of life stages seemed to fill a particular need. Personal problems could be attributed to universal developmental changes; predictable crises offered both security and spice to adult life.

The same period also saw the "graying of America," a dramatic increase in the proportion of men and women living beyond age 65, and a concomitant increase in their awareness of their economic and political power. Older people began to demand attention, and academics took up the challenge. Personality development offered an attractive alternative to studies of cognition, where decline, if not inevitable, was the general rule (Arenberg & Robertson-Tchabo, 1977).

But it is the nature of science to be self-correcting. Not only did scientific ideas generate theories of adult development; they also led to research. Instead of talking about what might be, or about what we want to be, we can use the research efforts of the past 40 years to see what really is going on. More and more, we believe, the findings are coalescing into a pattern, and the pattern is one of stability (Costa & McCrae, 1980c). Maddox (1968) showed that well-adjusted elderly people remained active. Havighurst, McDonald, Maculen, and Mazel (1979), who studied professional careers, were led to formulate what they called "continuity theory." Recently Neugarten (1982) has propounded the notion of *age irrelevance* to account for the fact that age is not a very useful predictor of social functioning. As we shall see later, within the field of personality research this emphasis on stability has been strongly seconded by the work of investigators like Jack Block (1981). It is beginning to appear as if James and Freud were right.

But if nothing happens with age, why write a book?

This reaction is shared by some of our colleagues in the field, and it is one with which we have often confronted ourselves. One answer would be to persuade people about stability, to disillusion those who are looking for some magic transformation with age, or to reassure those who fear that they face periods of developmental crisis and turmoil and would much prefer to continue the business of their lives.

There is also another, better answer. We have not said, nor will we say, that nothing of psychological importance occurs in adulthood. People live most of their lives in this period; they begin careers, raise children, fight wars, and make peace; they experience triumph and despair, boredom and love. Old age too has its share of new experience and new perspective on the old experience. All of this makes a fascinating story (Gullette, 1989). From our point of view, it is all the more fascinating since one of the keys to the story is the individual's personality. People stay much the same in their basic dispositions, but these enduring traits lead them to particular and ever-changing lives.

In Search of a Phenomenon

Most sciences start with a phenomenon and try to explain it. Astronomy arose from attempts to account for the regular changes observed in the moon and stars. Biology tries to explain how different species have come to exist and adapt so differently to their environments. Cultural anthropology began in efforts to explain the puzzling customs of preliterate societies, just as abnormal psychology developed from observation of the bizarre behavior of the mentally ill. But if we ask what students of aging and personality are trying to explain, we are likely to draw a blank. The field of adult personality development seems to have emerged as an afterthought, a logical extension of other branches of study.

Some researchers came to it by way of gerontology, the study of aging. We know that there are major changes in physiology with age, and the popular belief that old people begin to lose their memory has been confirmed by controlled longitudinal studies that demonstrate declines in certain, though not all, cognitive abilities (Salthouse, 1989). By analogy, some investigators began to wonder about personality. Does it too change with age? Is there a gradual decline in emotional or social functioning? Do older people become increasingly susceptible to mental illness, as they do to physical illness?

Researchers who began as students of personality had a somewhat different basis for their questions. We know (or think we know) that there are changes in personality in childhood and adolescence. Infants become emotionally responsive to familiar faces only around 30 days; at 8 months they are likely to develop separation anxiety when taken away from their parents. Middle childhood is a period of compliance for most children; adolescence is generally conceded to be a period of rebellion and turmoil. Data show that self-esteem is usually low in this period, and rises as people reach young adulthood (Bachman, O'Malley, & Johnston,

1978). Recklessness and sensation seeking also seem to decline after adolescence (Zuckerman, 1979).

These observable changes led to theories of child personality development, of which Freud's is historically the most influential. Psychologists trained in this tradition began to ask if the same kinds of developmental changes could be taking place in adulthood. If there were oral, anal, and genital stages in childhood, might there not be later psychosexual stages for adults?

This investigation by analogy or extension is in the highest tradition of science. Physicists look for (and find) subatomic particles that in some respects parallel known particles. Cognitive psychology has benefited from computer models. Often this procedure can serve to refocus our perspective and allow us to "see" phenomena we have never noticed before but that are obvious once our attention is called to them. The discoveries of life-span development may be equally convincing once they are made (indeed, we think they are).

The fact that aging and personality constitute a field in search of a phenomenon is itself an interesting phenomenon. What it seems to mean is that the changes in personality that occur in adulthood—if indeed there are any—are less dramatic than those of childhood. There are some stereotypes of old and young people, but these are notably inconsistent. Romantic idealism is thought to be characteristic of the young, but what about Don Quixote? Age purportedly brings a mellowing of the spirit—except to cranky old men.

We can agree that old people are less healthy than young ones and that they lose their hair, teeth, and hearing. We cannot seem to agree that they become more or less anxious, loving, or withdrawn. The field of aging and personality was intended to answer such questions.

One possible explanation for the lack of common knowledge about personality change in adulthood is that there *are* no changes. But before we jump to that conclusion, we must bear in mind the particular problems that a common-sense focus has in formulating ideas about aging. In order to detect a pattern, we need to see a phenomenon repeatedly. Some parts of what we see are the result of chance, some the result of an underlying regularity, and only repeated observations can tell which is which. The parents of a first baby are concerned with every change, not knowing what is normal development and what might be a sign of illness. By the third or fourth child, however, the pattern is familiar, and the experienced mother is something of an expert in child development.

But we do not live long enough to have repeated experience with adult development. We know our grandparents as old people, but we do not know what they were like as children. We can watch our parents grow old, but it is difficult to separate our own maturing perceptions from real changes in them. We can, of course, observe our own life and the lives of our friends, but we could expect to draw conclusions then only at the end of our lives. And we have grown up in a particular period of history whose twists and turns, rather than the aging process itself, may have made us what we are.

In short, common sense does not provide the distance, or perspective, from which to grasp any facts about adult development except the most obvious. Historical biographers, who can compare across the centuries, and anthropologists (Myerhoff & Simić, 1978), who can contrast cultures, can offer some insight. As psychologists, we base our approach on the premise that scientific measurement of personality characteristics in aging people can also provide a basis for answering this question. Quantitative investigations of large samples of people followed over a period of years can detect even very subtle changes with great objectivity. And psychologists have been concerned with issues of personality development long enough that we now have data following the same individuals over the greater part of their lives. This book is based, first and foremost, on the results of those studies. As we interpret them, they point clearly to the conclusion that personality forms part of the enduring core of the individual, a basis on which adaptation is made to an ever-changing life.

It is only fair to warn the reader that the interpretations we make are not universally shared. A number of theories of adult personality development have been proposed, and many researchers believe that they provide a more insightful account of adulthood than the stability view offers. The evidence on which the stability view rests, like all empirical evidence, is open to alternative interpretations, and a number of these have been advanced. In particular, as we will see in detail in Chapter 7, there is fundamental division on what exactly is meant by *personality*. It may turn out that what we call personality is stable, whereas what they call personality changes. Special attention will have to be paid to the issue of defining and measuring personality.

A Note on Psychotherapy

An account of some of our research published in the popular press was headlined, "Your personality—you're stuck with it" (Hale, 1981). As clearly as anything else, that phrase illustrates how our research is often seen, and why it is frequently unpopular. Our findings seem to be read as a sentence of doom for all people who are unhappy with themselves. But the findings do not necessarily mean that at all. We hope to show in the remainder of this book that the process of aging in itself does not bring about regular changes in personality, and that most people change little from age 30 to age 80 in some of the most central aspects of their social and emotional makeup. Most people do not change—but that does not mean they *cannot* change. It does suggest, however, that the change will not come of itself, nor will it come easily. Effective psychotherapy or major life experiences (such as war or religious conversion) may profoundly alter us, but usually this occurs only if we are ready for a change and willing to work to make it happen.

What is "effective psychotherapy?" Each major school of therapy is able to claim its own victories (e.g., Rogers & Dymond, 1954; Stuart, 1977) and recent research (VandenBos, 1986) confirms the value of psychotherapy in general. But virtually all psychotherapists would agree that real change in personality cannot be achieved at all without intensive and generally long-term efforts by skilled professionals who create very special circumstances and that even then the prospects of success are by no means certain.

When Does Adulthood Begin?

The claim that personality is stable in adulthood needs some clarification. Who, after all, is an adult? Legal definitions of adulthood vary widely, not only by state but by function. A woman is legally of an age to marry at 14 in many states; the driver's license is withheld until age 16, voting until 18, and drinking until 21. Insurance companies, with actuarial wisdom, charge higher rates for drivers under 25. William James and a generation of hippies set age 30 as the dividing point between youth and settled adulthood.

Most psychologists probably consider college students—at least by the time of graduation—full-fledged adults; and in many respects, of course, they are. There is reason to think, however, that personality development continues, at least for some individuals, for several more years (White, Spiesman, & Costos, 1983). Studies that trace individuals from college age into later adulthood almost invariably report some changes in the average levels of personality traits and more fluctuations for individuals than are found in studies of individuals who are initially older (Finn, 1986; Helson & Moane, 1987; Jessor, 1983; Mortimer, Finch, & Kumka, 1981). Haan, Millsap, and Hartka (1986) concluded from their study of personality that important changes may occur after high school:

> Great shifts in personality organization are ordinarily thought to occur *during* adolescence, but these findings suggest that more marked shifts occur, not during adolescence, but at its end when most people make the profound role shifts entailed by entry into full-time work and marriage. (p. 225)

What is the nature of the changes seen in the decade of the 20s? When we compare the personality scores of college students to those of adults on the NEO Personality Inventory (Costa & McCrae, 1985, 1989a), our measure of the five factors of personality, we find that students are somewhat higher than adults in Neuroticism, Extraversion, and Openness, and lower in Agreeableness and Conscientiousness. These differences suggest (although, as our discussion of cross-sectional research in Chapter 4 will explain, they do not *prove*) that college students mature and mellow a bit, becoming a little less emotional and flexible, but kinder and more responsible.

If we define adulthood as the period from age 18 on, studies like this make it clear that there is indeed adult development in several aspects of personality. We have adopted a different definition of adulthood. The data suggest to us that personality change is the exception rather than the rule after age 30; somewhere in the decade between 20 and 30, individuals attain a configuration of traits that will characterize them for years to come. From the perspective of the trait psychologist, adulthood begins at that point.

OTHER VIEWS: THEORIES OF CHANGE

A brief introduction to theories of change is an essential starting point for this book; much more will be said about the theories of Levinson and Gould in Chapter 8. Readers may want to consult the original sources for more extended (and perhaps more objective) accounts of these theories.

Among major personality theorists, only two made significant contributions to life-span theory: Jung and Erikson. The former left relatively unstructured ideas, but was very influential in turning attention to the later years. Erikson, on the other hand, produced an elaborate and finely articulated theory that has become the basis of considerable empirical work (e.g., Tesch & Cameron, 1987; Whitbourne, 1986a,b). His theory of eight stages of life is probably the single most important theory of adult personality development.

Jung, it will be recalled, objected philosophically to Freud's emphasis on sexuality. Jung proposed that sexual development was central to personality only in the young, in whom the function of procreation was vested. Past the age of 40 there must, he felt, be other sources of growth, other areas of concern to the individual. These were more likely to be spiritual than sexual, and instead of revolving around the social function of procreation, they concerned the individual's relation to self. *Individuation* was the term he coined to reflect the continuing process of self-discovery and self-development, which he hypothesized would occur in the second half of life.

One of the key concepts in individuation was a balancing of opposing traits. Jung (1923/1971) conceived of the self as having two sets of opposed functions for dealing with internal and external reality: thought versus feeling, and sensation versus intuition. At any time in the life of the individual, one or another of these functions would be dominant, and its opposite would be repressed. In order for there to be a full and complete expression of the self, however, the repressed side of the personality would also have to be allowed its chance. The psychological ideal was found in old age, when an integration of opposing functions would mark the culmination of development. Similarly, other personality structures, such as the persona and shadow (which represent socially acceptable and unacceptable aspects of the self) and the anima or amimus (the feminine side of men or masculine side of women) must also be integrated. In general, this view of adult personality would lead to the expectation that the manifest characteristics of the young person should change markedly with age, either becoming their own opposite or moderating in degree as they were integrated with their complements.

Jung's theories were based on his experience with psychiatric patients and on his own experience of aging, and were buttressed by his scholarly studies of such obscure fields as alchemy and the *I Ching*. Few psychologists have claimed fully to understand his ideas, and few subscribe to them *in toto*, but some of the basic notions, such as continued and personalized development and the rise of repressed sides of self, have left a profound mark on subsequent theories.

Erik Erikson's (1950) views of adulthood, on the other hand, have become received wisdom in all their details. Erikson belongs to the group of ego psychologists (along with Fromm, Horney, Rappaport, and Anna Freud) who began with classical psychoanalytic theory and in greater or lesser degree modified it to take into account features they believed had been slighted by Freud. Psychoanalytic theory is fundamentally biological in tone and leaves little room for the influences of culture or the individual's own efforts at growth and change. Erikson's solution to the problem of accounting for social and environmental influences on personality was to argue that the traditional psychosexual stages that formed the backbone of Freudian personality development were paralleled by psychosocial stages. In addition to oral conflicts, the infant was faced with the resolution of the issue of basic trust versus mistrust, and each person's resolution of this conflict was heavily shaped by the cultural traditions that dictated methods of child rearing. Corresponding social issues were postulated for anal, phallic, latency, and genital stages.

Having made the transition from sexual to social stages, Erikson found that he was free to extend the social stages beyond the limit of sexual development. He hypothesized that the young adult needed not only genital gratification but also psychological intimacy in order to form the lasting bonds needed for the establishment of family life. He or she was required to resolve the crisis of intimacy or be left with a pervading sense of isolation. In the period of child rearing and adult careers, a new issue—generativity—became salient. Individuals who do not adopt an orientation that fosters growth in their children and community succumb to a sense of stagnation and meaninglessness. Finally, in old age the approach of death and the completion of life tasks leave the individual with the realization that his or her life is over and that there will be no second chances. Poorly resolved, this crisis leads to bitterness and despair; well resolved, it brings about a sense of ego integrity and an acceptance of both life and death.

Erikson's model of development is *epigenetic*, which means that the resolution of each crisis depends on the outcome of former resolutions. The best preparation for ego integrity is a life marked by intimacy and generativity (as well as desirable outcomes of the crises of childhood). But Erikson also admits a considerable element of changeability: At each crisis there is a possibility of new success or failure. The opportunity to redeem a misspent life at any age is one of the more inviting aspects of this theory.

Most of the empirical research on Erikson's stages has been confined to the period of adolescence and the transition to adulthood (e.g., Constantinople, 1969; Whitbourne & Waterman, 1979), but occasional studies have also been conducted on middle-aged and elderly people. Erikson's ideas have been more widely adopted, sometimes in modified forms. Certainly the notion of stages of adulthood has become widespread, and the conception that orientation to life must change with point in the lifecourse seems unquestionable. (As Neugarten, 1968, notes, at some point in middle age, life begins to be measured in terms of time left to live rather than time lived.)

After the 1950s, research took the place of theorizing in this area. Even earlier one investigator had made significant contributions to the literature. Charlotte Bühler (1935) examined diaries and other personal records to chart the course of life in substantial samples of people. She noted a general "curve of life" including periods of growth, maintenance, and decline, and focused on the motivational changes that she believed occur with age. For the young person, instrumental strivings are central to daily activities; for the older person, these become much less important and are replaced by concerns for intrinsic values.

A large number of empirical studies were undertaken, in some cases to test the theories proposed by Erikson and Jung, in others simply to see what happened as people aged (Neugarten, 1977). Cross-sectional comparisons of young and old on a plethora of variables were conducted, retrospective accounts were collected from aged men and women, and a handful of longitudinal studies were launched. We will return to these studies in later chapters; they do not concern us here since they did not, in most cases, lead to theories of adult change. A few regularities were reported from the cross-sectional studies, including an increase in the level of introversion with age, but this change was rarely interpreted.

An exception to the atheoretical bent of these researches is found in the work of Neugarten and her colleagues. At least two significant theoretical concepts of change in adulthood emerged here, based in both cases on research using the Thematic Apperception Test (TAT), in which psychologists interpret the stories told by subjects in response to a standard set of pictures, some commonplace, some bizarre. Neugarten herself (1964) is responsible for the concept of *interiority*. She postulated that older individuals turn inward and consolidate their sense of self. The identity that the adolescent takes on and the adult acts on is further distilled in old age, and individuals become more and more like themselves. An increase in social introversion reported in some cross-sectional studies is sometimes taken as evidence of increased interiority, but even Neugarten (1968) admits that there seems to be no regular change in social and emotional functioning with age. Some intrapsychic process, not readily observable to an outsider, must be meant by the term *interiority*.

Similarly, Gutmann's (1964) concept of ego mastery styles is tied to intrapsychic changes inferred from TAT responses. Guttman finds evidence in his TAT stories for three styles of mastery: active, passive, and magical. The first is seen in stories that show the hero taking forceful action to solve problems; the second is inferred when the hero accepts conditions as they are and adapts to them; the last, magical mastery, is seen in stories in which the hero distorts the situation or fails to see obvious dangers and problems. A "magical" solution has lost contact with reality.

Gutmann proposes that there is a universal developmental sequence in mastery styles. Young men use active mastery; middle-aged men, passive mastery; and old men, magical mastery. Originally found in a sample of men from Kansas City, the same pattern reappears, according to Gutmann (1970, 1974), in rural Mexicans and in the Highland Druze of Israel. A somewhat different pattern is found in women, a tendency to use passive mastery appearing in young women, and active mastery in older ones. The crossover of the sexes is interpreted as change in masculinity–femininity, somewhat in conformity with Jung's notions of balancing. As women age they become more masculine in mastery style; as men age, they become more feminine.

It is imperative to note that an ego mastery style is the hypothesized basis for *experiencing* events; it is not the basis for overt action. Gutmann points out that among the Druze the oldest men are the Elders, who have great power in decision making and are vigorous and decisive in running their community. The significance of a magical mastery style is thus far more subtle than it might at first seem. The discrepancy between the overt and observable and the unconscious, intrapsychic, or inferable, has bedeviled personality psychology from the beginning; interiority and ego mastery styles are simply the gerontological version of far more pervasive perplexities.

George Vaillant (1977), a psychiatrist, proposed a theory of adult development based on the maturation of defenses. Defense mechanisms in one form or another have been central to many psychodynamic theories from Freud on; Vaillant built on this tradition by proposing that there are 18 basic defenses grouped into four levels that can be ranked in terms of psychological maturity. The least healthy are the psychotic mechanisms of Level I that alter reality for the user and include delusional projection, denial, and distortion. Level II mechanisms operate not by changing reality but by altering the user's distress, either experienced or anticipated. These immature defenses include projection, schizoid fantasy, hypochondriasis, passive aggression, acting out, and dissociation. Neurotic defenses (Level III) include reaction formation, isolation, displacement, and regression; and mature defenses (Level IV), which integrate reality and private feelings, include humor, altruism, sublimation, suppression, and anticipation. Working with the Grant Study of Adult Development, Vaillant and his colleagues studied the use of these mechanisms in a longitudinal sample of 95 Harvard alumni. An extensive file had been maintained for each subject, including transcripts about how they had dealt with recent problems and stressors. Vaillant abstracted over 1,700 vignettes from these files, and raters, blind to the age and identity of the subject, evaluated each to determine the kind of defense mechanism used. (It should be noted that in the psychoanalytic tradition, virtually all behavior, even the most rational and mature, is ultimately defensive, so all vignettes could be scored.)

When the responses were divided into three periods (less than 20, 20 to 35, and over 35), there were systematic changes in the use of the different categories of defense mechanism. Between adolescence and early adulthood there were clear increases in the use of mature mechanisms and decreases in the use of immature mechanisms; neurotic mechanisms did not show differences. This trend continued, though more weakly, in comparing early adulthood (20–35) with later adulthood (over 35). The data led Vaillant to see adult development in terms of ever more mature forms of defense. Note that this theory is supported by data only for the early years of adulthood—indeed, it may provide further evidence that full adulthood is not reached until age 30. Whether maturation of defenses continues into later life is still a matter of conjecture.

In the 1970s two major theories of adult development were generated at about the same time. (Sheehy's *Passages* was based on early formulations of these.) Levinson and his colleagues (1978) wrote on the *Seasons of a Man's Life*, whereas Gould (1978) called his work the study of *Transformations*. Both hold that there are distinct stages of personality development in young and middle adulthood, but the differences between the two theories are as notable as the similarities.

Levinson and his co-workers gave intensive interviews to 40 men—10 executives, workers, biologists, and novelists. In cooperation with these subjects, the researchers wrote a biography for each man that focused on changes in what Levinson calls the life structure. The life structure includes personality, but it also includes career, marriage, other relationships, values, and so on. According to the scheme worked out by these writers, adult life is divided into fixed and age-related stages. After the early career beginnings comes a period of reassessment at the age-30 transition. A much more searching reassessment comes at the midlife transition at age 40. In this period, often characterized as a midlife crisis, there is a period of inner turmoil that, according to Levinson, often seems to resemble neurosis. Dreams and aspirations that the young man had repressed in dealing with the realities of starting a career now come to the fore, and often a new career is launched that better addresses the long-denied needs.

Gould, whose version of adult development is more closely tied to personality, devises a version of psychoanalytic thought to explain the changes he thinks he sees in adults. At the heart of the theory is the basic insecurity of the child, faced with the uncertainties and dangers of the world. To cope with these fears, the child adopts a set of beliefs that Gould calls *illusions of safety*. Thus, children believe that their parents will always be there to take care of them; that there is no real evil or death in the world; that life is simple and controllable. Each of these illusions is comforting to the child, but each leads the adult to a distorted view of the world. Over the course of early adulthood, individuals must come to terms with these beliefs and abandon them to find a more realistic view of the world.

Gould considers that these illusions of safety, like psychodynamic defenses, are unconscious. Young adults are unaware that they assume that parents will always be there to help—in fact, they may explicitly deny such a belief. But, says Gould, they will act *as if* they harbored these delusions, and that is the key to the action of unconscious forces. Becoming an adult, attaining full adult consciousness, depends on outgrowing these illusions: a painful but salutary process. There is, according to Gould, a regular sequence in which the illusions are tackled and thus a rough correspondence to age, but there are fewer chronological absolutes in his system than in Levinson's.

*   *   *

This review of the major theories of adulthood reveals their major strength and one of their weaknesses. The strength lies in the sheer attractiveness of the proposition that individuals continue to grow and change as adults. Surely all the experience of years counts for something! Surely the universal changes in health, appearance, and intellectual functioning have some parallel in personality! Surely there must be some hope for individuals whose current life is not the kind they would want to repeat for the next 50 years!

The first, and in some respects the most troubling, weakness with the theories is their mutual inconsistency. A number of very thoughtful and insightful observers of humankind have contemplated the course of adult life and have pointed out patterns they seem to see. But these patterns as often contradict as support one another. Gould sees his patients coming closer and closer to reality; Gutmann detects a retreat from reality. Bühler sees the last phase of life as one of decline; Erikson sees it as the time for the development of wisdom. Levinson puts age limits on his stages of adult change; Neugarten hypothesizes a steady increase in interiority. The view that age brings maturation in forms of defense (Vaillant, 1977) conflicts with the conclusion that older people employ primitive defenses in dealing with stress (Pfeiffer, 1977). When observers from a dozen different perspectives see the same phenomenon, we begin to believe it is really there. When everyone reports something different, it is hard to know how to interpret it. And that is the time to turn away from personal impressions and look at the facts.

·2·

A TRAIT THEORY OF
PERSONALITY

Conflicts among theories of adult development pale in comparison with conflicts among theories of personality. At least gerontologists can all agree that they are interested in what happens to people as the years pass. The only common denominator of personality psychology is the attempt to provide a psychological account of the person as a whole. But schools of psychology are so different in the phenomena they emphasize—from stimulus–response bonds to unconscious archetypes to cognitive maps—that the resulting theories of personality are often incommensurable. We cannot cover all these approaches fully, nor do we think they all deserve attention. Instead, we will concentrate on trait models of personality, both because they are compatible with a wide variety of theoretical approaches, and because they have formed the basis for most research on personality. Personality measures, whatever their theoretical origins, are usually measures of traits.

Within the more limited scope of trait psychology there are still many controversies, but there is also evidence of real progress toward consensus in recent years. Questions about the cross-situational consistency of behavior (Mischel, 1968), the validity of trait measures (Fiske, 1974), and even the objective reality of traits themselves (Shweder, 1975) had thrown the field into crisis in the 1970s; there was a widespread belief that personality psychology was on its last legs.

If we held the same skeptical view today, we would certainly not be writing this book. The developments of the last 20 years have been little short of spectacular: Personality psychology has had a renaissance, with major advances in conceptualization, description, and measurement. The five-factor model has brought order and understanding to the endless list of specific traits. Life-span developmental psychology and longitudinal studies have made a major contribution to this rebirth by demonstrating the reality and significance of enduring dispositions.

The renaissance has been made possible only by a reformation in theory and research. Standards of research have become more rigorous, measures more critically scrutinized, replications demanded and provided. Correspondingly, theorists have become more willing to qualify and modify their positions on the basis of empirical findings. Perhaps for the first time, personality psychology has begun to be a real science.

Clearly, an entire volume could be devoted to the state of personality psychology today. At best, this chapter can only give some sense of the issues and an outline of the arguments—and the data—we think make a case for a particular model of personality. The model we will develop is central to the remainder of the book, for when we say that personality is stable, we mean personality as defined by that model. We will also discuss personality measurement, since measures and their interpretation allow us to check theories against the facts. We will offer our preferred theories, models, and methods in this chapter, but even in the current climate of emerging consensus, the reader should realize that our preferences are not universally shared. The issues we raise here will not be put to rest—indeed, they will recur throughout the remainder of the book. In Chapter 7, in particular, we will contrast trait psychology with ego psychologies.

Perspectives on Human Nature

As every student of personality theory knows, three major schools of psychology have been reflected in theories of personality: psychoanalytic, behaviorist, and humanistic. Psychoanalytic theories of personality (Freud, 1933, 1938) stress the individual's unconscious motivations, which must be inferred from such indirect sources as dreams, slips of the tongue, and fantasies. Behaviorist versions of personality theory (Dollard & Miller, 1950) limit themselves to observable behavior and invoke situational determinants, expectancies, and histories of reinforcement to explain behavior; more recently, social learning theories (e.g., Bandura,

1977), have acknowledged the role of cognitive processes in shaping behavior. Humanistic psychologies (Maddi & Costa, 1972), which arose in reaction to what were perceived as the irrational and mechanistic biases of psychoanalytic and behavioral theories, emphasize humankind's capacity to think, love, and grow. Each of these approaches has made valuable contributions to personality psychology, and we will have more to say about them later, especially in Chapter 7. Our current concern, however, is to draw attention away from them to an alternative approach to personality that we feel deserves more credit than it is normally given.

The major schools have been interpreted as representing three different philosophies of human nature that, for the sake of contrast, are often depicted in oversimplified form. These caricatures of human nature may not do justice to the intricacies of the theories themselves, especially in their contemporary forms, but they do highlight the basic concerns of each perspective. From the psychoanalytic tradition, we might infer that the individual is basically irrational, driven by animal instincts, with rational control maintained only by the countervailing forces of socially induced guilt and anxiety. From a behaviorist perspective, the individual is seen as less ominous and unpredictable; indeed, human nature is largely or wholly the result of experiences in the social environment that shape and reward certain behaviors. People are reactive, habit-bound, creatures of the environment they live in. Humanistic psychologists endow people with a far more pleasing aspect; love, creativity, and play are thought to be the quintessential features of human nature, and both irrationality and rigidity are interpreted as signs of the destructive influence of society.

How can it come to pass that theorists who look at the same phenomenon—human nature—draw such different conclusions about it?

One possibility that may account for this selective attention to the facts about human nature is that people are different. Freudians hold that man is naturally aggressive, and they have no trouble pointing to infamous examples of the kind of humanity they envision. Rogerians (Rogers, 1961) believe in the capacity for openness and love, and they, too, find exemplars of their ideas. (Maslow, 1954, studied such self-actualizing individuals as Abraham Lincoln and Eleanor Roosevelt as a kind of counterbalance to the case studies of patients that had formed the basis of Freudian psychology.) Despite the claim that people are able to transcend their environments, it is all too easy to find individuals who seem to be wholly a product of a history of reinforcements.

For decades the debate has raged about which of these is the true image of human nature. The idea that they might all contain an element of truth is a truism that has captured the imagination of almost no one. But it forms the basis of another school: the psychology of traits, or individual differences.

Are people basically selfish? Some are, some aren't.
Are human beings intrinsically creative? Some are, some aren't.

This position, which emphasizes the consistent differences of individuals, has always played a major role in both common sense and academic psychology. It might also be seen as a philosophy of human nature itself, one well suited to a pluralistic society. But it has not received much attention as a philosophical position, and from the beginning trait psychology has been regarded as a relatively minor part of personality theory: not as a fourth school, but only a set of personality measures, a few isolated studies, an appendix to one of the "true" schools.

One reason for this is that it has been possible to view individual differences simply as one aspect of an all-encompassing theory. To the degree that each of the other schools attempts to account for at least some individual differences, each incorporates the trait model. Classical psychoanalytic theory (Freud, 1938), for example, proposed that the resolution of psychosexual conflicts in childhood and the development of characteristic defenses led to enduring character traits, such as those typifying the anal personality. Neatness, punctuality, thrift, and cleanliness are often viewed as the outcome of a fixation during the anal-retentive stage of development. Maslow, a representative humanist, defined individual differences in terms of levels of basic motivation. Social learning theorists (Bandura, 1977), the contemporary descendants of behaviorists, might explain characteristics like masculinity or femininity as the result of role-modeling and socialization processes.

In short, every theory of personality is concerned with the differences as well as the similarities among people. But the concern tends to be secondary. Maddi (1980), who reviewed the major types of personality theory, discussed individual differences in terms of what he calls *peripheral* characteristics, in contrast to the *core* characteristics that form the heart of personality theory. Trait psychology would seem to be all periphery and no core; why settle for that when other schools promise both?

One reason is that other schools are less than fully successful in delivering a good model of individual differences. Each school leads to an emphasis on certain characteristics, often to the exclusion of others. Freudian theory, for example, is primarily concerned with neurosis and impulse control. It has an elaborate system for describing the varieties and degrees of maladjustment. But it fails to say much of significance on why some individuals are introverted, some extraverted. Psychoanalysts might well claim that, from their point of view, differences on this dimension are trivial. Other traits are trivial from other points of view. Only a system that grants the first place to individual differences will attempt to provide a comprehensive list of traits. And comprehensiveness is essential if we are interested in the area of personality and aging: How can we specify what characteristics do and do not change unless we know the full range of characteristics to look at?

BASIC PRINCIPLES OF TRAIT PSYCHOLOGY

In common speech, when asked to describe someone, we generally rely on trait terms. We say that one person is hard-working and aggressive, another is hostile and unimaginative, a third is shy but loyal to close friends. Learning how to use such words properly, as applied both to others and to oneself, is an important part of language acquisition. As naive psychologists, all English-speaking people subscribe to a trait theory of psychology. Personality trait terms are also central to most or all other human languages (Goldberg, 1981), probably because the language of traits is so useful in facilitating interaction with other people that every culture has invented it.

As scientists, trait psychologists have tried to go beyond the naive, common sense view of traits. But the best of them, like Gordon Allport (1937), have also acknowledged the contributions of the natural system. Human beings have been trying to understand and describe each other for thousands of years, and it would be presumptuous indeed to suppose that psychologists could start from scratch and come up with a better system in a few years. Trait researchers have borrowed from the common sense system in two respects: First, trait theories of personality have often begun by attempting to spell out the assumptions behind the use of trait words; and second, trait measures have been based in varying degrees of immediacy on the language of traits that has been built up over the centuries. We will return to that aspect later in this chapter.

We can define traits as *dimensions of individual differences in tendencies to show consistent patterns of thoughts, feelings, and actions*. Characterizing traits such as shyness and trust as *dimensions of individual differences* means that people can be ranked or ordered by the degree to which they show these traits. Some people are very trusting, most moderately trusting, but a few are quite suspicious. In fact, all the traits that we will be concerned with are found in varying degrees in all people, with distributions that approximate the familiar normal curve. Although some personality theories describe *types*—distinct groups of people characterized by a unique configuration of features—current research supports the view that most so-called types are merely extreme scorers on continuously-distributed trait dimensions (McCrae & Costa, 1989a; Widiger & Frances, 1985).

The more of a trait people have, the more likely they are to show the behavior it disposes toward, and thus the more frequently we are likely to see it. Similarly, the more the trait characterizes them, the more intensely they act and react in relevant situations. A very gregarious individual really likes to be around people, and frequently is. Frequency and intensity of the appropriate acts and feelings are the major signs from which we infer the level of the trait.

The word *tendencies* in our definition emphasizes the fact that traits are only dispositions, not absolute determinants. A great number of other factors go into the choice of a particular action or the occurence of a particular experience. Gregarious people like to talk, but they normally do not chatter on during moments of silent prayer. Well-adjusted people may not worry much, but even they are likely to be anxious when awaiting the results of a job interview or a medical procedure. The requirements of the social roles we play, the facts of the current situation, the mood of the moment, and acquired habits all join in shaping the choice of a particular act, word, or emotional reaction.

Although this qualification may seem obvious, many psychologists have been disturbed by the estimates of how weak personality dispositions can be. In most of the published literature, personality traits account for only about 5% to 10% of individual differences in actual behavior in any specific instance (Mischel, 1968). On the one hand, this fact is properly sobering for psychologists or laypeople who expect that a personality test will tell them precisely how a person is going to react in a particular situation. On the other hand, personality lasts a lifetime, whereas roles and moods and situations come and go, and the cumulative effects of personality are enormous.

By *patterns of thoughts, feelings, and actions* we mean to indicate both the breadth and the generality of traits. Traits should be distinguished from mere habits, repetitive, mechanical behaviors such as smoking or driving fast or saying "You know" after every sentence. Habits are specific learned behaviors; traits are generalized dispositions, finding expression in a variety of specific acts. Habits are thoughtless repetitions of earlier behavior; traits often lead people to develop entirely new behaviors, often after much thought and planning. Driving fast may simply be a habit, perhaps learned from observing the way friends or parents drive. But if the fast driver also likes loud music and rollercoasters, and perhaps experiments a bit with drugs, we begin to see a general pattern we can identify as excitement-seeking (Zuckerman, 1979). The excitement-seeker may spend weeks planning for a trip to Las Vegas—or he may decide to go on the spur of the moment. But in either case, going to Las Vegas is not likely to be simple habit. In many respects traits resemble motives rather than habits, and it is often unclear whether a disposition such as excitement-seeking should be called a trait or a motive. *Trait* appears to be the broader term, and indicates motivational, stylistic, and other aspects of human consistency.

The *consistent patterns* that indicate traits must be seen over time as well as across situations. This means that traits are to be distinguished from passing moods, transient states of mind, or the effects of temporary stress and strains. If an individual is anxious and hostile today but calm and good-natured tomorrow, we attribute these emotions to the situation—perhaps pressures at work or a quarrel with a spouse. Only when emotion, attitude, or style persists despite changes in circumstances do we infer the operation of a trait. Measures of personality traits are expected to show high retest reliability when administered on separate occasions days or weeks apart, because traits are characteristic not of situations, seasons, or times of day, but of the individual at a particular point in his or her life.

Short-term consistency does not preclude long-term change. In fact, there could be neither stability nor change without a consistent pattern to begin with. Personality change means that one consistent pattern is replaced by another. We will review the evidence for such changes in Chapters 4 and 5.

Note that our definition of traits says nothing about their origins. Psychodynamic theories emphasize interactions of children with their parents; social psychological theories may point to peer pressures. There is increasing evidence for the importance of genetic influences on many traits (Plomin & Daniels, 1987). Whatever their origin, by adulthood individuals can be characterized in terms of a variety of traits, and research on personality and aging can proceed from that point.

Similarly, we need not understand the physiological basis of traits in order to chart their development in later life. Most contemporary psychologists would acknowledge that there must be some neurophysiological or hormonal basis for personality, but it is unlikely that we will ever find a single region of the brain that controls Neuroticism, or a neurotransmitter that accounts for Extraversion, or a gene for Openness. The trait names do not refer to the underlying physiology, but to the abstract consistencies in the ways people act and experience and to whatever complex underlying causes they may have.

How Many Traits? Which Ones?

Any number of human characteristics fit the definition of traits. There are physical traits (tall, healthy), ability traits (intelligent, musical), and social traits (rich, famous). Our interest is in personality traits, which describe emotional, interpersonal, experiential, attitudinal, and motivational styles. One way to get a sense of the scope and variety of personality traits is by consulting the dictionary: The English language provides an embarrassment of riches to the trait psychologist. So important are descriptions of people that thousands of terms have evolved, distinguishing minute shades of meaning that delight the poet and confound the empirical scientist. One major approach to personality has focused on analyses of natural language trait terms (John, Angleitner, & Ostendorf, 1988).

The more common alternative has been to begin with psychological theory and the insights of trained clinicians and researchers. We do not expect chemists or anatomists to base their taxonomies on lay terminology, and many psychologists have disdained the common vocabulary of traits.

Theories of particular characteristics have often lead to the development of trait measures; hundreds of scales have been created in this way. Rokeach (1960) developed a questionnaire to measure his concept of dogmatism, and Crandall (1975) proposed an adjective checklist to assess Adler's (1938/1964) concept of social interest. There are dozens of scales intended to measure depression and others to assess closely related concepts such as loneliness and hopelessness. Many of these scales are technically excellent instruments, but their sheer number makes it difficult to comprehend the scope of personality variables.

In an attempt to bring some order to the field, several researchers have proposed trait *systems*, sometimes based on elaborate theories, sometimes simply reflecting a judicious choice of traits. Most have developed personality inventories to measure simultaneously all the traits in the system and thus provide a fuller personality profile than any single scale could give.

Jung's (1923/1971) theory of psychological types became the basis of many instruments. In particular, scales to measure the two Jungian attitudes of Introversion and Extraversion quickly became popular. In one of the earliest applications of factor analysis to personality research, Guilford and Guilford (1934) analyzed measures of introversion–extraversion and found that several different traits were represented. Guilford continued his factor analytic studies of personality and eventually developed an inventory of ten traits, the Guilford–Zimmerman Temperament Survey, or GZTS (Guilford, Zimmerman, & Guilford, 1976). Another factor analyst, Hans Eysenck, noted that Extraversion was one of two fundamental dimensions that recurred in analyses of many personality inventories. The second dimension was emotional instability or maladjustment; because it was seen most clearly in individuals traditionally diagnosed as neurotics, he called this dimension *Neuroticism*. Later Eysenck and Eysenck (1975) added a third dimension, Psychoticism, to their list of basic personality dimensions. In addition to Introversion–Extraversion, Jungian psychology calls attention to two other contrasts: Sensation versus Intuition, and Thinking versus Feeling. The Myers–Briggs Type Indicator or MBTI (Myers & McCaulley, 1985) measures these, as well as a contrast between Judging and Perceiving.

Henry Murray, whose 1938 volume, *Explorations in Personality*, is one of the classics of the field, was a psychodynamic theorist who viewed motivation as the key to personality. He and his colleagues at the Harvard Psychological Clinic identified a list of needs or motives they considered necessary for a reasonably complete description of the individual's personality. Needs for achievement, affiliation, and nurturance are among the list of 20 or so needs. Many instruments have been created to measures these needs, of which perhaps the best is Jackson's (1984) Personality Research Form, or PRF. Jack Block (1961) led another team of dynamically oriented psychologists and psychiatrists in an effort to develop a standard language for personality description. Instead of adopting a particular theory, their items were intended to provide a theoretically neutral language of description, useful to clinicians or researchers of any school. Further, they made a deliberate and sustained attempt to be comprehensive—to include *all* important personality characteristics. This is a crucial feature to which we will return later.

The psychiatrist Harry Stack Sullivan formulated an interpersonal theory of psychiatry that has had influences on two important trait systems. Students of interpersonal behavior (Leary, 1957; Wiggins, 1979) discovered that most traits that described styles of interacting with others could be arranged in a circular order around the two axes of Love or affiliation and Status or dominance. Figure 1 presents a diagram of this Interpersonal Circumplex. Individuals high on one trait (e.g., gregariousness) tend to be high on adjacent traits (dominance and warmth) and low on traits on the opposite side of the circle (aloofness). Concepts of

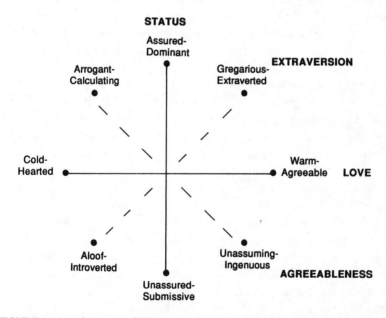

FIGURE 1. An adaptation of Wiggins et al.'s version of the Interpersonal Circumplex. The solid lines indicate the dimensions of Love and Status used in Wiggins' system; the broken lines indicate the dimensions of Extraversion and Agreeableness. Adapted by permission.

interpersonal interaction were also central to formulations of personality disorders (Millon, 1981; Widiger & Frances, 1985) and were ultimately incorporated in the American Psychiatric Association's official diagnostic system, the DSM-III. These personality disorders can be interpreted as extreme forms of normal personality traits.

The Quest for a Unified System

Historically, competition among these systems has been a preoccupation of personality psychologists, and the lack of a single, unified model has significantly hindered progress in the field. Researchers from different schools could not easily communicate, so results could not be compared. A study of age changes on the GZTS would not speak to the concerns of adherents to Murray's system of needs, so a separate study of age changes in needs might be required. Research efforts were at best inefficient.

If all the different systems really identified distinct parts of personality, as they appeared to do in principle, the search for a comprehensive model would be futile. But numerous studies have shown that there are important overlaps among the various systems. Although needs may seem to be quite different from personality disorders and from Jungian functions, the measures of these concepts have much in common. Neuroticism and Extraversion play a large role in many personality inventories—so much so that Wiggins (1968) called these the "Big Two." Unfortunately, the correspondences are often obscured by the labels psychologists have chosen for their scales. Two measures with the same label may measure different traits, and two measures of the same trait may have very different labels.

The identification of new traits might seem to be the equivalent of the entomologist's classification of insects or the astronomer's cataloguing of stars. In fact, it is something quite different. It is easy enough to identify a beetle from its picture and description or to characterize a star by its exact position in the sky. But we cannot pin up specimens of anxiety or personal insecurity or neuroticism or guilt-proneness and compare them, nor do we have a map of the "personality sphere" that we can use to check the location of a trait. How do we know whether the traits in one system are the same as those in another system under different names?

The only way we can tell if a scale measures a totally new trait or is merely some variation on a familiar one is by measuring a group of people on the proposed new trait as well as on all the older, known traits and seeing whether the measures of the new trait really give us some new information. (The technical name for the process is *discriminant validation*.) Since there are hundreds of scales in use, it is virtually impossible to measure all of them on an adequate sample of people and so settle the issue once and for all. But if we piece together all the research of the past 50 years in which a few traits have been measured jointly and compared, we can begin to see the outlines of the forest we are in. And once we have some notion of the major groups of personality traits, it becomes much easier to judge the contribution of new candidates. In short, we will have begun to map out the territory of personality and obtain the equivalent of the astronomer's map of the heavens and the entomologist's taxonomy of insects.

The major tool in this endeavor has been factor analysis, a mathematical technique for summarizing the associations among a group of variables in terms of a few underlying dimensions. The degree to which two traits go together, or covary, is assessed by the correlation coefficient, which is fairly easy to interpret. But as the number of traits increases, the combinations soon surpass the ability of the unaided mind to comprehend: When 35 trait scales are examined there are 595 different correlations; 50 scales yield 1,225 correlations. Factor analysis offers a way to determine how to group together sets of traits that are all related to each other and unrelated to other sets of traits. For example, anxiety, anger, and depression cluster together as part of the broader domain of Neuroticism; they are all relatively independent of traits such as sociability and cheerfulness, which are part of Extraversion.

It is its ability to condense and organize great quantities of information that makes factor analysis a natural instrument for researchers interested in studying the structure of traits. As an analytical tool, however, factor analysis is not infallible. Different researchers can arrive at different conclusions from the same data when they use factor analytic techniques differently. Our view is that factor analysis should be guided by what we already know about personality structure, just as experiments are guided by theoretically derived hypotheses. Used in this way, factor analysis has led to solid and replicable findings about the structure of traits.

Natural Language and the Five-Factor Model

One way to avoid the controversies of competing psychological theories is to turn to the description of personality offered by natural languages such as English. This approach draws on the folk wisdom embedded in the language, and the resulting system will be readily understood by all speakers of the language: You must be trained in Freudian theory to know what an anal-retentive character is, but everyone understands what *stubborn* and *stingy* mean. Most importantly, however, the argument can be made that natural language can be used to define the full scope of individual differences in personality. Personality differences are important in getting along with others, in work and play, in maintaining traditions and creating new ones. Every culture must have evolved words to represent these differences, and over the course of centuries, every important attribute or trait will surely have been noted and named (Norman, 1963). In their study of an unabridged dictionary, Allport and Odbert (1936) found about 18,000 such trait-descriptive terms—more than enough to occupy personality psychologists.

In fact, far more than enough—too many. Some screening, some clustering of synonyms is needed to make this language manageable. Allport and Odbert began that job by identifying about 4,000 terms that most clearly referred to personality traits. The next step was taken by Cattell (1946), who formed groups of synonyms from the 4,000 words, eventually identifying 35 clusters. These were used in a study of personality ratings; the 35 scales were factored and 12 dimensions were identified. Combined with four additional dimensions Cattell had found in studies of questionnaires, these became the basis of Cattell's personality inventory, the Sixteen Personality Factor Questionnaire or 16PF (Cattell, Eber, & Tatsuoka, 1970).

Our contributions to research on personality structure began with analyses of 16PF data on a sample of volunteers participating in a longitudinal study of aging conducted by the Veterans Administration in Boston (Costa & McCrae, 1976). After considering a range of possible solutions, we settled on what seemed to be both simple and adequate: a three-factor model. Two of the three dimensions were so similar to Eysenck's Neuroticism and Extraversion that we adopted those names; the third we called *Openness to Experience.*

Rokeach (1960), who was interested in the structure of ideas, had written about dogmatic individuals who were not open to new ideas or values. The clinician Carl Rogers (1961) had observed that some of his clients were out of touch with their own feelings, and he proposed that openness to inner experience was a criterion of good mental health. Coan (1972) created a measure of openness to fantasy and aesthetic experience, and Tellegen and Atkinson (1974) noted that the capacity to become deeply involved in experiences, which they called *openness to absorbing experience*, was characteristic of individuals who were easily hypnotized. We saw all of these traits as part of a single domain of Openness.

We created an inventory to measure specific traits, or facets, of each of these three domains and conducted research with it for several years. Although it worked well in many respects, it shared with most other trait systems the limitation that it was not comprehensive. We knew that some traits, such as conscientiousness, were not represented, but, like other researchers, we had no clear notion of what other traits might also be lacking. Ours was a good model as far as it went—but how far was that?

The quest for comprehensiveness led researchers back to the natural language. As long ago as 1961, two Air Force researchers, Tupes and Christal, had conducted a series of studies using the 35 rating scales devised by Cattell. Instead of the 12 factors Cattell had reported, they found only five—but they found them in several different samples. Warren Norman (1963) recognized the significance of this finding and, after replicating the five factors in his own studies, suggested that they constituted an "adequate taxonomy of personality traits." Interest in this model waned, however, until Goldberg (1981, 1982) started the project from scratch, going back to the dictionary and forming his own sets of synonyms—and replicating the five-factor model once again.

Norman had called the factors Extraversion or Surgency, Agreeableness, Conscientiousness, Emotional Stability, and Culture. When, in the 1980s, we began to reexamine this system, we found striking parallels to our own. Norman's Surgency was clearly our Extraversion, and his Emotional Stability was simply the opposite pole of our Neuroticism. If Norman's Culture matched our Openness, then our three-factor model could be nested within the five-factor model, and the claim that the latter was truly comprehensive would be considerably strengthened. Using adult men and women from the Baltimore Longitudinal Study of Aging (BLSA), we confirmed these hypotheses (McCrae & Costa, 1985, 1987) and quickly became advocates of the five-factor model. We developed scales to measure Agreeableness and Conscientiousness to supplement our original instrument and published it as the NEO Personality Inventory or NEO-PI (Costa & McCrae, 1985, 1989a).

*   *   *

If the five-factor model is a truly comprehensive taxonomy of personality traits, it has profound implications for the study of aging and personality. The task of looking for age changes, for example, is immensely simplified. Instead of being obliged to consider separately each of the 18,000 traits named in the English language and the hundreds of scales created by psychologists, we can concentrate on five broad groups of traits. By sampling traits from each domain, we could get a reasonable idea of how all traits were related to age.

To the extent that existing measures can be classified in terms of a taxonomy, the five-factor model can be used to summarize the existing literature and to look for similar patterns across different instruments. Further, the comprehensiveness of the model would ensure that our search for age changes was exhaustive. We would not need to worry that we had inadvertently omitted consideration of some trait that shows striking age changes. If we see maturation in some traits in a domain, we may wish to look carefully for changes in other traits in the same domain. Studies of aging often require decades of data collection, so researchers need to be very selective in the variables they choose to study. The five-factor model can help us formulate plausible hypotheses about which traits must be represented and which can be safely ignored.

But the five-factor model has many other applications in the psychology of aging, because it provides a framework for systematic research. Whether we are interested in the so-called midlife crisis, preferred age of retirement, adjustment to widowhood, or risk factors for dementia, we know we have fully considered the possible role of personality if and only if we have measured all five factors.

But is the claim to comprehensiveness justified? Does the five-factor model in fact encompass all the competing systems? This is an empirical question, and we must postpone our answer until we have considered how personality traits should be measured.

·3·

MEASURING PERSONALITY

From Concepts to Data

The whole trick of science is to test ideas against reality, and in order to do that, something has to be measured. We may suspect that salespeople are likely to be extraverts, but in order to prove it we have to be able to measure Extraversion to convince other people that we are measuring it successfully. If we can come that far, it is a relatively easy matter to see whether salespeople score higher than others on our measure, although we also have to be concerned with the representativeness of our sample, the magnitude of the difference we find, and any number of other problems in interpretation.

In many respects, trait theories of personality are among the easiest to operationalize (as the process of finding suitable measures for theoretical concepts is called). Traits are generalized dispositions, so we know we must look for evidence of consistent patterns of behavior or reactions across a range of situations. Traits endure over time, so we know that our measures must give us about the same results when applied at two different times, say a few weeks apart. Individuals vary in the degree to which they can be characterized by a trait, so we know our measure must show a range or distribution of scores.

Based on what we know about the domain, we would be able to measure Extraversion by getting answers to the following questions:

- How many close friends does this person have?
- How much does this person enjoy parties?

- Is this person often the leader of a group?
- How active and energetic is this person?
- How much does this person crave excitement?
- Is this person usually cheerful?

If we come up with a reasonable system for answering all these questions, say on a scale from 1 to 5, we can add up the numbers and assign a total score for Extraversion. Once we have the answers for a sample of people, we could begin to check the utility of our measure by asking some simple questions. First, do these items generally agree in the picture they give of the individual? That is, do people with many close friends also tend to be energetic and cheerful? This is called *internal consistency*, and it provides evidence that the different behaviors or reactions are actually part of a pattern, not just a collection of unrelated activities. If not, either we have a bad set of questions, or we have misunderstood the nature of Extraversion. Second, do the scores people get on one occasion parallel the scores they get at a later time? Are the extraverts of January still extraverts in March? This is called *retest reliability* and demonstrates that what is being measured is a trait, not a temporary state or mood of the individual.

There is little dispute about any of this. Most psychologists agree on what kinds of answers we need; the problem comes in deciding how we should get the answers. How do we know how much a person enjoys parties? We could ask the person for a self-report, but he or she may never have thought about it, or may lie to us, or may unconsciously distort the answer. We could ask friends for peer ratings, but they may not know how the person really feels and may have seen only one side of his or her personality. We could watch the person at a party and note how much he or she smiles, how long he or she stays, how excited and enthusiastic he or she seems to be; but his or her behavior at this party may be atypical. Perhaps the person has a toothache or does not get along with the host.

Behaviorally oriented psychologists would prefer the third strategy, behavioral observation, since it seems to be the most objective and scientific. But as we have pointed out, the contributions of dispositions to observable behavior are often overshadowed by the press of circumstances, and recent studies have shown that behavior has to be observed over many occasions before reliable inferences can be made about traits

(Epstein, 1979). In principle, repeated observation is perfectly reasonable; in practice, it is prohibitively expensive and time consuming.

Furthermore, observations of behavior, regardless of their number, may not be the most accurate source of answers regardless of their number. If we are really interested in the individual's dispositions, how the person feels may be much more relevant than how he or she acts. It may be necessary to put on a front, to play a role, to *seem* instead of *being*. A simple question asked in a way that allows for a candid answer, may give a far truer picture of real dispositions. In some areas, such as happiness, it can reasonably be argued that personal opinion is the *only* meaningful criterion.

It would hardly be an exaggeration to say that trait psychology has been floundering over these issues for the past 30 years. The great majority of researchers have been content to hand out questionnaires and trust the self-reports of their subjects, but their conclusions have been dismissed time and again because of objections about the kinds of errors to which self-report instruments are prone (Edwards, 1957; Berg, 1959). Behaviorists have scoffed at the idea that paper-and-pencil measures can be a substitute for the observations of real behavior. Psychodynamic theorists have objected that unconscious defense mechanisms or more or less conscious tendencies to present a socially desirable image of oneself make self-reports suspect. Social psychologists have contended that what counts is the perception of behavior by significant others and that, in consequence, only ratings should be trusted.

At last, however, there is some prospect that these controversies will be resolved. We know only too well that any single method of measurement, any source of answers to our questions, is subject to certain kinds of error and that consequently the surest results are those that can be seen using several different methods, as Campbell and Fiske (1959) noted long ago. But we are also beginning to see convincing evidence that, properly employed, many methods can give a reasonable approximation to the truth. A growing body of studies has shown that different methods do lead to the same conclusions about people.

One line of research has been concerned with correspondence between objective, observable behavior and self-reports. In one study (McGowan & Gormly, 1976), researchers followed a small group of college students and clocked their speed of walking. The fastest walkers were the ones who reported the highest activity level and who were rated by their peers as most energetic—not a particularly exciting result for the average reader, but a revelation for those psychologists who thought that self-reports were totally untrustworthy. Similarly, Small, Zeldin, and Savin-Williams (1983) recorded altruistic and dominant behaviors of small groups of teenagers on a summer camping trip and also asked the campers to rate each other on these two dimensions. They found remarkably high agreement between their behavior counts and the peer ratings. Another version of this line of research (Epstein, 1977) has demonstrated that as the sample of behavior increases, the correspondence between observations and self-reports increases to quite respectable levels. Research of this kind continues to support the validity of self-report measures, with an ever-increasing understanding of the reasons why self-reports and behavior ratings do not correspond perfectly (Moskowitz, 1988; Wright & Mischel, 1988).

Self-Reports and Ratings

The direct observation of behavior in the laboratory or in natural settings is invaluable as a way of anchoring our scales to rigorous scientific measurements, but as a technique of personality assessment it is both cumbersome and expensive. It would be virtually impossible to make sufficient observations on sufficient subjects over a sufficient number of years to approach the study of age and personality in this way.

Fortunately, there are alternatives. Self-report is the most widely used method; here individuals are asked to describe themselves by answering the items of a questionnaire or checking off adjectives that apply to them. Individuals have spent a lifetime getting to know themselves, and they alone can draw on the subjective experience that tells them whether they truly enjoy an activity or, deep down, harbor vague desires or anxieties. Provided that subjects are honest with themselves and with the researchers, self-report is probably the best way to measure personality.

That proviso, however, has always been disputed: Subjects may deceive themselves, or they may simply lie. For researchers concerned about these possibilities, there are three options honored by tradition: projective methods, which are supposed to allow the investigator to see behind the individual's facade; validity scales designed to detect faking or lying and adjust self-reports accordingly; and ratings from knowledgeable informants. We will postpone until Chapter 7 an evaluation of projective methods and focus for the moment on the other two approaches.

Ratings can be obtained from friends, neighbors, or fellow students, from parents or spouses, or from psychologists or other trained observers. In all these cases, the rater does not simply make a tally of behaviors, but instead interprets all the information he or she has about the person being rated—the target—as the basis for ascribing traits. Although friends and neighbors may be biased by favorable (or occasionally unfavorable) opinions of the target, they are less likely than the target to deceive themselves about the target's personality. Even more importantly, researchers who use peer ratings need not rely on any single view, but can ask several raters for their judgments, examine the agreement among these, and combine them into an average rating.

Rating studies have played an important role in personality theory. The five-factor model itself was first identified in studies of ratings (Norman, 1963; Tupes & Christal, 1961), and, as we will see, some important studies of age and personality have used peer, spouse, or expert ratings. In sheer quantity, however, self-report studies have far outnumbered rating studies, and perhaps the most important contribution of rating studies has been what they have been able to show about the validity of self-reports.

Rate yourself on the six Extraversion items listed earlier on a 1-to-5 scale, and then ask a friend who knows you well to rate you. You may be surprised at the differences of opinion. We would be guilty of failing to learn from decades of criticism if we did not acknowledge that there is a substantial element of illusion in the views we hold of others (Fiske, 1978) and in our idea of what their view of us is like (Swann, 1983). We easily and rapidly form opinions about others' personalities, often with little basis in fact. This is particularly true of those with whom we have only a passing acquaintance.

But these limitations should not cause us to despair. When knowledgeable raters are asked to assess a target's personality using reliable and valid trait measures, the results are generally encouraging (McCrae, 1982b). We asked subjects in the Baltimore Longitudinal Study of Aging to complete the self-report form of the NEO Personality Inventory; with their permission, we also obtained ratings from spouses and from one to four peers (friends and neighbors), using a rating form of the NEO-PI (McCrae & Costa, 1988c). The first column of Table 2 gives intraclass correlations between pairs of peers who rated the same target. All the correlations are statistically significant, showing that ratings are not

TABLE 2. *Correlations Between Peer Ratings, Spouse Ratings, and Self-Reports*

	Agreement between			
NEO-PI factor	Peer and peer	Peer and spouse	Peers and self	Spouse and self
Neuroticism	.36	.45	.37	.53
Extraversion	.41	.26	.44	.53
Openness	.46	.37	.63	.59
Agreeableness	.45	.49	.57	.60
Conscientiousness	.45	.41	.49	.57

Note. All correlations are significant at $p < .001$. N's = 144 to 719. Adapted from McCrae & Costa (1988c).

random impressions, but instead are reflections of characteristics on which independent observers can agree. The extent of agreement is substantial for all five factors: The median value of .45 means that almost half of the variance in rating scores is attributable to the trait itself (Ozer, 1985), the other half being error—that is, mistakes and biases in perception, careless responding, legitimate differences of opinion, and so on. The second column of the table shows that peers agree with spouses about as well as they agree among themselves. By averaging together two or more ratings we obtain even more trustworthy information about the target, as the errors of one observer are cancelled out by opposing errors in another.

What about agreement between self-reports and ratings? Can we "see oursels as ithers see us," as Robert Burns wished? The last two columns of Table 2 suggest that we can, with substantial correlations of self-reports with averaged peer ratings and with spouse ratings. The highest correlations are seen when self-reports are compared with spouse ratings. Perhaps husbands and wives know the targets more intimately than do friends or neighbors; perhaps they show higher agreement because couples discuss their personalities with each other and share their perceptions of themselves. In any case, this is one more piece of evidence that both ratings and self-reports are useful ways to measure personality, with at least as much truth as error.

Similar results and conclusions have been reported by many other researchers in recent years, as Table 3 shows. This research, conducted on a variety of samples using many different instruments, firmly estab-

TABLE 3. *Some Recent Studies Comparing Self-Reports and Peer Ratings*

Study	N	Subjects	Raters	Measures	Average correlation
Cheek (1982)	85	College men	3	4 adjective factors	.44
Amelang & Borkenau (1982)	321	Young adults	3	5 adjective factors	.58
Kammann et al. (1984)	60	Students	2	6 adjectives	.30
Paunonen (in Jackson, 1984)	90	Students	1	20 PRF scales	.52
Marsh et al. (1985)	151	Students	1	13 self-concept scales	.58
Woodruffe (1985)	66	Students	10	14 adjective scales	.58
Conley (1985)	378	Couples	5	4 adjective factors	.36
John (1988)	50	Individuals	4	96 adjectives	.31
Funder & Colvin (1988)	157	Students	2	100 CQS items	.27
McCrae & Costa (in press-c)	100	College men	4	5 NEO-PI factors	.59

Adapted from McCrae & Costa (1988c).

lishes the utility of both self-reports and ratings as methods of assessing personality.

The studies in Table 3 all date from the 1980s. Until that time there had been relatively few studies comparing self-reports and ratings. Ratings are cumbersome to obtain, because raters must be identified, contacted, and persuaded to participate and because some individuals may be unable or unwilling to provide the names of suitable raters. Researchers and clinicians have preferred the convenience of self-reports, even if they did not trust them. Consequently, a major tradition in personality assessment has sought ways to determine the validity of self-reports using special validity scales designed to outwit defensive or dishonest test takers, as a lawyer tries to trap a lying witness in a contradiction. Despite extraordinary efforts and ingenuity, however, it is far from clear that any of these scales really works—probably because most self-reports are reasonably honest to begin with.

Perhaps the most common strategy for creating validity scales was used by Edwards (1957), who had judges rate the social desirability of items on the MMPI, and selected a set of highly evaluative items. People who wished to make a good impression would answer *yes* to the desirable items and *no* to the undesirable ones. By summing the number of such responses, test takers could be assigned a Social Desirability score. High scores were considered by many psychologists as grounds for throwing out the test. Another MMPI scale, the K scale, was designed to assess defensiveness, and scores on the psychopathology scales were "corrected" by adding a fraction of the K scale score (McKinley, Hathaway, & Meehl, 1948). In theory, this addition compensated for the defensive denial of psychological problems.

In practice, however, these approaches are very problematic. Logically, a high score might result from an attempt, conscious or unconsicous, to make a good impression; but it might also result from honest answers by truly well-adjusted, agreeable, and conscientious people. It is desirable to be honest, and liars might falsely claim to be honest if asked—but so would truly honest people. A claim of honesty is inherently ambiguous.

Crowne and Marlowe (1964) believed they had a solution to this problem: They wrote items that would almost never be literally true, such as "Before voting, I thoroughly investigate the qualifications of all candidates." They reasoned that someone who answered *yes* to such items would clearly be lying. But test takers are not literalists; they are likely to say to themselves, "Surely these psychologists didn't mean to ask if I actually study the voting records of every single political candidate, from President to dogcatcher. No one does, so that would be a stupid question to ask. What they must have meant to ask was whether I am a concerned citizen who takes voting seriously. Since I am and I do, I guess I should answer *yes*."

Rational analyses of what subjects might be thinking when they respond will not suffice here; the only way to find out if validity scales succeed in identifying and correcting self-report biases is by empirical test. We can compare corrected and uncorrected self-reports with an impartial, external standard—say, observer ratings—to see whether correcting improves accuracy of self-reports. Several studies (Dicken, 1963; McCrae & Costa, 1983a; McCrae et al., 1989) convincingly show that the use of validity scales does nothing to improve the accuracy of self-reports in volunteer samples—indeed, it often impairs them. Most people apparently answer honestly, without any significant attempt to make themselves look good. It is possible that there is more defensiveness or socially desirable responding under other conditions, for example, when applying for a job. But that possibility need not concern us here. The studies of personality and age that we examine all use volunteer subjects with no motivation to fake their scores, and we are justified in putting considerable faith in these self-reports as one line of evidence.

A QUESTIONNAIRE MEASURE: THE NEO PERSONALITY INVENTORY

Any of the instruments in Table 3 might be suitable for the study of aging and personality. In fact, however, most of our research has used the NEO Personality Inventory or NEO-PI (Costa & McCrae, 1985, 1989a), and a more detailed description of the instrument may give a better sense of the process of measurement and the meaning of the major dimensions of personality.

The NEO-PI consists of 181 items, phrased either in the first person for self-reports (e.g., "I really like most people I meet") or in the third person for ratings (e.g., "She has a very active imagination"). Respondents read each item and decide on a 1 to 5 scale if they *strongly disagree, disagree,* don't know or are *neutral, agree,* or *strongly agree* with the statement. The responses are then summed to yield five basic domain scores for Neuroticism, Extraversion, Openness, Agreeableness, and Conscientiousness. When compared with data from normative samples that show how most people respond, these scores allow us to characterize the respondent. For example, an individual who scores higher than three-quarters of the normative sample on Agreeableness might be described as *compassionate, good-natured, and eager to cooperate and avoid conflict.* One who scored in the lower quarter of the distribution could be described as *hardheaded, skeptical, proud, and competitive.*

Table 1, in Chapter 1, listed some adjectives that describe low and high scorers on the five domains. In general, Neuroticism represents the proneness of the individual to experience unpleasant and disturbing emotions and to have corresponding disturbances in thoughts and actions (Vestre, 1984). Psychiatric patients who were traditionally diagnosed as neurotics tend to score very high on this dimension, but many individuals score high without having any psychiatric disorder: Neuroticism is a dimension of personality on which people vary only in degree. Extraversion is a more familiar term; it concerns differences in preference for social interaction and lively activity. Openness in our model should not be confused with self-disclosure (being willing to talk about one's inner feelings); instead, it refers to a receptiveness to new ideas, approaches, and experiences. People who are closed to experience are not necessarily defensive, nor are they necessarily narrow-minded in the sense of being judgmental and intolerant. Instead, they are characterized by a preference for the familiar, practical, and concrete, and a lack of interest in experience for its own sake.

Agreeableness is seen in selfless concern for others and in trusting and generous sentiments. Low Agreeableness (or Antagonism) is tough-minded and hard-headed. Although agreeable people are nicer than antagonistic people, antagonism, too, has its virtues. We want surgeons to be ruthless in cutting out disease and lawyers to be aggressive in our defense. Conscientiousness is a dimension of individual differences in organization and achievement. Highly conscientious people are dutiful and self-disciplined, but also ambitious and hardworking, sometimes to the point of being "workaholics." Men and women low in Conscientiousness are more lackadaisical and easy-going and less exacting with themselves or others.

The NEO-PI was developed over a 10-year period, but in the first years we were concerned with only three domains—Neuroticism, Extraversion, and Openness (whence the name, "NEO"). For these three domains we also developed measures of more specific traits, which we have called *facets*, because they reflect specific sides or aspects of the broader domains. Each of the N, E, and O domain scales is composed of six subscales that measure these specific facets.

The Eighteen NEO Facets

Anxiety and hostility, the first two facets of Neuroticism, are the dispositional forms of two fundamental emotions: fear and anger. Everyone experiences these emotions from time to time, but the frequency and intensity with which they are felt varies from one person to another. Individuals high in the trait of anxiety are nervous, high-strung, and tense. They are prone to worry; they dwell on what might go wrong. Hostile people show a corresponding proneness to experience anger. They tend to be irritable and ill-tempered, and may prove hard to get along with.

Two different emotions, sorrow and shame, form the basis of the traits of depression and self-consciousness. As a trait, depression is the disposition to experience sadness, hopelessness, loneliness; depressed people often have feelings of guilt and of diminished self-worth. Individuals high in self-consciousness are more prone to the emotion of shame or embarrassment. They are particularly sensitive to ridicule and teasing, because they often feel inferior to others. (Self-consciousness is often called shyness, but it should be noted that people who are shy in this respect do not necessarily avoid people. Introverts often claim to be shy when in fact they simply do not care to interact with others; they use shyness as an excuse.)

Two of the facets of Neuroticism are more often manifest in behaviors than in emotional states. Impulsiveness is the tendency to give in to temptations and to be overwhelmed by desires. Because they have so little control (or perhaps because they experience such strong urges), impulsive people tend to overeat and overspend, to drink and smoke, gamble, and perhaps use drugs. Vulnerability designates an inability to deal adequately with stress. Vulnerable people tend to panic in emergencies, to break down, and to become dependent on others for help.

Some individuals will be anxious but not hostile, or self-conscious but not impulsive. But in general, those high in Neuroticism are likely to be high in *each* of these traits. They are prone to violent and negative emotions that interfere with their ability to deal with their problems and to get along with others. We can envision the kind of chain of events such people may experience: In social situations they are anxious and embarrassed, and their frustration in dealing with others may make them hostile, further complicating matters. In compensation, they turn to the use of alcohol or food, and the long-term results are likely to be depressing. Although the emotions and impulses which disturb them may not occur simultaneously, they succeed one another with distressing regularity.

The facets of Extraversion can be subdivided into three interpersonal and three temperamental traits. Warmth, or attachment, refers to a friendly, compassionate, intimately involved style of personal interaction; by contrast, cold individuals are more likely to be formal and impersonal, with weak attachments to most other people. Warmth and gregariousness (or the desire to be with other people) together make up what is sometimes called sociability. Gregarious people like crowds; they seem to relish sheer quantity of social stimulation. Assertive people are natural leaders, easily taking charge, making up their own minds, and readily expressing their feelings and desires.

The three forms of Extraversion we have called temperamental are activity, excitement-seeking, and positive emotions. Extraverts like to keep busy, acting vigorously and talking rapidly; they are energetic and forceful. They also prefer environments that stimulate them, often going in search of excitement. Fast cars, flashy clothes, risky undertakings hold an attraction for them. The active and exciting life of extraverts is reflected emotionally in the experience of positive emotions. Joy, delight, zest, and jocularity are part of the package of traits in the domain of Extraversion. Once again, all these dispositions are synergistic, working together to form a personality syndrome. Activity leads to excitement and excitement to happiness; the happy person finds others easier to get along with, and congeniality easily turns to leadership.

We measure Openness to Experience in six different areas. In fantasy Openness implies a vivid imagination and a tendency to develop elaborate daydreams; in aesthetics it is seen in sensitivity to art and beauty. Aesthetic experience is perhaps the epitome of Openness, since it is pure experience for its own sake; we know from studies of occupational interests that a preference for artistic activities is especially characteristic of open people (Costa, McCrae, & Holland, 1984). As Rogers might have predicted, open individuals experience their own feelings strongly, and they value the experience, seeing it as a source of meaning in life.

Openness to action is the opposite of rigidity: open people are willing to try a new dish or see a new movie or travel to a foreign country. Openness to ideas and values is also part of the domain; open people are curious and value knowledge for its own sake. Perhaps because they are willing to think of different possibilities and to empathize with others in other circumstances, they tend to be liberal in values, admitting that what is right and wrong for one person may not be applicable in other circumstances.

Facets of A and C

The NEO-PI does not measure specific facets of Agreeableness and Conscientiousness; only global domain scales are included. But it would certainly be possible to measure more specific aspects of these two domains, and future revisions of the NEO-PI will probably include such scales.

A review of the literature (Costa, McCrae, & Dembroski, 1989) suggests several aspects of Agreeableness that might be included as facets. Agreeable people are trusting, believing the best of others and rarely suspecting hidden intents. Age changes in trust would be of particular interest because Erikson (1950) regarded this as the earliest and most fundamental outcome of psychosocial development. According to his views, those who do not develop trust can never really advance toward industry, identity, and intimacy. Just as agreeable people trust others, so they are themselves trustworthy, straightforward, frank, and candid. Agreeable individuals are meek, deferring to others rather than aggressively pushing for their own ends; they are also modest in their assessment of their own abilities and importance. The selflessness of agreeable people is seen in their considerateness, altruism, and desire to help others. Attitudinally, agreeable people are tender-minded and sentimental, an easy touch for charities and good causes.

Different facets of Conscientiousness can also be discerned. Conscientious people are rational, informed, and generally think of themselves as being high in competence. Part of their success results from their organization and orderliness, which make them efficient in work. They are high in the need for achievement, striving for excellence in everything they do; and they are necessarily high in self-discipline to be able to accomplish their goals. In some respects, conscientious people are inhibited, adhering scrupulously to their moral precepts and rigorously fulfilling their social and civic duties. Finally, they are deliberate, making plans in advance and thinking carefully before acting. Theirs is a life clearly directed along the paths they choose to pursue.

Making Distinctions

It is not difficult to see the relationships among traits within a single domain. But it can be difficult to make the distinctions between and among domains that the facts demand. Human beings have a tendency to evaluate ideas and organize them in terms of good and bad. It is easy to see Neuroticism as bad and Extraversion, Openness, Agreeableness, and Conscientiousness as good, and then to assume that individuals high in Neuroticism are likely to be introverted, closed, antagonistic, and unreliable. It doesn't work that way. The five domains are independent; consequently, an individual high in Neuroticism is as likely to be introverted as extraverted, closed as open. Five dimensions cannot be collapsed into one without serious distortions.

One way to make the necessary conceptual distinctions is to con-centrate on the opposite poles, the low ends, of the traits we are discussing. Introverts are cold, but not hostile; loners, but not self-conscious; not particularly cheerful, but not necessarily depressed either. Individuals who are closed to experience are not necessarily maladjusted; in fact, they are somewhat less likely to experience violent emotions by virtue of their lesser sensitivity to emotions of all kinds. They may not care to travel to strange places and meet unusual people, but they are just as likely as open people to seek excitement and crowds of people—as long as both are of the familiar variety.

There is another mistake in contrasting "good" and "bad" dimensions of personality: We may be mistaken about which is which. From the individual's point of view, there are distinct advantages to being well-adjusted and extraverted. Such people usually report themselves to be the happiest, most satisfied with life (Costa & McCrae, 1980a). But from society's point of view, all kinds of people are necessary: those who work well with others and those who can finish a task on their own; those who come up with creative new ways of doing things and those who maintain the best solutions of the past. There are probably even advantages to be found in Neuroticism, since a society of extremely easy-going individuals might not compete well with other societies of suspicious and hostile individuals. Cultures need members fit for war as well as peace, work as well as play, and some theorists (Hogan, 1979) have even suggested that such societal advantages may account for individual differences in an evolutionary sense: Human beings have evolved consistent differences because this range of characteristics is useful in the survival of the social group.

THE COMPREHENSIVENESS OF THE FIVE-FACTOR MODEL

We know that the five-factor model encompasses the lay conception of personality as embodied in the trait names of the English language and that the NEO-PI provides both self-report and rating measures of the factors (McCrae & Costa, 1985, 1987). We can now turn to the question of whether the five-factor model is truly comprehensive: Can it account for the traits identified by other psychological systems? A series of studies using the NEO-PI along with other instruments points to an affirmative answer.

Perhaps the most impressive evidence of comprehensiveness comes from analyses of the California Q-Set or CQS, developed by several panels of psychologists and psychiatrists who explicitly tried to include every important aspect of personality suggested by their psychodynamic orientation (Block, 1961). We know that their selection was not biased by the five-factor model, because they had completed their work before it was first reported (Tupes & Christal, 1961).

In our study, we had 403 men and women from the BLSA describe themselves using the CQS; when we analyzed the 100 items, we found five factors whose defining items are given in Table 4. It was clear to us that these were essentially the same factors that we measured in the NEO-PI, and correlations between the CQS factors and NEO-PI scales confirmed this hypothesis. The five-factor model organizes CQS items as well as it organizes trait names.

One particularly elegant way to demonstrate convergences between two instruments is by factoring the scales from both instruments together

TABLE 4. *California Q-Set Items Defining the Five Factors*

Factor	Low scorer	High scorer
Neuroticism	Calm, relaxed	Thin-skinned
	Satisfied with self	Basically anxious
	Clear-cut personality	Irritable
	Prides self on objectivity	Guilt-prone
Extraversion	Emotionally bland	Talkative
	Avoids close relationships	Gregarious
	Overcontrol of impulses	Socially poised
	Submissive	Behaves assertively
Openness	Favors conservative values	Values intellectual matters
	Judges in conventional terms	Rebellious, nonconforming
	Uncomfortable with complexities	Unusual thought processes
	Moralistic	Introspective
Agreeableness	Critical, skeptical	Sympathetic, considerate
	Shows condescending behavior	Warm, compassionate
	Tries to push limits	Arouses liking
	Expresses hostility directly	Behaves in a giving way
Conscientiousness	Eroticizes situations	Behaves ethically
	Unable to delay gratification	Dependable, responsible
	Self-indulgent	Productive
	Engages in fantasy, daydreams	Has high aspiration level

Adapted from McCrae, Costa, & Busch (1986).

in a joint analysis. When Wiggins' revised Interpersonal Adjective Scales (IAS-R) were factored along with NEO-PI factors, all the IAS-R (Wiggins et al., 1988) scales showed their highest loading on the Extraversion and Agreeableness factors (McCrae & Costa, 1989c). As Figure 1 (p. 27) shows, the traits of the interpersonal circle can be arranged around these two dimensions. From this diagram it appears that the traditional axes labeled "Love" and "Status" are intermediate between E and A. In other words, both systems describe the same circle of traits, but they do so from slightly different starting points.

Joint factor analysis (Costa & McCrae, 1988a) was also useful in understanding Murray's (1938) needs as measured by Jackson's (1984) Personality Research Form (PRF). Table 5 gives factor loadings; by concentrating on the larger loadings (in boldface), the relationship between needs and personality factors can be seen. These data (from a group of people originally recruited to provide ratings on our BLSA subjects) suggest that individuals high in Neuroticism worry about others' opinions of them (need for Social Recognition), are defensive and guarded (need for Defendence), and want care and sympathy (need for Succorance). Extraverts need social contact (Affiliation), attention (Exhibition), and fun (Play). Open individuals appreciate variety (Change), intellectual stimulation (Understanding), and aesthetic experiences (Sentience), and are adventurous (low Harmavoidance) and unconventional (Autonomy). Individuals high in Agreeableness enjoy helping others (Nurturance) and tend to be self-effacing and modest (Abasement); by contrast, antagonistic people are domineering (Dominance) and quarrelsome (Aggression). Those who score high in Conscientiousness value organization (Order) and accomplishment (Achievement) and are persistent (Endurance), careful (low Impulsiveness), and deliberate (need for Cognitive Structure).

Table 5 also shows something else: Many of the needs have high loadings on two or more factors. Nurturance, for example, is related to both Extravertion and Agreeableness; Aggression is related to both Neuroticism and (low) Agreeableness. These findings are perfectly reasonable (McCrae & Costa, 1989b). We expect nurturant people to be both sociable and selfless and aggressive people to be both angry and selfish. But joint loadings like this make the correspondence between needs and the five factors less obvious. Researchers who begin by thinking in terms of nurturance and aggression are unlikely to come up with the dimensions of Extraversion, Agreeableness, and Neuroticism, even though these dimensions make perfect sense in hindsight. Perhaps this is one of the reasons why the five-factor model was not discovered sooner.

Similar analyses have shown that the scales in the Guilford–Zimmerman Temperament Survey (GZTS), the Eysenck Personality Questionnaire (EPQ), and the Myers–Briggs Type Indicator (MBTI) can also be related to the basic five factors (McCrae, 1989). Table 6 shows how the scales can be classified. Note that the EPQ contains no measure of Openness, the MBTI no measure of Neuroticism, and the GZTS a disproportionate number of scales measuring Neuroticism and Extra-

TABLE 5. *Joint Factor Analysis of NEO-PI Factors and PRF Scales*

	Varimax-rotated principal components				
Variable	N	E	O	A	C
NEO-PI Factors					
Neuroticism	81	−17	02	09	−14
Extraversion	13	83	13	−03	13
Openness	−09	−07	78	04	−11
Agreeableness	−01	15	−18	72	−23
Conscientiousness	08	−15	00	23	77
PRF Needs					
Abasement	06	−14	12	58	08
Achievement	05	03	46	02	64
Affiliation	04	83	−13	19	11
Aggression	43	07	14	−68	−21
Autonomy	−42	−33	47	−26	−10
Change	−06	21	60	−12	−11
Cognitive Structure	19	07	−23	−30	52
Defendence	53	−07	−13	−48	−05
Dominance	00	38	45	−46	32
Endurance	−16	07	33	15	52
Exhibition	05	65	23	−31	−03
Harm avoidance	21	05	−52	32	09
Impulsivity	29	11	24	03	−61
Nurturance	25	49	10	55	06
Order	−05	12	−25	−17	64
Play	−13	65	07	−06	−37
Sentience	11	29	53	13	−09
Social Recognition	60	34	−10	−19	10
Succorance	53	40	−34	18	−14
Understanding	−02	00	64	10	16
Desirability	−35	45	07	10	54

Adapted from Costa & McCrae (1988a).

TABLE 6. *Classification of Traits from Alternative Systems*

Instrument	Neuroticism	Extraversion	Openness	Agreeableness	Conscientiousness
GZTS	−Emotional Stability −Objectivity −Friendliness −Personal Relations −Masculinity	General Activity −Restraint Ascendance Sociability	Thoughtfulness	Friendliness	Restraint
EPQ	Neuroticism	Extraversion		−Psychoticism	−Psychoticism
MBTI		Extraversion	Intuition	Feeling	Judgment

Note. Minus signs indicate that the scale measures the opposite of the factor.

version. The five factors appear to be both necessary and sufficient for describing the basic dimensions of personality; no other system is as complete and yet as parsimonious.

Finally, research in progress indicates that the Axis-II diagnostic categories for personality disorders may also be classifiable in terms of the five factors. Wiggins and Pincus (in press), for example, have shown that scales which measure schizoid disorders are closely related to Introversion, whereas those measuring histrionic disorders are related to Extraversion. Borderline disorders are characterized by high Neuroticism, dependent disorders by high Agreeableness. Individuals high in Conscientiousness appear to be prone to compulsive disorders. Only Openness is not clearly implicated in the current list of personality disorders, and perhaps future research will suggest that there are also pathological forms of Openness and Closedness.

* * *

The meaningfulness of trait psychology and the validity of trait measures are crucial to all the other arguments about aging and personality we will offer, because the great majority of empirical studies of aging and personality employ these kinds of measures. In Chapter 7 we will return to the theories of personality to consider alternative conceptions of personality and its assessment.

In the meantime we will assume that we have provided adequate justification for looking seriously at what happens to traits over the adult life course. We have argued that traits are indispensable for laypeople and for psychological theorists; that there is growing agreement about how many important groups of traits there are; and that there is encouraging evidence that several ways of measuring personality all lead to similar descriptions of people, and thus are dependable bases for inferences about aging and personality. We can now turn to the data on aging. What effects do aging and the accumulation of experience have on personality traits?

·4·

THE SEARCH FOR GROWTH OR DECLINE IN PERSONALITY

If we want to know whether personality changes across the adult years, the most straightforward way of proceeding would seem to be to measure personality in young and old people and see if there are any noticeable differences. This simple prescription turns out to be more complex than one might at first imagine. There are several excellent discussions of measuring change and disentangling aging, birth cohort, and time-of-measurement effects (e.g., Kausler, 1982; Schaie, 1977), complete with diagrams and statistical formulas. Our purpose here is not to teach methodology, but to show why a question as apparently straightforward as "Does personality change with age?" is not straightforward at all, and to review evidence on whether personality grows or declines with age.

Growth and decline are the most obvious and fundamental of developmental processes. Children grow taller each year until they reach adult stature; thereafter they remain at about the same height for many years, until in old age the settling of bones in the vertebral column makes them shrink somewhat. Many biological functions, notably sexuality, show similar curves, as do some, though by no means all, of the intellectual functions, such as short-term memory and spatial visualization abilities.

Many physical, biological, and social functions, however, do not exhibit the pattern of growth and decline. Some characteristics, like gender or eye color, are established by birth, and show no significant change across the life span. Variables of another class go through a period of growth, but show little or no decline. Vocabulary, for example, tends to grow dramatically in childhood and then to level out after the end of formal education, with little change thereafter.

These trends do not exhaust the possibilities. Perhaps growth in personality is unlimited, like the physical growth of some fish. Perhaps the pattern of change is not a simple up or down, but a complicated pattern of peaks and troughs—a possibility suggested by some of the stage theories we have mentioned. Rather than belabor the possible, let us turn to the facts and see if we can simply *describe* the age trends in personality dimensions. Later we can worry about what they mean, or where they come from.

CROSS-SECTIONAL STUDIES OF PERSONALITY DIFFERENCES

There are some fairly obvious ways of going about looking for this kind of age trend. First, we can measure an individual's personality now, and then return in 10, or 20, or 40 years to measure it again. We could then tell what net change, if any, had occurred in the meantime for each individual. This is a longitudinal design, in many respects the best way to study aging. The major problem with longitudinal studies is quite simple: They take too long. Few scientists are willing to wait 10 years for results, let alone 40. Gardeners may be willing to plant trees now that will not bear fruit for 10 years, but few researchers see themselves as gardeners. In fairness, there are some differences. Gardners know that if they wait patiently they will be rewarded with apples or cherries or plums. Researchers never know what they will find out, or if the results will turn out to be interesting or informative. If they knew the answers, they would not need to ask the questions.

What one really wants is some shortcut method of answering the question of age changes, and the cross-sectional method is invaluable as that kind of tool. In cross-sectional designs, one takes a group of younger people and a group of older people and compares them on the traits of interest. We might observe that 40% of men over 60 were bald, whereas only 2% of men under 30 were. Hence, it would seem, baldness is age-related. This is an example of the kind of cross-sectional observation we all make, and it is almost certainly a correct conclusion.

Studies that compare groups of different ages are called *cross-sectional* because they take a slice at one time of individuals of various ages. Note that this strategy has a number of advantages. For example, if we measure enough people, we can look not only at young versus old, but at much finer groupings: we can contrast people 38 to 43 years old with people 44 to 49 years old to see if the former are showing signs of a midlife crisis. We can search for a curve of growth and decline by decade or year to say at exactly what point there is a peak in creativity or productivity or depression. In a matter of weeks or months a researcher can estimate the effects of age on whatever variable he or she is interested in studying.

By this method, thousands of studies on age and personality have been conducted and hundreds published in the scientific literature. In 1977 Neugarten reviewed the findings that had been reported: egocentrism, dependency, introversion, dogmatism, rigidity, cautiousness, conformity, ego strength, risk-taking, need for achievement, locus of control, creativity, hope, the self-concept, social responsibility, morale, dreaming, and attitudes toward aging were all found to be different in different age groups. However, the studies rarely agreed with each other: Some researchers found that older people are more dogmatic, some that they are less. (Doubtless other researchers have found no age differences at all, but it is sometimes difficult to find a journal that will publish such "uninteresting" results.) Only introversion, according to Neugarten, seems to show a consistent pattern of increase in the latter half of life.

In updating Neugarten's review we can take advantage of the five-factor model to organize results, and we can test the replicability of findings by comparing age effects for different scales that measure each of the five domains. We will focus on three large-scale studies that use instruments that cover all or most of the five domains. Siegler, George, and Okun (1979) studied a sample of 331 men and women initially aged 54 to 70 who completed the 16PF. Douglas and Arenberg (1978) examined age differences on the GZTS among two groups of men in the BLSA: 605 men tested between 1958 and 1968, and 310 men tested between 1968 and 1974. Subjects ranged in age from 17 to 98, so age differences anywhere in adulthood should be apparent. In our study of the PRF (Costa & McCrae, 1988a), we examined age correlates in a sample of 296 men and women aged 22 to 90 who were friends and neighbors of BLSA participants. (A significant positive correlation of a scale with age would suggest that the trait increases with age; a negative correlation suggests that the trait declines.)

Four scales in the 16PF—low Emotional Stability, Suspiciousness, Tension, and Guilt-proneness—measure aspects of Neuroticism; none of them showed cross-sectional age differences. Four GZTS scales—Emotional Stability, Objectivity, Personal Relations, and Masculinity—tap emotional adjustment, the polar opposite of Neuroticism. Masculinity was slightly lower for older subjects in both samples studied by Douglas and Arenberg, whereas Personal Relations was slightly higher; there were no differences in Emotional Stability or Objectivity in either sample. Age was also uncorrelated with PRF scales related to Neuroticism: Social Recognition, Defendence, and Succorance. Apparently there are few age differences in Neuroticism.

There is some evidence of age differences in Extraversion. GZTS General Activity and Ascendance were lower in older BLSA men in both samples, as was Sociability in the first BLSA sample. Age was also negatively related to PRF needs for Exhibition and Play. However, there were no age differences in the need for Affiliation, nor in any of the 16PF Extraversion scales: Warmth, Assertiveness, Surgency, Adventurousness, and Group-Dependence.

Age trends in Openness are mixed. Needs for Change and Sentience appeared to decline with age, whereas the need for Understanding increased. GZTS Thoughtfulness also increased, but there were no age differences in needs for Harmavoidance or Autonomy or in 16PF scales measuring aesthetic sensitivity, imaginativeness, and liberal thinking.

Agreeableness is not measured by the 16PF scales, but GZTS Friendliness was a bit higher among older subjects, as was the need for Abasement. Needs for Dominance and Aggression appeared to decline with age. All these data point to a cross-sectional increase in Agreeableness.

Although GZTS Restraint was higher for older men in both of Douglas and Arenberg's samples, other measures of Conscientiousness—16PF Superego Strength and Self-Control and PRF needs for Achievement, Order, Endurance, Cognitive Structure, and low Implusiveness— showed no relationship to age.

There are several different ways to interpret these studies, and most of the interpretations would be championed by one writer or another. One reasonable reading of the literature would be that there are age-related declines in some aspects of Extraversion and increases in Agreeableness, but that most other aspects of personality remain constant across the life span. But many researchers in the field would be skeptical about this conclusion. They would point out that cross-sectional findings may result from many causes besides maturation. One alternative interpretation is provided by sampling bias.

Sampling Bias

Virtually all psychological research makes use of sampling and statistical inference in reaching its conclusions. We do not give personality tests to *all* 80-year-olds and *all* 30-year-olds; we give them to some few whom we can persuade to take them. Yet the conclusions we are interested in are not limited to the group we happen to have measured, but concern aging in general or 80-year-olds in general. A great deal of acute mathematical thinking has gone into the development of statistical tests that allow us to determine whether the differences we see between two random samples are real or simply a chance outcome of the particular group of people we happened to examine. In general, the larger the sample, the better the estimate of the true score for the population, the whole group about which we want to make generalizations. Samples of about 2,000 are routinely used to estimate the feelings of 200,000,000 Americans on such issues as the energy crisis or the liklihood of an economic depression.

Sampling itself, then, is not a problem for science. The trouble comes in the requirement that the sample be *random.* If we could go through the records of the Census Bureau, selecting every 100,000th citizen, we would be in a good position to make the best of a cross-sectional study. But samples tend to be quite different in real life. In practice, we find a sample by asking the cooperation of a senior citizens' group, or advertising in the paper, or asking our friends if they or their parents would participate in our study. This is sometimes called haphazard sampling, since it is neither really random, nor exactly systematic.

In the early days of gerontological research, some dreadfully flawed conclusions were reached because of this problem. Old people were selected from nursing homes, since there were few Senior Citizens' clubs in those days; young people, of course, came from the colleges at which the researchers worked. The so-called age differences that emerged from these studies painted a dismal picture of old age: The older people were less intelligent, less mentally healthy, rigid, depressed, and so on. The fact that college students represented the elite of their generation, whereas nursing home residents were by and large the worst-off of theirs, was somehow forgotten. If we were to extrapolate from these cross-sectional findings, we would discover for example that by the time we are in our 80s we will only have had an 8th-grade education! Errors this obvious are rarely made today. But sampling still presents problems, at the magnitude of which we can often only guess.

Part of the problem stems from the fact that researchers tend to be specialists. Personality psychologists are expert at constructing scales, but tend to be less concerned with sampling. Sociologists and epidemiologists are meticulous about their sampling strategies, but may have limited knowledge about psychometrics and are often constrained by the time limitations imposed by the interview format they favor. Rarely does a gerontologist combine both sets of skills in looking for age differences, so real progress often depends on collaborative work among many scientists from different disciplines.

A good example is the National Health and Nutrition Examination Survey I Follow-up Study, or NHANES (Cornoni-Huntley et al., 1983). Originally designed to provide basic information on Americans' health, this survey was made the basis for a nationally representative study of aging. Over 10,000 adults ranging in age from 35 to 85 were surveyed between 1981 and 1984; included in the interviews were short scales to measure Neuroticism, Extraversion, and Openness (Costa & McCrae, 1986b).

Figure 2 summarizes the results of cross-sectional analyses for black and white men and women. It is obvious that the lines are essentially flat, showing only trivial declines across five decades. (Because of the huge sample size, even these slight effects are statistically significant.) Data from this representative sample replicate other cross-sectional findings of lower Extraversion among older subjects, but they also underscore the limited magnitude of the age differences. It would be a little foolish to concoct a theory of age and personality around the effects seen in Figure 2.

Agreeableness and Conscientiousness were not included in the NHANES study, so we do not know what pattern they would have shown in a representative sample. Even if the cross-sectional increases in Agreeableness we reviewed earlier had been replicated, however, it could be argued that the effect was the result of another artifact, selective mortality. There are preliminary but intriguing data suggesting that antagonistic hostility is associated with heart disease (Costa et al., 1989): Young and middle-aged men who are very low in Agreeableness appear to be at higher risk for experiencing a heart attack. It is possible, therefore, that Agreeableness is higher among older groups only because

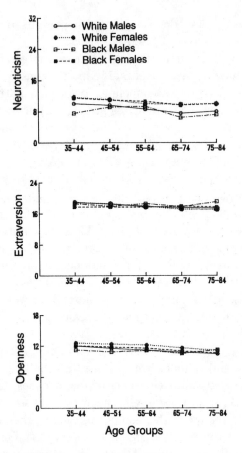

FIGURE 2. Mean levels of Neuroticism, Extraversion, and Openness to Experience for 10-year age groups of white men, black men, white women, and black women, aged from 35 to 84 years. Adapted from Costa et al. (1986).

the most disagreeable members of their generation have already died. Agreeableness itself need not increase with age in order to find a cross-sectional age difference.

Cohort Effects

Spurious age difference in cross-sectional studies can also result from generational or birth-cohort effects. When we make cross-sectional comparisons, we are in effect assuming that the young people of today will eventually come to resemble the current generation of older people. In some respects, such as the increased incidence of baldness, they almost certainly will. But we do not know whether they will also have the same attitudes, same habits, or the same personality as today's elderly. In short, we do not know whether personality is shaped more by aging or by cohort factors, by intrinsic maturation or by the social history of specific generations of people.

In the early days of personality theory, under the influence of Freud's models of development, it was assumed that personality was formed early in life as the result of a complex series of interactions between child and parents. Overly rigorous forms of toilet training and general discipline were held to be the source of fixations, inhibitions, and neuroses in later life. Whereas Freud himself never advocated such a simple relationship, many psychologists, pediatricians, and educators came to the conclusion that we would all be more emotionally healthy if we were given more freedom as children. Dr. Benjamin Spock's (1946) immensely influential writings on child care took a step in this direction, and books such as Neill's (1977) *Summerhill* showed what childhood could be like in an atmosphere of freedom. Over the past half-century, corporal punishment has almost disappeared from schools and has certainly declined in most households. Today, many psychologists and educators are calling for a return to firmer discipline, just as Neill tried to distinguish between "freedom" and "license."

The point is not that today's form of discipline is better or worse than that enjoyed by children 50 years ago: The point is that it is demonstrably different. According to the basic tenets of some forms of personality theory, this difference in the treatment of children ought to have the most dramatic consequences for their adult personality. If child rearing changes across generations and if adult personality depends on child rearing, different generations should show major differences in personality. These differences, however, would reflect not the action of aging but the accident of birth into a particular generation.

This confusion of generational or birth-cohort differences with age changes is not merely hypothetical. There are a number of documented cases in which cohort differences have been shown to be responsible for cross-sectional findings. Bones in the leg, for example, are typically a bit shorter in older men than younger. This is not a maturational effect, however, but a cohort effect (Friedlander et al., 1977). More recent generations of children have had better diets and have as a result grown taller in childhood and adolescence. Somewhat closer to the topic at hand, generational differences have also been shown to account for most of the age differences in vocabulary that have been reported (Schaie & Labouvie-Vief, 1974). Most vocabulary is learned in formal schooling, and today's adults had much more of that than their grandparents did.

If we return to the cross-sectional studies we have reviewed, we may now want to revise our conclusions. Perhaps the consistent decline in Extraversion is the result of changing styles of child rearing. When children were taught to speak only when spoken to, they may have developed lifelong habits of reticence. The formal interactions of children with their parents may have put a permanent damper on interpersonal warmth and spontaneity. Thus, the older generation we see now may be more introverted not because of age, but because of what passed for good breeding a few decades ago. Today's outspoken, uninhibited children may turn out to be outspoken, uninhibited oldsters half a century from now.

On the other hand, it is also possible that very different processes are going on under the camouflage of age differences. If there are such significant changes in child rearing, shouldn't we be seeing many and massive age differences when we compare distant generations? Or is it possible that the absence of consistent age differences is the result not of stability but of equal and opposite effects of aging and cohort? This perplexing idea, which plays a central role in many arguments about aging research, deserves a bit more discussion.

Suppose that, as progressives hope, the change in child-rearing practices over the past 50 years has really had the beneficial effects that it was supposed to: Suppose that today's young adults are mentally and emotionally healthier than the young adults of 1930. Suppose further that, in the process of living and learning how to adapt, all people tend to grow in mental health with the years and to overcome the handicaps of a less-than-optimal upbringing. Then we would say that society as a whole is getting healthier and healthier, as each new generation starts off better, and as each individual, every day in every way, gets better and better. Note that under this optimistic set of assumptions, there would be little evidence of age differences when cross-sectional comparisons were made: The older individuals would have risen from a level of poor mental health to good mental health, but they would not now differ from young adults whose good mental health is the result of enlightened child rearing practices. Thus two major effects on well-being—one linked to socialization, one to aging—could jointly give the appearance of "no differences."

Lest the reader be unduly encouraged by this hypothesis, note that the opposite set of premises could yield the same conclusion. Perhaps what we have seen in the past years is the decline of civilization, a breakdown of discipline that leaves each successive generation with fewer and weaker inner resources. If at the same time aging has the same deleterious effects on mental health as on physical health, then all of us are getting worse with each passing day. And yet, again, a comparison of young with old people would show equal levels of mental health—or, in this case, mental illness.

Alternative interpretations like these are the despair of social scientists and have prompted many to abandon altogether the cross-sectional study. These researchers prefer to study aging as an ongoing process in individuals. They conduct longitudinal research.

LONGITUDINAL DESIGNS: TRACKING CHANGES OVER TIME

Most of the problems associated with cross-sectional studies can be solved by using the other major method of aging research, longitudinal studies. In these, a group of individuals is selected and measured at one time, then followed and measured repeatedly over a period of years, perhaps for decades. In contrast to the age differences estimated by cross-sectional studies, longitudinal studies estimate age *changes*. That is, they can see directly how the individuals under study have changed and at what point the changes occur. (As we will see, this does not necessarily mean that the changes are *caused by* aging.)

The major appeal of the longitudinal design is its ability to separate changes from generational effects. People only live once. They may absorb in their youth the characteristic tone of their generation, but having done so, they retain it for life. Longitudinal changes cannot be the result of generational differences, nor is there much evidence to suggest that individuals of different generations change in different ways or at different rates, at least with regard to personality.

In contrast to the hundreds of cross-sectional studies, there are only a handful of longitudinal studies of adult personality. The reasons should be clear: It is extremely difficult to keep track of people over a period of many years, and the rewards of longitudinal research are remote. In fact, virtually all the studies to be reported demonstrate the altruism of a set of foresighted scientists who began the measurement of personality in studies others would eventually report.

These studies vary considerably in the kinds of individuals studied, the methods and instruments used to measure personality, and the intervals at which measurements were made. They are quite consistent, however, in their conclusions: There is little or no evidence of longitudinal change in personality characteristics in the period of adulthood, from 30 to 80 years of age. Let us turn to some of the specifics. We will review longitudinal analyses of the 16PF because the results are typical, and because the existence of two independent studies makes informative comparisons possible.

Stability in the 16PF

Our early research on aging and personality was conducted in conjunction with a longitudinal program sponsored by the Veterans Administration in Boston, the Normative Aging Study (Costa & McCrae, 1978). The participants in this project are 2,000 men, mostly veterans, ranging in age from 25 to 90 years. Most are white, and long-term residents of the Boston area. Although there are relatively few individuals from the lowest socioeconomic levels, there is a reasonable representation of subjects with a high school education and beyond. Of course, as in all such studies, the participants are volunteers; in this case they have volunteered to return to the clinic every 5 years for tests. They also complete questionnaires mailed to them at home as the need arises. In addition to medical examinations, the men have been given occasional assessments of personality and cognitive abilities. Between 1965 and 1967 about half the participants were given Cattell's 16PF.

In 1975, we readministered a form of the 16PF to a group of 139 men, originally aged 25 to 82. Among other things we were interested in seeing if there were systematic declines or increases in the traits measured by the 16PF. Of the 16 scales, two, intelligence and social independence, were significantly higher at the second administration; 14 showed no evidence of change over the 10-year interval studied. Tension, adventurousness, liberal thinking, tender-mindedness, and superego strength—among other traits—neither increased nor decreased for the average man in this sample. In retrospect, we view this as the major finding of the study. At the time, however, we were as curious as everyone else about the changes. The scales that absorbed our attention were the two that changed. But as we examined our findings in detail, it became clear that they were probably *not* the elusive age changes we had been seeking.

In 1975 the participants scored higher on measures of intellectual brightness and social independence. We suspect the increase in intelligence scores was probably a matter of testing. When people are given the same test twice, they tend to do better the second time, even though they are not actually any more intelligent—this is known as a practice effect. In addition, the test was given at the laboratory on the first occasion, under timed conditions; in 1975, the men completed the test at home, at their own pace. Allowing more time may have improved scores. We concluded that it was unlikely that the men had actually become more intelligent with age. In any case, we do not regard intelligence as an aspect of personality, and we leave it to our colleagues in cognitive aging to chart the course of mental abilities in adulthood.

The longitudinal change in the social independence scale was more puzzling. For one thing, there were no cross-sectional differences in this trait. That probably meant that, if real longitudinal changes were taking place, they were not showing up in cross-sectional comparisons because they were somehow obscured by generational differences. It is precisely because of the possibility of such confusions that researchers turn to longitudinal designs; when they find evidence of them, however, it is usually an unpleasant surprise. We were faced with the prospect of explaining not only why individuals became less dependent on the approval of social groups as they aged, but also why different generations (or, as we will see, times of measurement) also influenced this variable.

Before exerting our creativity in looking for an explanation of this curious finding, we should be sure there is really something here to explain. The fundamental principle of science is reproducibility: A phenomenon must be dependable, regardless of how or by whom it is observed. Few phenomena in the psychological sciences show the invariance of the laws of physics, because our constructs are more abstract and less easily and accurately measured. But we have a right to demand that results be generally replicable—that most investigators will report the same general findings and that we can show them ourselves using different measures or different groups of people. The fact is that many so-called findings in psychology are the results of chance, and even the statistical methods that psychologists adopt do not protect them from drawing the wrong conclusions once in a while. One alternative, therefore, is to ascribe the longitudinal change in social independence to pure chance. The finding may be meaningless, a fluke.

There is some basis for thinking that this might be so. Social independence is an aspect of introversion, and our finding might be taken as evidence that individuals become more introverted with age—an interpretation that supports some theories of aging. But the 16PF also has several scales that tap other forms of Extraversion, and none of these other scales showed a similar change in our sample. If we wanted to find evidence of change (as many developmentalists do), we might argue that independence happens to be the only aspect of Extraversion that shows maturational change. In principle there is nothing wrong with this hypothesis. If all Extraversion scales behaved identically, there would be no reason to measure them separately. But notice that in order to claim this longitudinal change as an age effect, we have to make two rather cumbersome assumptions: first, that the maturational changes do not show up in cross-sectional studies because of some mysterious confounding of generational differences with age changes; and second, that there is something special about independence that distinguishes it from other, closely related scales that show neither the maturational changes nor the generational differences. Possible, but unlikely.

Fortunately, there is a much more direct way to find out if this was a chance result. An independent longitudinal study carried on at Duke University over a period of 8 years also employed the 16PF, although in a slightly shorter, simplified form (Siegler et al., 1979). Researchers there looked for age changes and differences in a sample of men and women initially over 46 years old, who represented not only a different geographical region but also a somewhat broader range of socioeconomic status. These researchers also reported that their subjects improved on the second testing of intelligence, but they found neither cross-sectional differences nor longitudinal changes in social independence. Thus, the apparent decline in Extraversion is not replicated across methods (it is found in longitudinal, but not cross-sectional analyses), facets (social independence, but not other Extraversion scales), or samples (Boston but not Duke). Since replication is the foundation of scientific inference, the case for change in that personality trait seems closed.

The Duke investigators also reported an anomalous finding: Although there were no cross-sectional differences in guilt-proneness, a scale that measures an aspect of Neuroticism, they found that with time men tended to score lower and women higher on this scale. None of the other Neuroticism scales showed the same pattern, nor did the men in the Boston study become less guilt-prone with age. Again, we conclude that this finding can best be ascribed to chance.

Most importantly the Duke study confirmed the Boston study in finding overwhelming evidence of stability. It found no longitudinal changes in the degrees to which subjects were outgoing, emotionally stable, assertive, happy-go-lucky, conscientious, adventurous, tender-minded, suspicious, imaginative, shrewd, liberal-thinking, independent, controlled, or tense.

SEQUENTIAL STRATEGIES: AVOIDING PRACTICE AND TIME EFFECTS

Longitudinal methods, we have pointed out, are free from some of the problems of cross-sectional studies, but they have other problems of their own. One of these we have already encountered in discussing the changes in intelligence seen in the Boston and Duke studies. When individuals take the same test repeatedly, they may answer differently simply as a result of exposure to the test. When an ability test is in question, this is called a *practice effect,* and that term has also been used to describe other effects of repeated measurement. For example, people may find a personality test less threatening the second time and give more candid answers. Or they may find it boring and become careless. These differences might show up as "longitudinal changes" when the results of the first and second tests are compared, even though they have nothing to do with the aging process.

On the other hand, some critics have pointed out that individuals often like to give an impression of consistency. They may recall what they said the first time when asked to respond again, and they may try to give the same answers. This would give the impression of stability even in the face of real change.

Test makers are painfully aware of this problem, and have come up with a few partial solutions. One is to use a different but similar test the second time—a so-called parallel form. This is the solution adopted, for example, by the Educational Testing Service when students take the Scholastic Aptitude Test on more than one occasion. Since each test is different in content, there is no direct possibility of remembering the questions and figuring out the answers between tests. But most students will score a little higher the second time they take the test, probably because they feel more comfortable with the process. Parallel-form testing is not a perfect solution.

If we are really concerned with the growth and change of a particular individual, the problem of practice effects is unavoidable. But if we are only interested in finding out whether people change with age, an alternative strategy has been advocated by a number of prominent developmental methodologists (Schaie, 1977; Baltes et al., 1977). Suppose we take a random sample of individuals born in 1900 and randomly divide them into two groups. We know from the laws of statistics that, if we have a large enough sample, the two halves are unlikely to be different on any variable we choose to measure; they are equally representative of the population of men and women born in 1900. Next, suppose we measure the personality of the first group in 1960, but do nothing to the second group. If we return in 1980 to measure the first group, we will have the standard longitudinal design, and we will never quite know if the differences we find (or fail to find) are the result of aging or of practice effects. However, if in 1980 we measure the *second* group and compare it with the first group as measured in 1960, the difference cannot be the result of practice (because the second group has never taken the test) and may therefore be a consequence of aging itself. (Incidentally, if we measure both groups in 1980, we can compare changes for the groups with and without practice and so estimate what the pure practice effects are. That is extremely useful information for other investigators who need to know whether they should worry about practice effects or whether they can safely ignore them.)

This design, in which different individuals born at the same time are measured at two or more different times, is known as a "cross-sequential design with independent samples," or, as we will call it, a *cross-sequential design*. Douglas and Arenberg (1978) reported cross-sequential analyses on the GZTS scales. Their two samples were collected at successive intervals (1958 to 1968, and 1968 to 1974), making this kind of analysis possible. Their second sample scored lower than their first on Emotional Stability, Personal Relations, and Masculinity, suggesting an increase in Neuroticism. Note that this finding appears to contradict the small cross-sectional decline in Neuroticism shown in Figure 2. None of the other GZTS scales showed significant cross-sequential effects.

A related design is called *time-sequential:* Here individuals of the same age are measured at different times. Sixty-year-olds, for example, might be surveyed in 1960 and in 1980. The differences could not be caused by aging itself, since both groups are the same age. They could, however, be the result of generational differences, since the 60-year-olds of 1960 were born at the turn of the century, whereas the 60-year-olds of 1980 were born in 1920. A great deal of ingenuity went into the invention of these designs, and they elegantly solve some of the vexing problems of aging research. But they too are ambiguous, for a reason that has not yet been mentioned.

Take as an example attitudes toward women. Suppose we had asked a national sample of 20-year-olds in 1960 if they believed that women should have their own career, freedom of choice in family planning, or the right to participate in professional sports. Relatively few would have endorsed these aspirations. But if we asked the same questions of a different group from the same cohort (now 40-year-olds) in 1980, we can anticipate that a much larger proportion would agree (Costa & McCrae, 1982). We know this is not a cohort effect, or generational difference, since all these individuals were born in the same year. We know it is not a practice effect, since the respondents in our second sample have never been interviewed before. But surely we would not conclude that it was an aging effect, that individuals adopt increasingly liberal attitudes toward women as they grow older. It is more likely that we would insist the *times* had changed and almost everyone had modified opinions on these issues as a result of the Women's Movement. This would be a clear example of what is known as a *time-of-measurement effect.*

Pollsters are as plagued by time-of-measurement problems as educators are by practice effects. Some theorists (Baltes & Nesselroade, 1972) have claimed that these problems are less crucial to personality investigators, because personality is unlikely to be shifted by temporary historical movements or swings in attitude. Perhaps so, perhaps not. In view of how little we know about adult personality, many would argue that it is not safe to make that assumption. What we need is a design that avoids the problems of the cross-sequential design—one that can compare people at different ages but in which we can rule out the possibility that time of measurement is responsible for the apparent effect. Is there any way to do this?

There is one way. We can eliminate time-of-measurement effects (and practice effects) if we measure all our subjects once, at one time. Of course, in order to see the effects of age, we would have to measure simultaneously individuals of different age groups. And this, lo and behold, is nothing other than the cross-sectional design with which we started. We have come full circle.

This curious circumambulation has bedeviled researchers for years and left the field in some perplexity. A number of additional designs of greater complexity have been proposed to break out of the circle, but astute critics have always been able to weave them back in. The fact is that individuals are always born in one and only one generation, and they always grow older during a certain historical period when things are changing in a certain way and to a certain degree. Short of cloning people to raise them in different circumstances, we find no way out of the dilemma. Time, cohort, and aging are inextricably confounded.

AN INTEGRATED APPROACH

We might at this point abandon all hope and move to another field of study. Alternatively we can adopt a more constructive point of view (Costa & McCrae, 1982). Although there is no way to be sure that we interpret an effect correctly, there are ways to improve our chances. For example, when we see the same direction and magnitude of an effect in cross-sectional, cross-sequential, and longitudinal studies, it becomes highly likely that a real aging effect has been found. Exactly this pattern is found when analyses of health problems are conducted (Costa & McCrae, 1980b). All types of analyses pointed to an increased frequency in men of sensory, genitourinary, and cardiovascular complaints with age. These results are hardly surprising, but they do demonstrate that the analyses work when a true maturational effect is there to be found.

The Douglas and Arenberg study of GZTS scales and a more recent study of NEO-PI scales provide examples of the kinds of inference that can be made when multiple analyses are conducted in the same sample.

Longitudinal analyses of the GZTS showed that 5 of the 10 scales declined between the first administration and the second, some 7 years later. But the results of other analyses indicated that only two of these were likely to be aging effects. Thoughtfulness and personal relations shared a pattern of effects in longitudinal, cross-sequential, and time-sequential designs, but not in the cross-sectional analysis. The longitudinal effect may have been the result of aging, time, or practice; the cross-sequential of aging or time; and the time-sequential of cohort or time. The one common element in the three designs is time of measurement, so it seems likely that, during the decade of the 1960s, participants become less thoughtful and less trusting of others. This line of reasoning is confirmed by the failure to find any cross-sectional differences in thoughtfulness or personal relations: When everyone is measured at the same time, there are no age or cohort differences.

Friendliness shows a more complex pattern. Like thoughtfulness and personal relations, it declined in the three designs that share time of measurement as an effect, but it also showed a cross-sectional *increase*. Douglas and Arenberg (1978) interpreted this as evidence not of maturation, but of long-term cultural change: "successive cohorts and individuals became more easily aroused to hostility and tended to be less agreeable" (p. 745). Certainly we would want to see replications of this finding before accepting it as valid.

Only two traits survived this screening: masculinity and activity level, both of which declined with age in cross-sectional, longitudinal, and cross-sequential designs, but showed no effect in the time-sequential analysis. Results were just what one would expect if there were maturational changes in masculinity and activity, and the only alternative explanations involved complicated and improbable combinations of practice, time of measurement, and cohort effects.

However, the changes in both activity level and masculinity on the GZTS are extremely small. For the statistician, the statement that they amount to about one-eighth of a standard deviation over 7 years communicates that point. For others, another comparison may make it more forcefully. The observed rate of decrease in masculinity was 0.41 items every 6.6 years. We once computed that at this rate it would take our older subjects, initially 75 years old, 136 years to reach the same level of femininity as the average college woman. Psychologists may speak of the feminization of older men, but the reader should recall that the process would be fully completed only if men lived 211 years!

Even more extensive analyses were conducted on NEO-PI scales in a 6-year longitudinal study of 983 men and women ranging in age from 21 to 96 (Costa & McCrae, 1988b). In addition to self-reports, we conducted some parallel analyses on spouse rating of 167 men and women. (Because we had spouse ratings of A and C only at the second time period, we were unable to do longitudinal analyses on these scales; and because we did not recruit a new sample of spouse raters, we were not able to conduct cross-sequential analyses of ratings.) The results of cross-sectional, longitudinal, and cross-sequential analyses are summarized in Table 7. In this table, minus signs suggest a decline with age, plus signs an increase, and zeros no effect; stronger effects are indicated by more signs. However, none of the effects accounts for as much as 10% of the variance in personality scores; age and aging are weakly related to personality at best.

Although it might appear that there are several age effects, a closer inspection of the table shows very little *consistent* evidence of maturational effects—indeed, not a single scale shows unequivocal evidence of change. Total Neuroticism, for example appears to decline in cross-sectional analyses of both self-reports and spouse ratings. It also declines over time in self-reports. But according to husbands and wives, rated Neuroticism actually increased over the 6-year period! No effect was seen in the cross-sequential analyses.

All the other studies we have discussed—and almost all in the literature—are based on self-reports, and systematic biases in self-reports might account for the general lack of age changes reported. It could be argued that external observers may more accurately perceive and report true aging effects. The analyses of spouse ratings summarized in Table 7, however, confirm the absence of strong and clear maturational effects for the three domains of Neuroticism, Extraversion, and Openness. Longitudinal studies of Agreeableness and Conscientiousness using spouse or peer ratings are still needed, but results from other domains give us no reason to distrust self-reports.

TABLE 7. *Age Effects from Analyses of NEO-PI Domain Scales*

	Cross-sectional		Longitudinal		Cross-sequential
NEO-PI Scale	Self-report	Spouse rating	Self-report	Spouse rating	Self-report
Neuroticism	− −	− − −	−	+	0
Extraversion	− − −	− − −	0	0	+
Openness	− − −	− −	0	0	+
Agreeableness	+	0	− − −		− − −
Conscientiousness	0	+ + +	−		−

Note. Minus signs indicate a negative assocation of the variable with age; plus signs indicate a positive association. Effects accounting for less than 2% of the variance are marked with one sign; those accounting for 2% to 5% are marked with two signs; and those accounting for more than 5% are marked with three signs. Zeros indicate nonsignificant effects. Longitudinal analyses of Agreeableness and Conscientiousness were conducted only for self-reports. Adapted from Costa & McCrae (1988b).

It is worth considering what different conclusions would be drawn if the different analyses summarized in Table 7 had been done in separate studies. The researchers who conducted cross-sectional studies would have reported decreases in N, E, and O and increases in A and C; the researchers who conducted the cross-sequential analyses would have found increases in E and O and declines in A and C! Neither set of conclusions would have been replicated by the longitudinal researchers. The moral seems to be that so many factors—sampling, cohort differences, practice effects, time of measurement artifacts, selective mortality—affect results that most so-called aging effects are probably spurious. Only when several types of evidence are considered together can reasonable conclusions be drawn.

One consistent pattern was found when the facets of N, E, and O were separately analyzed. NEO-PI Activity showed evidence of decline in four of the five analyses. Because another scale measuring this trait also showed declines in the Douglas and Arenberg (1978) study, it seems reasonable to conclude that as people age, there is a maturational decline in the pace and vigor of life. However, here too the effect is small and does not outweigh other sources of individual differences. Many 70-year-olds are more active than many 30-year-olds.

As this chapter makes clear, the simple question of "What happens with age?" is far from easy to answer. In many areas of gerontology, the separation of cohort, time of measurement, and practice effects from true maturational changes may require a lifetime of work. In personality, the problem is greatly simplified by the nature of the variables studied. No matter how you view it, the only consistent evidence points to predominant stability. With age, adults as a group neither increase nor decrease much in any of the traits identified by major personality instruments.

IMPLICATIONS: DEBUNKING SOME MYTHS OF AGING

What does the evidence of stability in personality mean for our view of aging? For some reason, when we say we find no evidence of growth or decline in personality, people hear only "no growth" and regard us as the bearers of bad news. But there is good news here, too. Perhaps it is unfortunate that people do not continue to grow and develop in adulthood, but surely it is reassuring to find that they do not decline. In view of popular and prevalent conceptions of aging, this is by far the more important implication.

In the past few years socially conscious individuals have attempted to create positive stereotypes of aging, reminding us that the aged are revered in many cultures for their experience and wisdom. Octogenerian musicians and actors and artists are showered with honors, and their current productions are uncritically acclaimed. In many ways, this new-found respect for the aged is just compensation for decades of neglect. But it often seems that there is something condescending and infantalizing about the status we grant them, as if the elderly needed special consideration. Skinner (1983) noted that the mindless veneration with which the ideas of older scholars and scientists are received reinforces platitudinous thinking and contributes to a decline in creativity.

We might even suspect that many people bend over backwards to think well of the elderly because at a deeper level they fear that age is nothing but decline. There are real losses in physical strength and vigor, in sexual interest, and in certain intellectual abilities, for which it is necessary to make allowances. But there are no significant declines in personality.

We need not worry that we will become crotchety and hypochondriacal with age, or that only firm resignation can save us from despair and the fear of death. We need not anticipate increasing social isolation and emotional withdrawal from the world. There is no reason to think that our interests will atrophy or that our values and opinions will become increasingly rigid and conservative.

And just as we need not dread our own future, so we need not pity others who have already reached an advanced age. The elderly are no more emotionally vulnerable or ideologically rigid than anyone else, and giving them special treatment in these areas is unnecessary and probably unwise. Older individuals are entitled to all the respect due any human being, but genuine respect means seeing them as they really are. With regard to personality they are no different from any other adults.

*   *   *

We contrasted longitudinal with cross-sectional studies by pointing out that the former traces development over time in the same individuals. And yet we have not presented data from a single individual so far; only from groups of individuals averaged at two points in time. Surely out of a large group of people there must be some who change: a few who learn and grow from their experiences, a few who fall into dispair or stagnation. Age does not bring universal decline or growth in personality traits, but perhaps it brings idiosyncratic changes that mirror the unique life courses of aging men and women. Longitudinal studies can address such questions, but only with a different kind of analysis. We turn to these issues next.

·5·

THE COURSE OF PERSONALITY
IN THE INDIVIDUAL

We have used the word *stability* repeatedly with the assumption that its meaning is obvious. But in fact, stability has several meanings, and a discussion of them is a necessary prologue to a fuller look at the data on personality and aging. Different kinds of statistical tests and sometimes different methods of collecting data are necessary when one is looking for different types of stability and change. Some kinds of stability are frankly uninteresting; others form the basis for a whole new way of thinking about the course of human lives.

*Two Different Questions: Stability and Change in Groups
and in Individuals*

In Chapter 4 we reviewed at some length the evidence of stability of mean levels of personality traits. In the simplest case, the cross-sectional study, we found that old people generally scored neither higher nor lower than young people on a variety of personality measures. This failure to find change in personality contrasts with the evidence of age-related changes in a number of functions. In childhood, for example, intelligence, vocabulary, and physical size and strength obviously increase through adolesence. In later adulthood, declines in strength, memory, and hearing are equally well documented. Most personality traits, on the other hand, do not show a pattern of rising or falling as people age.

In all these examples, whether of change or stability, we are comparing the average levels of groups of individuals. There are good reasons for concentrating on the average (or mean) level of a trait when we are interested in the effects of age. We know that most traits show a wide distribution, with some individuals high, some low, and many inter-mediate in the degree to which they manifest the trait. We can rarely make assertions of the form "All 80-year olds are higher in X than all 70-year-olds." If a psychologist is careless enough to say that old people have poor memories, he or she is sure to hear dozens of stories about old people with good memories or young people with worse ones. When so pressed, the psychologist is likely to rephrase the statement to say that, *on the average*, old people have poorer memories. "Of course," he might continue, "some people have better memories, some worse; they may have been born that way, or they may have developed skills through practice or education. Medications or illnesses or psychological states may interfere with memory performance. But I'm not interested in any of those things. I'm interested in the effects of age on memory. So my strategy is to measure a large group of people, some old, some young. Some of the old ones will be naturally bright, some naturally not so bright; some will be well-educated, some poorly educated. When I look at the group average, all those differences will cancel each other out. The only thing all these people have in common, and thus the only thing that will be characteristic of the group average, is the fact that they are older. The same logic applies to the young group. When I compare the average older subject with the average younger subject, any differences must be due to age."

We have already challenged the assumption that the only respect in which two such groups differed systematically was age, pointing out that they might well also differ in average education, health status, or other features. But if we can assume that those other characteristics have been controlled through a careful selection of subjects, the logic of cross-sectional comparisons is sound. Individual differences in memory are attributable either to age or to some other factors. The interest in studies of this sort is always in age as a source of individual differences; other differences are something of a nuisance, a source of possible confusion. In statistical models, they contribute to what is called an *error term*. In fact, if everyone started out with the exactly the same capacity for memory, it would be much easier to see the effects of age.

But people do not start off with the same abilities, just as they do not start off with the same levels of anxiety or assertiveness or openness to ideas. In early adulthood we find wide variation in all the personality traits of interest to us. We find the same range of differences among old people. We know from the studies in Chapter 4 that people on the average do not change much during adulthood; but so far we have said very little about what *individuals* do. Ms. Smith may be docile and traditional as a newlywed, but 30 years later she may have become assertive and unconventional. Mr. Jones may be interested in automotive mechanics and sports during his twenties, but be devoted to Bible readings by the time he is sixty. Then again, Ms. Smith may still be docile and traditional and Mr. Jones still interested in sports when both are past 70.

This is a question of stability or change not of a group of people, but of individuals. The study of changes in individuals is considerably more complicated and correspondingly more interesting than the study of changes in groups. If the group as a whole changes, we can be sure that at least some of the individuals have changed, but the converse is not necessarily true. The average level of the group may not be altered even though *all* the individuals change—if, for example, there are as many who increase as decrease. Finding out that groups are stable, then, does not rule out the possibility that individuals change; and, in fact, a number of fascinating possibilities for individual development are consistent with the findings of group stability.

There is a major methodological difference between the study of groups and the study of individuals. To make inferences about mean changes with age, we need only compare groups of different ages (provided we can be relatively sure they do not differ in any other characteristics). Any two groups of people will do, so the cross-sectional design is a convenient, if not foolproof, method of obtaining a quick answer. We need not wait for the passage of time.

But a study of individual changes requires that we examine the same person at two or more ages: Longitudinal studies with repeated measurements of the same subjects are essential. As a result, the evidence available on which to base conclusions is much slimmer, and of much more recent vintage. Only in the past decade have more than a handful of studies been published in which longitudinal data on personality were reported. Fortunately, all these studies have been in substantial agreement, and so we can draw our conclusions with considerable confidence.

There is, however, one approach in this area that parallels the cross-sectional study as a quick method of seeing what changes occur to an

individual over the life span. In the retrospective study, people are asked
to recall what they were like at earlier ages and compare their present
state. On the whole, psychologists have been extremely leery of this kind
of research (e.g., Halverson, 1988). Memory, they maintain, has ways of
playing tricks on people. In fact, a number of studies have shown that
people can and do distort the past, whether consciously or not. Many
more people, for example, "remember" voting for the winning candidate
than election results could possibly allow. There has been very little
research comparing memories of earlier personality with actual records.
However, the recent harvest of longitudinal findings allows us to compare retrospective reports with objective facts. As we will see, they
suggest that conclusions based on retrospective reports generally square
with prospective longitudinal findings.

DEVELOPMENTAL PATTERNS IN INDIVIDUALS

Although most personality theorists assume that adult personality is in
some way an outgrowth or developmental continuation of earlier personality, other views are also possible. We have already encountered (and,
we hope, countered) the critical view that wholly denies the reality of
personality, assigning to it the status of a social myth or a metaphysical
existence like that of the soul. So elusive and insubstantial an entity
could hardly be said either to change or to stay the same, and the whole
issue would be banished from the realm of scientific inquiry. A more
moderate position might hold that personality is like mood—a real
enough phenomenon, but one that comes and goes according to laws so
obscure that it seems completely random. Finally, a number of contemporary psychologists would probably conceptualize personality as
largely a function of the recent environment. They might see Extraversion, for example, as a set of learned responses to social situations. One's
environment may change radically as one goes from parents' home to
college to one work situation and then another and finally to a retirement
home. In some of these situations the person may be rewarded for
friendliness, leadership, and energetic behavior. In others, independence,
compliance, or quiet may be preferred and reinforced. After months or
years in such circumstances, the individual may come to internalize the
system of rewards and punishments, to assume the qualities promoted by
the environment. Personality may change.

Note that this kind of change is not necessarily age-related. Chance may play a large role (Bandura, 1982). What are neighbors like? What jobs are available? What does the family expect, and what are the effects of remarriage or of having or losing children? Conceivably one might be an introvert at 20, 40, and 60 and an extravert at 30, 50, and 70. Later personality might not be predictable at all from earlier personality. If there were any continuity in personality, it could be attributed to the stability of supporting environments. If the life structure remains the same, personality will too; but a change in the first could lead to a change in the second.

This extreme environmentalist position, compatible with older versions of social learning theory, is appealing neither to personality theorists nor developmentalists. It locates the origin of behavior in external circumstances, temporarily internalized, but easily replaced when circumstances change. Personality psychologists like to believe that personality is an intrinsic part of the person, changeable perhaps, but not quite so readily and with so little regard for the qualities that the individual brings to his or her exchanges with the environment. Developmentalists would also take exception to the social learning view, since they see personality as something that unfolds more or less naturally, each phase an outgrowth of earlier developments. Personality is something with a history, they would say, not simply a mirror of current events.

Of course, the fact that the environmentalist view of personality is distasteful to those interested in personality and aging does not in the least mean that it is wrong. Ten years ago, in fact, a majority of psychologists would probably have said that it was correct (many still would). At that time there were few studies that could really address the issue, but a number have since appeared.

True or false, the environmentalist view is certainly less beguiling than developmental theories, with their sometimes elaborate chains of growth, unfolding, and transformation. Central to the idea of development is the notion of *continuity:* In any developmental sequence, a single organism goes through a series of changes, each an expression of the same underlying entity. The butterfly is the natural outgrowth of the caterpillar, as different as the two are in form and function. The environment may hasten or retard, facilitate or damage the transformation, but caterpillars will never turn into spiders no matter what environments we impose on them. The same basic genetic material endures through and is manifest in successive stages of development.

Most of the theorizing about the course of personality in the individual has been offered by child developmentalists (Block & Block, 1980; Kagan & Moss, 1962; Thomas et al., 1968) interested in accounting for personality from the period of infancy through adolescence, although a few theorists have carried the idea through adulthood. The attempt to account for the origins of personality in childhood is immensely attractive, since childhood seems to be the time when the most could be done to change or improve lifelong patterns of adjustment. At the same time, it is an extraordinarily ambitious undertaking. It is easy enough to chart the course of Extraversion, say, in an adult: Simply have him or her fill out a questionnaire every 10 years or so. But we cannot ask a 5 year old to complete a questionnaire; we cannot ask an infant even a few simple questions. How, then, do we measure personality?—by observations of behavior? What kind of infant behavior corresponds to openness to aesthetic experience? Is it even meaningful to ask about this dimension of personality before adolescence?

Fortunately, we do not need to solve these problems here. Other writers, more knowledgeable in the area, have struggled with them and offered their own answers. The issue concerns us here, however, because the same answers may be useful in conceptualizing the course of personality in adulthood.

One of the more elaborate models has been labeled *heterotypic* (or *different-form*) *continuity* (Kagan, 1971). Just as an insect goes through four distinct but developmentally related stages, so too may personality evolve through a succession of distinct phases. Sociability in adulthood may be the consequence not of sociability in childhood, but of some very different trait—say, academic interests. If we watched an unsociable but intellectual child develop into a warm and friendly adult, we might believe that we had seen a failure of continuity. But if we watched a whole group of intellectual children become sociable adults, we would believe we had discovered a pattern, a kind of dispositional metamorphosis. (We might then attempt to explain the transformation: Perhaps the social advantages of a good education lead to a more congenial environment in adulthood, making the person more friendly. Or perhaps both academic pursuits in childhood and sociability in adulthood reflect an underlying tendency to please significant others in one's life. Speculations on what might account for such relationships are endless and endlessly intriguing, which may account for the popularity of this model with many developmentalists.) Almost any trait in childhood might develop into almost any other; and of course the changes need not be limited to childhood. Young adults may develop into older adults with quite different, but quite predictable, sets of traits (Livson, 1973).

For a time—before additional data disillusioned us—we thought we had found just such a pattern (Costa & McCrae, 1976). In looking at cross-sectional data on several aspects of openness to experience, we seemed to see a shift in the aspects of experience to which open men were open. In young men, when youthful romanticism was at its peak, openness was expressed as a sensitivity to feelings and to aesthetic experiences. In middle age, when the responsibilities of raising a family and furthering a career were uppermost, the same openness was seen in a more intellectual form, of which curiosity and a willingness to reformulate traditional values were the hallmarks. Finally, in the wisdom of old age, the open person was sensitized to both feelings and thoughts, both beauty and truth. Since differentiation and subsequent integration are familiar developmental processes (Werner, 1948), this sequence seemed to provide a classic case of personality development in adulthood.

We had to abandon this model soon after we proposed it, because we found that later and better data offered no support for it whatsoever. Individuals who are open to feelings and aesthetic experiences tend also to be open to ideas and values (and actions and fantasy) at *all* ages in adulthood. This is as true for women as for men, our later studies showed (McCrae & Costa, 1983a). Age, it now appears, has nothing to do with it.

The heterotypic continuity model has most frequently been discussed by researchers interested in personality development in early childhood, when observable behavior (such as the smiles or cries of an infant) may bear only the vaguest resemblance to later personality traits such as sociability or anxiety. Its use there may or may not be justified—a good deal more research is needed before we will know for certain.

One version, however, is familiar to students of adult personality development. As we noted in the Chapter 1, Jung (1923/1971, 1933) proposed one of the first models of adult personality development as part of his vast and intricate psychology of personality. Instead of traits, he described various functions or structures in the psyche that governed the flow of behavior and experience. The anima and animus, for example, are parts of the self corresponding to the feminine part of the man, the masculine part of the woman. Thought and feeling, sensation and intuition are functions of the mind for perceiving and evaluating reality. The persona is the part of our personality we show to others; the shadow, the part we conceal. All these and more form the self; and the goal of adult life is the full development and expression—the individuation—of the self.

For Jung, most of these functions and structures are opposites and cannot operate simultaneously. We cannot at once be masculine and feminine, intuitive and logical, courteous and contemptuous. If all these are to be expressed, they will have to take turns. Jung proposed that this balancing process would take a lifetime; he hypothesized that the functions that dominated youth would be replaced by their opposites in old age. The aggressive, forceful young man would become docile and passive with age; the passive young woman would become aggressive. Gutmann (1970), you may recall, proposed this particular transformation as a general rule.

It is somewhat hazardous to suppose that the functions hypothesized by Jung correspond to anything as straightforward as traits, but the notion of balancing might easily be applied to them. Instead of supposing, as the heterotypic continuity model does, that any trait may give rise to any other trait, we might suppose that each trait will lead into its own opposite. We can then predict what an individual's personality will be like in old age by reversing the characteristics seen in youth. Introvert will be extravert, open will be closed, agreeable will be antagonistic.

Finally, there is one more model, one more possible developmental sequence: There may be no change at all. Depressed youth may become depressed elderly; talkative oldsters may once have been talkative youngsters. It may seem strange to speak of development when there is no change, so perhaps this should be distinguished as a personological rather than a developmental model. But it shares with developmental schemes the central notion of continuity. Personality, according to this theory, is not at the mercy of the immediate environment; indeed, it withstands all the shocks of life and of aging. Catastrophic events—illnesses, wars, great losses—may alter personality, as may effective therapeutic intervention. But according to stability theory, the natural course of personality in adulthood is unchanging.

INVESTIGATING THE COURSE OF PERSONALITY TRAITS

Cross-sectional studies of personality traits tell us nothing at all about their natural histories. For that, we must trace the levels of traits through the lives of aging individuals. If we are interested in formulating general principles and not simply writing individual biographies, we have to have data from reasonably large samples of individuals. And if we have enough information to draw valid conclusions, we probably have too much to be able to understand it by simply inspecting it with the unaided mind. We have to resort to statistical summaries of the data, and of these the most important for the present purpose is the correlation coefficient.

The correlation coefficient, which expresses the direction and strength of the association between two variables as a number between −1.0 and +1.0, is fundamental to trait psychology, being used to express reliability and validity and forming the basis for factor analysis. It also provides the basic metric of personality stability: A stability coefficient is simply the correlation of a measure administered at one time with the same measure administered at a later time. (Note that this is also the operational definition of a retest reliability coefficient, although this latter term is usually used when the retest interval is a matter of days or weeks rather than years. We will return later to conceptual differences between the two coefficients and some implications for estimating true stability.)

Although they are familiar, correlation coefficients can be difficult to interpret. What, for example, is a high or good or impressive or strong correlation? What is moderate? What modest or weak? These disarmingly simple questions are the source of profound controversy in psychology. Being human, researchers tend to consider the correlations that support their point of view "strong," and the correlations that support other positions "weak." Even the most unbiased judgment, however, must somehow take into account a range of considerations, including the expected magnitude of association, the size of correlations typically found in that field of research, the relative size of other correlations, and the reliability of the measuring instruments.

In a few cases standards have become generally accepted. Reliability coefficients for personality tests, for example, are supposed to be in the vicinity of .70 to .90; most researchers would look askance at a test whose internal consistency was .40. In the prediction of behavior from a personality test, on the other hand, .40 would be quite respectable. One statistician, Jacob Cohen (1969), offered his expectations for psychological research in a set of rules-of-thumb: .10 is weak, .30 is moderate, and .50 or better is a strong correlation. It may be useful to the reader to consider a few familiar examples. The correlation of aptitude tests with college grades is about .40 to .60 (Edwards, 1954); height and weight show a correlation of roughly .70 (Peatman, 1947); and self-reports of anxiety and depression correlate about .60 in the BLSA.

If we obtain a set of measurements of personality traits and several years later measure the same set of people once more on the same set of traits, we would have the minimum information necessary to begin to evaluate the alternative theoretical positions we have described above. From the correlation of each trait at the first time with each trait at the second, we could test quite specific hypotheses about personality development.

If the environmentalist position is correct in positing that personality is freely reshaped by changing circumstances, there should be little or no correlation between any of the traits at the first time and any of the traits at the second. If sufficient time has elapsed to allow many individuals in the sample to move, change jobs, marry, or have children, we should expect substantial change in personality for many people in unpredictable directions. Thus, personality at Time 2 should be unrelated to personality at Time 1. We might expect modest correlations (say .30) between corresponding traits at the two times because some individuals would have remained in the same environments, which might have sustained the traits.

The heterotypic continuity model would predict high correlations somewhere, but it might not be possible to predict just where they would occur. Extraversion at Time 1 might be strongly correlated at Time 2 with Openness or with Agreeableness or with Conscientiousness. The distinctive feature of this model is that we would *not* expect Extraversion at Time 1 to be correlated chiefly with Extraversion at Time 2. It is principally for this reason that we would not want to conduct a study in which *only* Extraversion was measured at two times: If the heterotypic continuity model is correct, we would miss important evidence of personality continuity and transformation because we would not have assessed the trait into which Extraversion metamorphosed. By measuring all five personality factors, we are in a position to give a definitive test of the heterotypic continuity model in adulthood.

The balancing model of personality development is somewhat easier to evaluate, because we know the direction of the change we are supposed to expect. If we measure traits at the beginning of adulthood and then again at the end, we would expect a strong correlation between corresponding measurements of each trait—but we would hypothesize that the correlation would be *negative*. The extreme introvert would have become the extreme extravert, the feminine person would have become masculine, the open individual would have become closed. The predictions of this model, however, are somewhat harder to anticipate if the time span between measurements is a matter of years instead of decades, since individuals may not yet have reached a point of crossover. We would, however, expect great variability among individuals at the beginning and end of adulthood, but similarity among the middle-aged, all of whom are nearing the central crossover point.

Finally, the predictions of the stability model are straightforward: If personality traits are relatively unchanging over the years, there should be high positive correlations between corresponding traits over the two times; and the correlations of each trait with itself over time should be higher than the correlations across time between different traits. In other words, the same pattern that we call retest reliability when the test is readministered after a month would be seen as stability of personality if it were readministered after a decade.

Longitudinal Evidence

Many of the studies we described in Chapter 4 as sources of longitudinal evidence about changes in the average levels of traits have also provided evidence about the course of traits in individuals. Let us begin with an examination of data from the Baltimore Longitudinal Study of Aging for the 114 men who took the GZTS on three occasions about 6 years apart (Costa, McCrae, & Arenberg, 1980). Table 8 gives the observed intercorrelations among the 10 traits across 12 years from the first to the third administration.

Several things are immediately apparent from an examination of this table. Most obvious are the correlations, shown in boldface, that indicate the stability of individual traits. These correlations, ranging from .68 to .85, are extraordinarily high. Most psychologists might expect to see correlations this high if the measures were administered 12 days apart, but not 12 years; and in fact, the stability coefficients presented here are somewhat higher than the short-term reliabilities reported in the test manual (Guilford et al., 1976). Since the mean levels change very little (as we saw in Chapter 4), it becomes clear that most individuals obtain almost exactly the same scores on these tests on two different occasions separated by 12 years.

TABLE 8. *Correlations Among GZTS Scales Over 12 Years*

Third administration	First administration									
	1.	2.	3.	4.	5.	6.	7.	8.	9.	10.
1. General Activity	**.80**	−.13	.38	.27	.22	.21	−.15	−.01	−.03	−.09
2. Restraint	−.13	**.71**	−.21	−.33	−.03	−.05	.13	.18	.01	.04
3. Ascendance	.38	−.19	**.85**	.58	.33	.29	−.13	.16	.10	.04
4. Sociability	.29	−.33	.54	**.75**	.21	.28	−.01	−.06	.04	−.13
5. Emotional Stability	.15	−.02	.39	.35	**.71**	.66	.35	−.20	.37	.13
6. Objectivity	.06	−.02	.30	.30	.51	**.74**	.48	−.16	.37	.24
7. Friendliness	−.24	.15	−.23	−.04	.27	.41	**.77**	−.21	.35	.18
8. Thoughtfulness	.11	.16	.11	−.03	−.16	.18	−.28	**.71**	−.29	−.09
9. Personal Relations	−.12	−.05	.07	.05	.13	.25	.23	−.13	**.68**	.34
10. Masculinity	−.03	−.07	.11	−.04	.19	.32	.17	−.12	.24	**.73**

Note. Correlations greater than ±.24 are significant at $p < .01$. N = 114.

What about the alternative models of personality development? We need only consider the continuity models, because the data seem sharply inconsistent with any positions that do not recognize the continuity of personality. It is hardly believable to suggest that external environments have remained unchanged over the 12-year period—that would be far more puzzling than the stability of personality. Within the continuity models, the choice seems equally clear. The Jungian notion of balancing would predict *negative* correlations for the retest of traits over long intervals and zero correlations for moderate intervals; the correlations in Table 8 are strongly *positive*.

The heterotypic continuity model also fails to account for the results in Table 8. True, there are some sizable correlations between traits at the first administration and different traits at the third. For example, ascendance predicts later sociability with an impressive correlation of .54. But before concluding that ascendance *develops into* sociability, we should note that the reverse is equally true: sociability predicts ascendance 12 years later with a correlation of .58. Finally (although it is not shown in Table 8), the correlation of ascendance with sociability when both are measured at the same time is .64 at the first administration and .58 at the third administration. In short, regardless of when either is measured, the correlation of these two traits is about .6, a fact that is not in the least surprising when one recalls that both are facets of the domain of Extraversion. In the same way, strong predictive correlations are found between different traits in the domain of Neuroticism such as emotional stablity and objectivity. But none of the heterotypic correlations is as strong as the correlation of each trait with itself over time, and none of the predictive correlations cross the boundaries of their own domains. Extraversion does not predict Neuroticism; masculinity does not predict restraint.

If the data in Table 8 were the only evidence of this exceptional degree of stability in personality, we would quite properly be skeptical, but a number of other studies have reported similar findings. In the Boston study we found 10-year stability coefficients of .69 for Neuroticism and .84 for Extraversion (Costa & McCrae, 1977). Researchers at Duke University (Siegler et al., 1979) found correlations of about .50 for 8-year intervals, using a test with somewhat lower reliability. As long ago as 1955, Strong showed that occupational interests (which are closely related to personality dispositions) were highly stable after the age of 25.

A number of other longitudinal studies have been reported; they are summarized in Table 9. The correlations reported here uniformly support the stability position, although many of them are lower than those seen in Table 8, for several reasons. Some subjects were college age when testing began and had not reached psychological maturity. Finn (1986), for example, found substantially higher retest correlations for subjects initially aged 43 to 53 than for those initially 17 to 25. Differences in instrument are also important. The MMPI scales studied by Leon and her colleagues (1979) were intended to assess psychopathology, not personality traits, and so are not fully appropriate for a study of personality in a psychiatrically normal sample. Block's (1977) results, using a standard personality inventory in a large group of men and women initially over age 30, are precisely in line with the findings in Table 8.

The 6-year longitudinal study of the NEO-PI discussed in Chapter 4 (Costa & McCrae, 1988a) is also the basis for an analysis of the stability of individual differences. Table 10 presents stability coefficients for men and women subdivided into two age groups, as well as for the total sample for all NEO-PI scales. (Note that the stability coefficients for A and C are based on a 3-year retest interval, because A and C were not measured until 1983.) These correlations, ranging from .55 to .87, are all significant and all testify to extraordinary stability of personality, in men and in women, in early adulthood and in late.

The results in Tables 8 to 10 provide consistent evidence of high levels of stability over intervals of up to 30 years. Consider what that means.

TABLE 9. *Stability Coefficients from Recent Longitudinal Studies Using Self-Reports*

Study	Instrument	N	Sex	Initial age	Retest interval	Correlations Range	Median
Block (1977)	CPI	219	M, F	31–38	10		.71
Leon et al.	MMPI	71	M	45–54	13	.07–.82	.50
(1979)				58–67	17	.03–.76	.52
Mortimer et al.	Self-	368	M	Seniors	10	.51–.63	.55
(1981)	concept						
Conley (1985)	KLS factors	378	M, F	18–35	20	.34–.57	.46
Howard & Bray	EPPS	266	M	Young	20	.31–.54	.42
(1988)	GAMIN	264		managers	20	.45–.61	.57
Stevens &	EPPS	85	M, F	College	12	−.05–.58	.34
Truss (1985)		92	M, F	students	20	−.01–.79	.44
Finn (1986)	MMPI	96	M	17–25	30	−.14–.58	.35
	factors	78	M	43–53	30	.10–.88	.56
Helson &	CPI	81	F	21	22	.21–.58	.37
Moane (1987)				27	16	.40–.70	.51
	ACL	78	F	27	16	.49–.72	.61

Note. CPI, California Psychological Inventory; MMPI, Minnesota Multiphasic Personality Inventory; KLS, Kelly Longitudinal Study; EPPS, Edwards Personal Preference Schedule; GAMIN, Guilford/Martin Inventory of Factors; ACL, Adjective Check List. Adapted from Costa & McCrae (1989b).

In the course of 30 years, most adults will have undergone radical changes in their life structures. They may have married, divorced, remarried. They have probably moved their residence several times. Many people will have experienced job changes, layoffs, promotions, and retirement. Close friends and confidants will have died or moved away or become alienated. Children will have been born, grown up, married, begun a family of their own. The individual will have aged biologically, with changes in appearance, health, vigor, memory, and sensory abilities. Wars, depressions, and social movements will have come and gone. Most people will have read dozens of books, seen hundreds of movies, watched thousands of hours of television. *And yet, most will not have changed appreciably in their standing on any of the five dimensions of personality.*

TABLE 10. *Stability of NEO-PI Scales for Younger and Older Men and Women*

NEO-PI scale	Age 25 to 56 years		Age 57 to 84 years		Total
	Men	Women	Men	Women	
Neuroticism	.78	.85	.82	.81	.83
Anxiety	.74	.72	.72	.75	.75
Hostility	.74	.74	.75	.72	.74
Depression	.62	.77	.71	.66	.70
Self-Consciousness	.74	.81	.79	.78	.79
Impulsiveness	.66	.65	.70	.67	.70
Vulnerability	.73	.76	.60	.75	.73
Extraversion	.84	.75	.86	.73	.82
Warmth	.74	.66	.74	.66	.72
Gregariousness	.76	.69	.76	.68	.73
Assertiveness	.73	.75	.84	.79	.79
Activity	.72	.74	.77	.74	.75
Excitement Seeking	.69	.61	.79	.63	.73
Positive Emotions	.80	.65	.69	.69	.73
Openness	.87	.84	.81	.73	.83
Fantasy	.77	.74	.69	.63	.73
Aesthetics	.75	.83	.81	.67	.79
Feelings	.72	.61	.64	.62	.68
Actions	.75	.73	.66	.58	.70
Ideas	.78	.84	.78	.75	.79
Values	.77	.69	.70	.67	.71
Agreeableness	.64	.60	.59	.55	.63
Conscientiousness	.82	.84	.76	.71	.79

Note. All correlations are significant at $p < .001$. N's = 63 to 127 for sub-samples. Retest interval is 6 years for N, E, and O scales; 3 years for short forms of A and C scales. Adapted from Costa & McCrae (1988b).

*   *   *

The idea that personality should be so deeply and permanently ingrained is revolutionary in a scientific climate in which change, growth, and development are the watchwords. Not surprisingly, therefore, a number of psychologists have challenged the basic findings.

When unanticipated results are found, there is a strong tendency to dismiss them. This reluctance to accept an unforeseen result is not really a result of closed-mindedness, nor is it unscientific. On the contrary, the essence of science is to look critically at observations and conclusions. Every scientist knows that there is more than one explanation for any phenomenon, and is rightfully wary of accepting the first account that offers itself. True, the high correlations between personality scores at two different times are just what one would expect if personality is actually highly stable. But there are a number of other ways in which the same correlations could be observed that are entirely consistent with major change in personality. Until these rival hypotheses can be ruled out, it is premature to accept the conclusion of stability.

·6·

STABILITY RECONSIDERED: QUALIFICATIONS AND RIVAL HYPOTHESES

METHODOLOGICAL ISSUES IN THE ASSESSMENT OF STABILITY

The first and most fundamental challenge to any interpretation of data is the notion of chance: Perhaps the high stability coefficients were flukes. In this particular case that argument is extremely weak. Statistically, the likelihood of observing correlations of this size in samples this large purely by chance is less than one in 10,000. And it would be coincidence indeed if we happened to exceed these odds for measures of all five domains of personality. No scientist would seriously suggest that these are chance results.

If the only data were from the study of the GZTS in the BLSA, one might argue that the results are not generalizable to other segments of the population. Women were not included in that study; blacks and other nonwhites were greatly underrepresented; education, social class, and intelligence were markedly higher in the BLSA study than they are in the full population: Perhaps these characteristics somehow explain the observed stability. However, our conclusions are not based on Table 8 alone. Similar evidence comes from a variety of studies of men and women. There is strong replicability of results over samples that are considerably more diverse and representative than the BLSA.

The same argument—and the same answer—applies to considerations of measures. If stability were found only when the Guilford–Zimmerman Temperament Survey was used, we would begin to suspect that GZTS scores, not personality dispositions, were stable, and we would then try to determine what peculiarity about the GZTS accounted for its constancy. But highly similar results have been seen with the 16PF and the NEO-PI; in fact, almost every personality inventory that has been longitudinally examined has shown exceptional levels of stability.

And so the attack shifts ground. If it is not a specific personality test that accounts for stability, perhaps it is the nature of personality tests themselves. All of the instruments examined in Tables 8 to 10 are self-report inventories, in which we base our assessment of the individual on the ways in which he or she responds to a series of more or less straightforward questions. It has been known for some time that the scores we obtain in this way are not pure indicators of personality. Instead, any of several *response sets* may be operating, and these are likely to cloud the issue (Jackson & Messick, 1961). Some individuals agree to almost any characterization of them you offer, some reject them all. The former are called *yea-sayers*, or acquiescers, the latter *nay-sayers*. Some people are extreme responders. They tend to express their beliefs about themselves and other things strongly. Other people are more noncommittal, and frequently use the "neutral" or "don't know" response category. Social desirability has been the bane of many test constructors: How do we know that individuals are not lying in order to make themselves look good? How do we know that respondents are not fooling themselves as well as us?

Other response sets have also been noted: tendencies to respond carelessly, to try to make a bad impression (out of a kind of test-taking perverseness), to answer consistently. Study after study has documented the potential threat that each of these may pose to a straightforward interpretation of data, and scales have been incorporated into many prominent personality inventories in order to screen out the worst offenders. From time to time critics have alleged that paper-and-pencil tests may be explainable completely in terms of these stylistic (and substantively insignificant) sets (Berg, 1959), but careful analyses have consistently shown that this "nothing but" interpretation is far too extreme. Still, it is possible that the very high levels of stability in Tables 8 and 10 are inflated by response sets.

Consider first the possibility that subjects are motivated to respond consistently from administration to administration: They recall how they answered questions the first time, and repeat their performance on subsequent administrations despite real changes in their personality. This possibility is frequently advanced, but it becomes more and more implausible on examination. Why would people be so concerned with maintaining the appearance of consistency? A few subjects might be obsessed with maintaining an image, but it is hard to believe that nearly everyone in the sample would be (though that would be necessary to account for the observed coefficients). Further, even if they wanted to, is it likely that subjects *could* repeat their earlier performance? Informally, subjects often report that they do not even remember taking the test before—are we to believe that they somehow recall how they answered each particular question?

This deliberate consistency hypothesis is almost too implausible to entertain, so it is fortunate for us that it has already been tested. Woodruff and Birren (1972) retested a sample of individuals who had completed a personality measure 25 years before when they were in college. In addition to being given a simple readministration, the subjects were also asked to fill out the questionnaire *as they believed they had filled it out 25 years earlier*. In terms of average level, the original responses were closer to the readministration responses than they were to the subject's recollections of the original responses. Woodruff (1983) demonstrated this even more forcefully when she examined the correlations between real and recalled responses. The correlation between original scores and later recollections was low and statistically nonsignificant. By contrast, there was a strong and highly significant correlation between original responses and personality as measured 25 years later. We get a more accurate picture of what people were like 25 years ago by asking what they are like today than by asking them to recall how they were; memories, it seems, are not as stable as personality.

A more plausible interpretation of a response set explanation would be the following analogy: When individuals take a test, they employ a characteristic set of response styles that operate much like habits. Just as one never forgets how to ride a bicycle, so one may never forget the habits of test responding. When subjects retake the test years later, the same habits are activated and the same results obtained. Thus, there may be stability, but it is stability of response style, not personality.

This is not as strong an argument as it may at first seem. It might account for the convergence between scores on the same trait at two times, but it cannot explain the divergence between scores on different traits. The scales of the GZTS differ much more in content than in the response styles they are likely to elicit. Thus, the low correlations between unlike traits (e.g., sociability and thoughtfulness, $r = -.06$) are easily explained if content determines responses, but hard to explain if response sets determine responses. And if response sets do not account for scale scores at one time, they cannot account for the stability of scale scores across time. It is, however, still possible that stability is exaggerated by consistency of response habits.

Because response sets (including random responding, uncertainty, social desirability, and acquiescence) can be measured in the GZTS, we conducted empirical tests of this possibility (Costa et al., 1983). We found that there is indeed a certain consistency of response style across administrations, but it is less pronounced than the consistency of individual traits. And when we analyzed the data to eliminate the effects of this consistency, we found that the stability coefficients remained essentially unchanged. Artifacts of response set do not account for stability of personality.

The Self-Concept and Stability

A much more interesting and reasonable rival hypothesis was suggested to us by Seymour Epstein. He drew attention to the distinction between personality and the self-concept, between what we are really like and what we believe we are like. He suggested that we may develop a view of ourselves early in adulthood and cling to that picture over the years, despite changes in our real nature. Rosenberg (1979) expressed the same idea this way:

> The power and persistence of the self-consistency motive may be quite remarkable. People who have developed self-pictures early in life frequently continue to hold to these self-views long after the actual self has changed radically . . . [T]he person who grows gruff and irritable with the passing years may still think of himself as "basically" kindly, cheerful, and well-disposed; thus behavior which has become chronic is either unrecognized or is perceived as a temporary aberration from the true self.

Psychologists and sociologists have long known that we do have a self-concept, a theory of what we are like (Epstein, 1973), and that it seems to guide our behavior. It is this theory of ourselves that we draw on when we are asked to describe ourselves, whether to a friend or on a questionnaire. There has been considerable dispute about how we develop a self-concept, whether or not self-concepts are accurate, and what the possibilities are for change in the self-concept during adulthood. According to one view, the self-concept may be crystallized early in life and remain unchanged thereafter.

Stories abound about middle-aged men who take up tennis or jogging after 20 years of inactivity and have to revise drastically their image of themselves as athletes. Normally they make these revisions fairly quickly. They have to; they can't fool their bodies. But could they still imagine they were adventurous when they had lost their sense of daring? Could they still believe they were hostile when they had been mellowed by experience and age? Would anything in their intrapsychic or social experience *force* them to revise their self-concept, the way their exhaustion forces them to acknowledge the limits of their physical endurance?

Until we can answer these questions, the possiblity remains that all that we have demonstrated is the stability of self-concept. Further, this critique would apply equally to all studies, longitudinal and cross-sectional, that have relied on self-reports. In short, it would pull the rug out from under most of the claims of stability we have reviewed in this book and would allow the proponents of change to say, "See? People *do* change with age and with experience, just as we've told you. Only they don't *realize* they've changed."

In this case we cannot rely on evidence from self-reports, since they are themselves in question. We have to get beyond self-reports, which are determined by the self-concept, if we want to see the agreement between the self-concept and the true personality. For this we must turn to someone else's assessment of personality, and in our case we had available personality ratings made by the husbands and wives of 281 of our subjects (McCrae & Costa, 1982). We assumed that spouses were reasonable judges of personality (we had data to support that assumption), but we also argued that the spouses would be much more able than the individuals themselves to detect any changes that age had brought. We may be blind to changes in ourselves, but others who must deal with us on a daily basis are unlikely to overlook important changes in our personality.

By comparing self-reports with spouse ratings, we can get some idea of whether the self-concept has really been crystallized. Among young people the self-concept should still be quite accurate, a good reflection of what the person is really like. Consequently there should be good agreement between self-reports and spouse ratings among young couples. But if personality changes with age while the self-concept is frozen, self-reports will give increasingly inaccurate pictures of personality. Correspondingly, the agreement between self-reports and spouse ratings will become poorer and poorer. Among older couples there may be no agreement at all.

These would be the consequences if personality changed while the self-concept did not. When we examined the correlations between self and spouse for young, middle-aged, and elderly couples, however, we found no decrease in agreement with age. (In fact, the only significant difference was that there was more agreement—not less—about Extraversion in older men.) This finding provides some powerful evidence that personality does not change and that crystallization of the self-concept cannot itself account for the correlations seen in studies of self-report inventories.

There are other pieces of evidence as well. Jack Block (1971, 1981) has reported on a remarkable series of longitudinal studies conducted in Berkeley. Personality records have been kept on about 200 boys and girls over a period now approaching 50 years. These records include test scores, teachers' notes, biographical sketches, and many other documents. For each of four time periods (junior high, senior high, the 30s, and 40s) independent judges reviewed these records and rated the subjects on the California Q-Set, which, as we have seen, measures aspects of all five domains of personality. Different judges were used for each time period, and yet, when individuals were compared across time, remarkable evidence of stability in personality was found.

In another study on the parents of these subjects, judges provided ratings across an interval of 40 years, from ages 30 to 70 (Mussen et al., 1980). Again, despite the differences in judges and the unreliability of single-item scales, most of the ratings showed significant correlation across time.

For the domains of N, E, and O we now have 6-year longitudinal spouse ratings for 167 subjects. Table 11 gives stability coefficients for men and women separately and combined; all these correlations are significant and quite comparable in magnitude to those found in studies of self-reports. Husbands' and wives' views of their spouses' personalities confirm the essential stability of personality.

TABLE 11. *Stability Coefficients for Spouse Ratings of Men and Women*

NEO-PI scale	Men	Women	Total
Neuroticism	.77	.86	.83
Anxiety	.67	.82	.75
Hostility	.76	.81	.78
Depression	.69	.74	.72
Self-consciousness	.65	.77	.76
Impulsiveness	.70	.81	.75
Vulnerability	.62	.70	.68
Extraversion	.78	.77	.77
Warmth	.76	.70	.75
Gregariousness	.71	.72	.73
Assertiveness	.68	.75	.72
Activity	.72	.63	.68
Excitement Seeking	.65	.75	.69
Positive Emotions	.78	.77	.77
Openness	.82	.78	.80
Fantasy	.73	.73	.73
Aesthetics	.83	.70	.79
Feelings	.71	.65	.70
Actions	.78	.69	.75
Ideas	.75	.72	.75
Values	.81	.72	.76

Note. All correlations are significant at $p < .001$. Adapted from Costa & McCrae (1988b).

Critics could, of course, argue that spouses form a crystallized "spouse concept" that is the source of apparent stability, but such arguments become increasingly implausible. It is far more parsimonious and plausible to admit that personality really is stable.

Accounting for Variance and Correcting for Unreliability

The typical 10-year stability coefficient of .71 reported by Block (1977) can be interpreted to mean that 50% (or .71 squared) of the variance in scale scores at Time 2 can be predicted by Time 1 scores. Some critics of the stability position have asked about the remaining 50%: Isn't it fair to say that there are equal amounts of stability and change?

This argument would be sound if personality scales were perfect indicators of personality. But even the best instruments are fallible. When a subject encounters the NEO-PI item, "I really like most people

I meet," he or she must choose among five options, from "strongly disagree" to "strongly agree." If the subject happens to recall meeting several disagreeable people lately, he or she may respond "disagree." On a second administration, the subject may place more weight on his or her generally friendly response to people and "agree" with the item. The subject's personality has remained the same, but his or her reading of the item has changed. It is for this reason that scales combining many items are generally more accurate than those that include only a few: Random errors tend to cancel out when many items are used. (An illustration of this principle is seen in Tables 10 and 11, where the longer domain scales show higher stability coefficients than their component facet scales.)

There are also other sources of error in filling out questionnaires. Respondents may be living through a difficult period, perhaps looking for work or adjusting to a divorce; their temporary mood may color their perception of themselves. Problems with physical health may also affect responses. Whatever the causes, test scores tend to fluctuate from day to day for reasons that are unrelated to personality change. Traditionally, scales are evaluated in part by their ability to give relatively constant or *reliable* scores despite these influences. This property is assessed by repeating the measure a few days or weeks later for a sample of people and correlating the first and second set of scores. Since it can be assumed that no true personality change has occurred in the interval, retest correlations less than 1.0 can be interpreted as evidence of unreliability. Personality scales normally have retest reliabilities in the range of .70 to .90.

In longitudinal studies, the correlations between the initial and later administrations of the test are less than 1.0, lowered both by the day-to-day fluctuations of questionnaire responses and by whatever true change has occurred. Retest reliability puts an upper limit on stability: We cannot expect to find high correlations over a period of years if we do not observe them over a period of days. It is therefore reasonable to ask how close to this upper limit stability coefficients reach and what proportion of possible stability they show. Dividing stability coefficients by short-term retest reliabilities gives an estimate of the stability of the *true score*, the actual level of the traits that we try to infer from our tests.

This procedure, disattenuating correlations, leads to considerably higher estimates of stability. When corrected for attenuation resulting from unreliability, 12-year stability estimates for the GZTS scales shown in Table 8 ranged from .80 to 1.00 (Costa et al., 1980); the 6-year stability estimates for N, E, and O scales for the NEO-PI were .95, .90, and .97, respectively (Costa & McCrae, 1988b). Such analyses suggest that if we had perfect measures we would find near-perfect stability of personality traits. The 50% of variance not predictable from earlier scores is not true change; it is merely error of measurement.

RETROSPECTION AND SELF-PERCEIVED CHANGE

In Chapter 5 we mentioned that retrospection—asking individuals to recall how they were and how they have changed—was a simple but suspect method of examining stability or change in personality. We said that we could not be sure whether the reports would be accurate reflections of reality or distortions of memory. By now, however, we have a reasonable idea of what reality must have been like for most people: We know that stability rather than change predominates when prospective longitudinal studies are conducted. So is there any reason to reconsider retrospective reports?

In fact, there is. They serve, to begin with, as one more source of data, one more way to bolster or cast doubt on our findings of constancy. But equally importantly, they let us know something about how individuals view their own lives. If most individuals were to claim that they had changed dramatically when all the evidence points to the opposite conclusion, this would suggest that memory does indeed play tricks on us, and the function of these tricks would be of considerable interest. It might also explain why critics find the notion of stability in personality so counterintuitive.

Most people, in fact, can point to aspects of themselves that have changed in the past few years, and the reader may have been protesting on the basis of these exceptions throughout this book. But three things should be borne in mind in considering this kind of evidence. First, in one important sense retrospection is different from any of the kinds of studies we have reviewed. Statistics are usually interpreted in terms of individual differences; that is, they compare one individual with others. Saying that a person is warm means, in a certain sense, that he or she is warmer than most other people; saying that warmth does not change with age means that he or she will continue to be warmer than most people throughout life. But if we ask an individual if he has changed, he will be making comparisons between himself as he was and himself as he is now. He is likely to be far more sensitive to these changes than we are. We might find that he has risen from the 55th to the 58th percentile in warmth—a change we would call trivial. From his perspective, however, this change may be extremely important and the contrast very vivid.

Second, as perceptual psychologists would remind us, our attention is attracted by movement and contrast, not by stability and sameness. If a person is unchanged in characteristic levels of anxiety, hostility, asser-tiveness, excitement seeking, and openness to feelings and values, but has changed in gregariousness, he or she is much more likely to notice and remark on the change in that one element than on the stability in the other six. Our prediction of stability would be confirmed in 85% of the cases, but we would be judged wrong because of the one exception. Stability is not absolute, but it is far more pervasive than many people realize.

Finally, the question of sampling arises again. Readers under age 30 probably *have* experienced some personality changes in recent years, but they should not assume that this pattern will continue. Regardless of age, readers of this book (and life-span developmental psychologists) are probably not representative of humanity in general. They are, for the most part, intelligent, perceptive, and curious individuals. And almost certainly they are interested in seeing what changes age and experience will bring to them. In short, they begin with a bias toward finding change and the mental acuity to spot it, no matter how subtle or small it may be. Most people are neither predisposed nor skilled enough to recognize such changes.

We first discovered this when we began to investigate the so-called midlife crisis (Costa & McCrae, 1978). At that time we assumed we would find abundant evidence of a crisis; we simply wanted to document it. (See Chapter 8 for a fuller discussion of this study.) At the end of a standard questionnaire we asked that subjects comment in their own words on the ways in which they felt they had changed in the past 10 years. Subject after subject returned the questionnaire with words to the effect of "no changes worth mentioning." A few subjects did find some change to comment on; the great majority did not.

Gold, Andres, and Schwartzman (1987) recently came to the same conclusion in their study of self-perceived change. They administered the Eysenck Personality Inventory to 362 elderly men and women. One month later they readministered the questionnaire to half the sample as a control group; the other half—the experimental group—were asked to discuss their life and circumstances at age 40, and then to complete the questionnaire to describe their personality at age 40. The responses of the experimental group suggested that they perceived themselves as having been slightly more extraverted at age 40 than currently, but individual differences were highly stable. Recalled Neuroticism correlated .79 with current Neuroticism in the experimental group; the one-month reliability observed for the control group was .82. The corresponding values for Extraversion were .75 and .79. By the logic of correcting for attenuation, we could argue that these subjects perceived about 95% stability between ages 40 and 75.

Most people, then, do not see much change in their own dispositions in adulthood, but it is possible that the minority who do perceive differences are correct: Perhaps they really have mellowed or matured with age. To test this possibility we conducted a small study of self-perceived change in conjunction with our 6-year longitudinal study of self-reports and spouse ratings on the NEO-PI (Costa & McCrae, 1989). At the end of our packet of questionnaires we asked subjects to:

> Think back over the last 6 years to the way you were in 1980. Consider your basic feelings, attitudes, and ways of relating to people—your whole personality. Overall, do you think you have (a) changed a good deal in your personality? (b) changed a little in your personality? or (c) stayed pretty much the same since 1980?

We found that a bare majority (51%) believed they had stayed "pretty much the same," and another third (35%) thought they had changed "a little." But a substantial minority—14 percent—felt that they had changed significantly in personality; these individuals would probably take exception to our conclusions about stability.

Are these perceptions veridical, or are they distorted by tricks of perception or memory? One way to examine this question is by comparing stability coefficients within the three perceived change groups. If perceptions of change are accurate, we should see the highest stability coefficients in the "same" group and the lowest coefficients in the "changed a good deal" group. We have both self-reports and spouse ratings to test this hypothesis. But Table 12 provides no support for the hypothesis: None of the five personality factors is consistently less stable among individuals who believed they had changed "a good deal."

In addition to the global change item, we also asked subjects, "Spec-

TABLE 12. *Stability Coefficients Within Perceived Change Groups*

Perceived change

NEO-PI scale	"A good deal"	"A little"	"The same"
Self-Reports			
Neuroticism	.77	.79	.86
Extraversion	.66	.80	.86
Openness	.86	.83	.82
Agreeableness	.70	.56	.62
Conscientiousness	.80	.71	.81
Spouse Ratings			
Neuroticism	.86	.79	.84
Extraversion	.79	.79	.72
Openness	.90	.88	.71

Note. N's = 36 to 182 for self-reports, 13 to 71 for spouse ratings. All correlations are significant at p < .01. Adapted from Costa & McCrae (1989b).

ifically, compared to how you were 6 years ago, how lively, cheerful, and sociable are you now?" to assess perceived change in Extraversion. Similar items asked about the other four dimensions, and subjects could respond with "more", "less", or "same". We found that subjects who believe they were more extraverted or neurotic actually did score slightly higher on these two scales in 1986, but spouse ratings did not confirm the changes; perhaps there was a small but real change in self-concept, although not in true personality. There was no evidence from either self-reports or spouse ratings to substantiate self-perceived changes in O, A, or C. For the most part, it appears that perceptions of change in personality are misperceptions. Most people think they are stable, and those who think they have changed are probably wrong.

With the benefit of hindsight and the results of many longitudinal, prospective studies, it is interesting to consider results from an early retrospective study. Reichard, Livson and Peterson (1962), in one of the seminal books on personality and aging, interviewed a number of retired men to find out how they were adapting to old age and retirement. The interviewers spent a good deal of time taking life histories of their subjects so that they could note patterns of adjustment across the lifespan. Their conclusion? "The histories of our aging workers suggest that their personality characteristics changed very little throughout their lives" (p. 163).

CASE STUDIES IN STABILITY

The same individuals must be studied at least twice in order to calculate the stability coefficients we have focused so much attention on. But these coefficients are still group statistics, showing the extent to which the same ordering of individuals along a dimension is maintained over time. A less scientific but perhaps more easily grasped way to examine stability or change is by comparing the personality profiles of individuals at two time periods. Figures 3 to 5 provide examples of individuals in our studies tested in 1980 and again in 1986 (Costa, 1986). In these Figures, the 1980 scores are joined by broken lines, the 1986 scores by solid lines.

Figure 3 gives the NEO-PI profile of a woman who described herself as a homemaker; she was 62 when she completed the second administration. The first five columns of the profile show her standing on the five domains; we can see that she is average in Neuroticism and Agreeableness, low in Extraversion and Openness, and high in Conscientiousness (A and C were measured only in 1986). Her facet scores are given in the next three sets of columns. It is clear that her scores are almost identical on the two occasions; even the relatively fine distinctions within facets are preserved, most strikingly for Extraversion. The only notable change is an increase from average to very high in Openness to Values. Does this represent a temporary change in attitudes, or a permanent rethinking that may lead to greater openness in other areas? Future studies may provide an answer. Overall, her introverted, unadventurous personality seems consistent with her occupation.

Case 2 (Figure 4) is a retired minister and college professor who is well-adjusted, average in Extraversion and Agreeableness, and high in Openness and Conscientiousness. His scores show relatively more change, particularly in facet scales, but stability predominates at the broader level of domain scales. Although he seems to be somewhat lower in several facets of Openness at the second administration, he compensates by higher Openness to Fantasy.

A 64-year-old social worker provides our third case (Figure 5). Consistent with her profession, we can see that she is a very sociable person, high in warmth and gregariousness. Like the minister, she shows some fluctuation for facet scales, but her domain scores are almost identical in 1980 and 1986.

These profiles are typical, showing neither the most stable nor the most unstable of individuals in our sample. Scale scores are not identical on

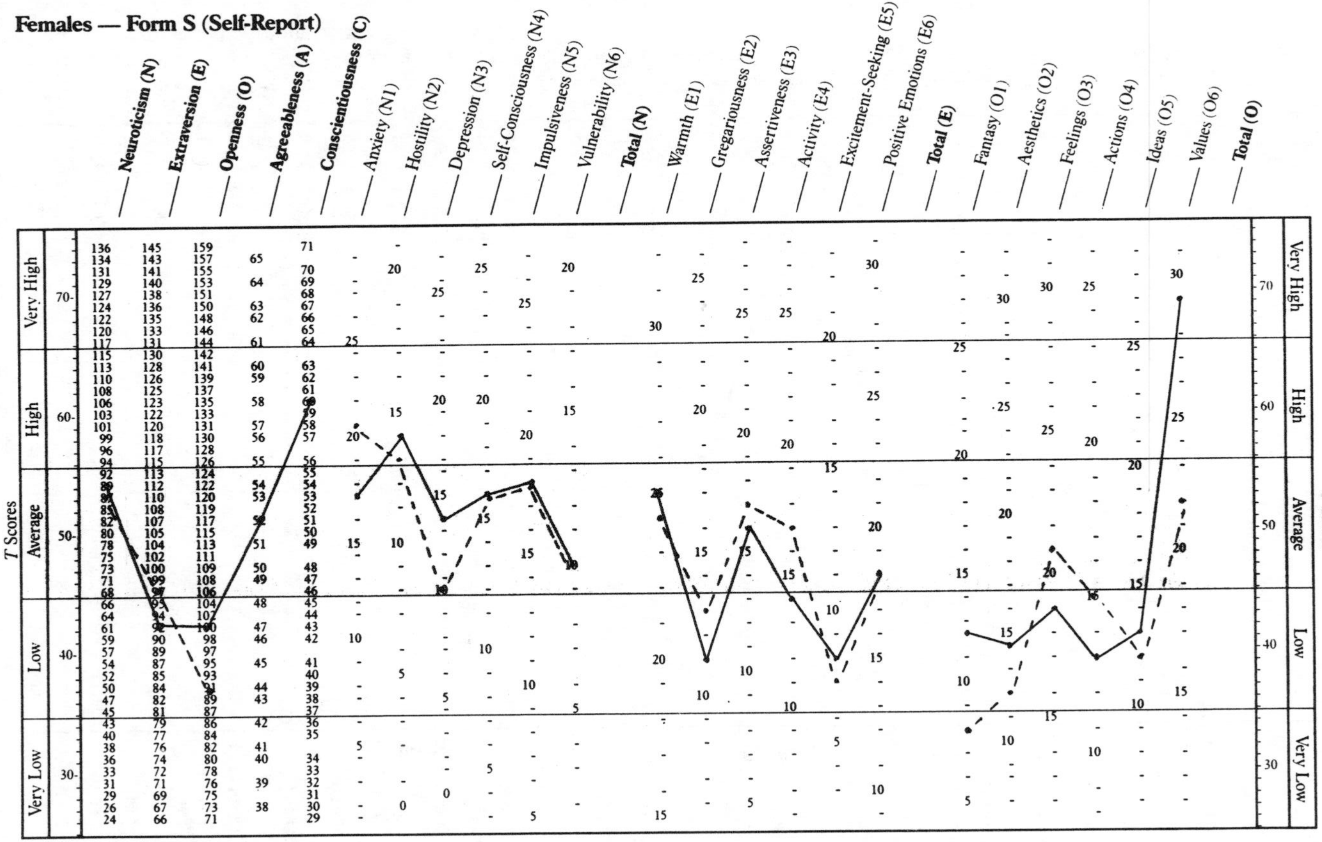

FIGURE 3. Personality profile for Case 1, a 62-year-old homemaker. Profile reproduced by special permission of the publisher, Psychological Assessment Resources, Inc., Odessa, Florida 33549, from the NEO Personality Inventory, Copyright 1978, 1985, 1989 by PAR, Inc. Further reproduction is prohibited without permission of PAR, Inc.

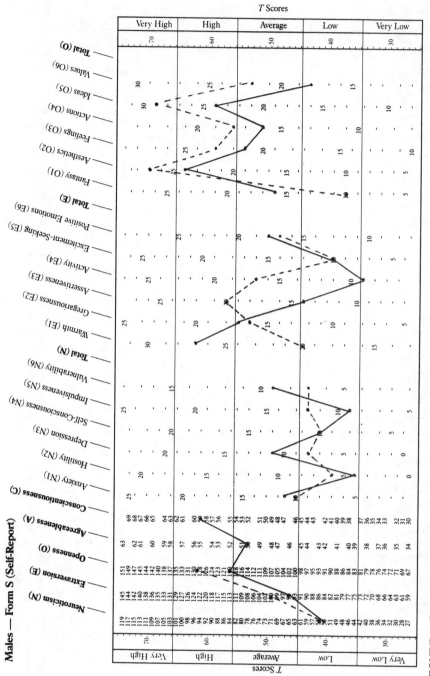

FIGURE 4. Personality profile for Case 2, an 87-year-old minister. Profile reproduced by special permission of the publisher, Psychological Assessment Resources, Inc., Odessa, Florida 33549, from the NEO Personality Inventory, Copyright 1978, 1985, 1989 by PAR, Inc. Further reproductin is prohibited without permission of PAR, Inc.

104

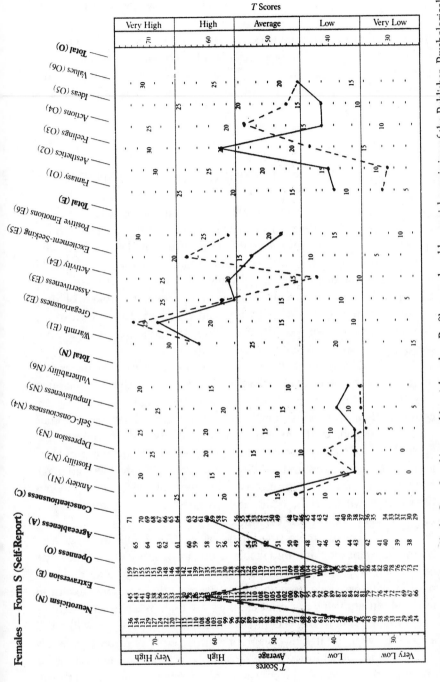

FIGURE 5. Personality profile for Case 3, a 64-year-old social worker. Profile reproduced by special permission of the Publisher, Psychological Assessment Resources, Inc., Odessa, Florida 33549, from the NEO Personality Inventory, Copyright 1978, 1985, 1989 by PAR, Inc. Further reproduction is prohibited without permission of PAR, Inc.

the two occasions, but then we know that scale scores are rarely identical even when the interval between tests is only a few weeks. Over the 6-year interval covered here, the resemblence in personality profiles is un-mistakable. These people are still the same individuals with the same unique configuration of traits.

IMPLICATIONS: PLANNING FOR THE FUTURE

Imagine the chaos that would result if personality were *not* stable! How could we commit ourselves to marriage if the qualities we loved in our spouse were subject to change at any time? Who would go to the trouble of completing medical school without the faith that they would still be interested in medicine years later? How could we vote for politicians if their past diligence and conscientiousness were not a token of their future performance? On what basis would we decide to retire early and move to Florida if we thought that at any moment we might become compulsive workers with boundless energy?

With the exception of those closest to us (whom we may never give up trying to change), we expect people to stay just as they are. Good or bad, we want them to be dependable and predictable, so that we can count on them in making plans for our own future. They feel the same way about us; one of the explanations for stability is the social pressure applied to keep everyone in his or her place. We can shape our own lives, attain our dreams, and find fulfillment for ourselves only if we can make realistic plans for the future. Since so much of life depends on our interactions with others, being able to guess how they are likely to respond years from now is essential.

The same is even more true for ourselves. Continuity in personality is a requirement for planning a viable future; it is also a source of the sense of identity. When, in Erikson's last stage, we review our lives and take stock of what we have been and done, we must do so to some extent in terms of our enduring dispositions. If we are high in Conscientiousness, we will take pride in our accomplishments; if we are low, we will recall all the fun we had. Lifelong dreams of writing poetry or fostering a family or dominating an industry make sense only in terms of the basic needs and traits they express. The constancy of personality is a unifying thread that gives meaning to our lives.

*   *   *

Once we begin to think in terms of stability, it becomes increasingly intuitive. Our parents and grandparents do not seem to change, although our understanding of them may alter greatly as we grow up. History tells us that Beethoven was a rebel at age 20 and at age 50, that Chairman Mao did not grow conservative with age. Hospital and prison records show that tendencies towards mental illness and antisocial behavior are dishearteningly stable. One begins to wonder how the idea of adult development ever arose to begin with.

But are we perhaps missing the whole point? Granted, emotional, interpersonal, and experiential styles may be relatively fixed, but are these the real cores of personality? Or are they instead peripheral characteristics whose stability is no more remarkable or noteworthy than stability in color of eyes or size of feet? Perhaps what is needed is not a different form of personality test or a different personality rater, but a wholly different conception of personality, in which it is seen not as trait but as process. Perhaps processes change with age.

·7·

A DIFFERENT VIEW: EGO PSYCHOLOGIES AND PROJECTIVE METHODS

The finding of stability in discrete traits we have discussed is not likely to be impressive to those who think of personality in terms other than traits. Behaviorists in general do not think of personality at all. They are interested in studying—and especially in controlling—behavior, and traits offer little promise of a way to reshape behavior; in fact, they may represent the greatest resistance to change.

Our concern in this chapter, however, will be with a different set of approaches to personality: the psychodynamic psychologies that see personality not as a collection of traits, each operating more or less independently to influence behavior, but as an *organization* of needs, motives, dispositions, habits, and abilities, an organization generally thought to be in the service of certain overarching goals. Depending on the version of psychodynamic theory, these goals might be set by biological instincts, the dictates of culture, or the individual's own experience and convictions.

In this chapter we also turn to an evaluation of projective methods, a form of personality assessment frequently advocated by ego psychologists. Do they make satisfactory substitutes for self-report inventories, or do they provide unique insights? Or does a careful consideration lead to a rejection of projective techniques altogether?

DYNAMIC OR EGO PSYCHOLOGIES

To the student of personality theory, it may seem strange to group together the theories of Freud, Jung, Rogers, Murray, Loevinger, Maslow—even Allport—as ego psychologies (in contrast to trait psychologies), but from a certain perspective it is perfectly reasonable. All these writers assume that individuals possess a variety of different and potentially conflicting tendencies, and all assume that the major business of personality theory is to explain how and why all these impulses are channeled and directed into the routine, purposeful, or occasionally irrational behavior we engage in, or the stream of consciousness we experience. Although the term *self* is sometimes used, *ego* is the word most frequently chosen to represent the aspect of the mind or personality that does the organizing.

We cannot hope in a few pages to provide adequate sketches of the theories we will be discussing—dozens of textbooks in personality theory do that already. We would, however, like to try to indicate some of the features they share that set them apart from trait theories. For our purposes we will emphasize the similarities of ego psychologies and minimize the profound differences, which are perhaps better known.

For Freud (1933), the ego develops as a mediator among fierce and primitive instinctual impulses (the id), punitive prohibitions internalized in childhood (the superego), and the social realities of the world. It operates through a series of tricks called *defense mechanisms*, and is ultimately very much at the mercy of the powers it attempts to control. This division of the psyche is at least as old as Plato, who wrote of appetite, passion, and reason as the elements of human nature, and who held that the ideal was the harmonious balancing of these parts. Freud's framework also seems to parallel the different emphases that have distinguished psychological schools in this century, since it acknowledges the importance of inborn tendencies and environmental pressures, as well as the capacity of cognitive processes—reason and individual choice—to moderate both these influences. In short, it seems likely that every complete psychology will have to deal with these issues in some form; one of Freud's major contributions was to formulate the 20th-century version of an age-old question. Many of the important personality theorists have made their primary contributions by modifying previous descriptions of the nature or significance of one of the three structures.

Murray (1938) uses the same general scheme of dynamic control, but changes the cast of characters considerably. Instead of describing primitive impulses, he endows human beings with a range of needs, some inborn, some acquired; and he proposes that the ego is a strong agent, not a figurehead, in most people, who use reason rather than defense to come up with solutions, compromises, plans, and schedules. Murray also proposed that the superego, the agent of morality within the individual, is not wholly unconscious and immutable. He felt that maturation, or what we would today call *moral development* (Kohlberg, 1971) was not only possible but the general rule.

Allport, Murray's contemporary at Harvard, developed two theories of personality, which he never clearly integrated. He is perhaps best known for his work as a trait psychologist (1966), but he also developed a dynamic theory of personality (1955). He emphasized the purposeful nature of human conduct and the significance of overarching goals, or *propriate strivings*, that guide and organize life.

Maslow (1954) was also a motivational theorist; his major thesis was that there are broad classes of needs that organize individuals' lives. The history of satisfaction of these needs determines the person's progress through a set sequence of motivations, ranging from the physical through the social to the transcendental needs of the self-actualizing person. In the writings of humanists like Maslow, the element of conflict, central to Freudian thought, is minimized and characterizes maladjusted individuals rather than the natural human condition.

Developmental Sequences

In addition to their similar emphasis on the process of resolving conflicts and satisfying needs, most of the major theorists of personality explicitly include theories of human development. Some, like Freud, with his psychosexual stages, or Maslow, with his motivational levels, deal with changes in the nature of the motivational tendencies, the forces that are to be channeled. Others concentrate on growth in the structures that organize the fundamental tendencies. Most assert that higher processes such as reason, empathy, and self-control allow mastery of raw impulses in ever more sophisticated ways.

Loevinger (1966) has proposed a theory of what she calls ego development. She distinguishes six stages each qualitatively different from the others. The impulsive stage is characteristic only of infants and perhaps of severely disturbed adults, but the other stages are found at all ages. Although each person is supposed to go through the same sequence of stages, many do not outgrow the early ones. In theory, the process is irreversible: Once mature, one can never again think and act in a truly immature way.

The stages Loevinger proposes are perhaps most easily characterized in terms of socialization. Individuals in the early stages are *preconventional*; they want their own way and have few scruples about how they get it. The rules of society are for them merely obstacles to their desires, and although they may follow rules when they know they would be caught otherwise, they have no real allegiance to them. Individuals at the conventional stages—where most adults function—have a very different attitude. They believe wholeheartedly in the need for and wisdom of rules, as determined by religion, law, or local standards of taste and etiquette. *Conforming* persons do what they are told without much question; they follows rituals and forms without necessarily understanding them, and they are motivated by the desire to maintain the good opinion of their fellows. *Conscientious* men and women, in the next higher stage, are also loyal to their country and faith, but are more thoughtful in their interpretation. They are guided by principles, not customs, and are beholden mostly to their own consciences. At the same time, the principles they follow are dictated by society, and they do not venture to question them. (Note that this usage of "conscientious" is different from ours; probably people scoring high on the Conscientiousness factor would also be classified at or above the Conscientious level of ego development, but that is an empirical question that has not yet been addressed.)

At the two highest stages of ego development are individuals who can be considered *postconventional*. They have internalized the principles of their social environment, but they have also transcended them. They, too, are guided by principles, but by principles of their own devising; and they are not unwilling to defy social customs that conflict with what they believe is a higher law. Great social reformers and founders of religions are usually at this level, but so are many ordinary individuals who do not choose to make a career out of their ethical opinions.

This description of Loevinger's stages is, of course, a great over-simplification, in part because it fails to show the importance of emotional and cognitive changes that accompany the moral development.

The form of thought necessary to articulate one's own moral principle is far more sophisticated than that required to say "I want it!" Sensitivity to others' feelings or to one's own unspoken fears or desires is also a far cry from the raw lust or rage that can characterize individuals at the lower ego levels. Progressive levels of ego development, then, are characterized by increasing complexity, differentiation, and integration of thoughts, feelings, and actions.

Dynamic Dispositions

Dynamic theorists often prefer to speak of needs or motives rather than of traits. Motives and needs are dynamic in the sense that they drive behavior, urging us on to do whatever is necessary to achieve certain goals. Some needs, like the need for oxygen, are universal; others, like the need for achievement, characterize only some people or vary in the degree to which they are important to individuals. Motivational psychologists are concerned with the universal ways in which needs are experienced, acquired, and expressed, whereas personality theorists are generally interested in identifying the needs or motives that typify or characterize an individual, usually in contrast to others. Thus, we say that Smith is high in the need for achievement, whereas Jones is low in the need for achievement but high in the need for affiliation.

If this description of needs sounds familiar, it is because it is very similar to the definition previously offered for traits. We showed in Table 5 that the Murray needs measured by Jackson's PRF can be classified within the five-factor model. Some theorists, such as Guilford (1959), regard motives as a class of traits. The only real problem with this conceptualization is that it suggests that there is a clear boundary between motivational and other traits. The distinction between motivational and temperamental traits, or between adaptive and expressive traits (Allport, 1937), is in many respects artificial. Traits as we measure them seem to form a syndrome of motives, moods, expressive and adaptive behavior, and attitudes. The hostile individual, for example, may be high in the need for aggression, often experience the emotion of anger, have a gruff tone of voice, use direct attack as a way of solving problems, and believe that people will always do their best to cause him trouble. The person high in openness to aesthetics may desire to collect art, enjoy beautiful objects, have an artistic handwriting, take lessons to learn painting, and believe the government should support the arts. Traits, then, can be said to have motivational as well as other components. Recall that *disposition* is another word for both *trait* and *motive*. Given the similarities between the two, it seems somewhat silly to decry the "static" nature of traits.

CONTRASTING TRAITS WITH EGO PROCESSES

Trait theories do share with dynamic theories a concern for motivation. But in other respects the two approaches differ, and it is important to consider these differences in judging whether personality changes with age. The most significant differences have to do with the role of ego processes in resolving conflicts and organizing behavior over time.

Conflict and Its Resolution

Dynamic theories of personality tend to emphasize the interaction of the elements they postulate. Freud's instinctive urges are forever battling against irrational prohibitions and rational restraints for expression. Each bit of behavior we observe and each passing thought in our mind is held to be the end result of this perpetual conflict. At one moment the forces of the ego are in control; the next, a slip of the tongue or pen reveals a momentary breech in the defensive armor. Rarely can any behavior be understood as the expression of any single internal tendency. Instead, drives may merge together (as sex and aggression do in sadism) or may be transformed by defense mechanisms into their opposite or may represent a compromise between the dictates of the superego and the cravings of the id. It hardly comes as a surprise to Freudians when personality traits do not predict behavior very well, since behavior is a function of the constantly changing relative strengths of a host of actively competing forces.

As usual, Freudian theory presents this view in its extreme form, holding that *all* behavior is defensive and that conflict is inevitable. Later theorists, like Rogers and Maslow, took a less grim view of the human condition, believing that conflict was not inherent in human nature. But many personality theories recognize the need to explain the mechanisms by which conflicts between impulses or principles are resolved when they do arise.

At each moment we are capable of acting and experiencing in only a very limited way. We are not at liberty to express our assertiveness or indulge our anxiety continually, even if we would like to. We are limited by the opportunities the environment presents, the demands that society and the persons we interact with place on us, and sometimes the competing pressures of incompatible traits: Excitement-seeking bids us to drive faster, anxiety urges us to slow down. It is obvious that choices must be made—consciously, unconsciously, or by habit—and it is clear that these choices are not, by and large, random. Sane, mature individuals are not buffeted by internal and external pressures like leaves in the wind. With more or less success, they coordinate their behavior and routinely resolve conflicts. The mechanisms for resolving conflict are an important part of the ego.

For psychoanalysts, conflict is usually resolved through the use of defense mechanisms (A. Freud, 1936). Wishes or memories that would create too much guilt or anxiety because of their conflict with internalized prohibitions are repressed, transformed, or disguised. The individual is not even aware that a conflict exists, except when the transformations fail or lead to neurotic symptoms. Whether or not one accepts the accounts offered by analysts, it is certainly true that individuals do learn to control their impulses. Sometimes suppression—deliberate and conscious inhibition—is involved, but often the offending desires never reach consciousness. Children cry when they do not get what they want; adults may feel frustrated, but it rarely occurs to them to cry.

Murray and Kluckhohn (1953) describe a number of more rational ways to resolve conflicts between tendencies. Using reason, foresight, and self-control, the individual with a strong ego is able to choose between competing courses of action, resist temptations that would lead to undesirable consequences, and resolve the conflicting claims of social pressures, personal preferences, and external necessity. Resolving conflicts need not mean the application of rigid self-control. There are usually opportunities for compromise or for creative solutions. Two needs may be fused (that is, both may be satisfied by the same behavior, as when a neurotic extravert talks about his imaginary illnesses); or one might be used in the service of another, as when a person closed to values uses her assertiveness to force a conservative position on a group.

Temporal Organization

Another way to resolve conflicts is to allow each tendency expression at a different time. By creating—and sticking to—routines or *schedules* (as

Murray calls them) we can manage to satisfy all or most of our needs on a regular basis. Organizing behavior in time is an essential and distinctive feature of ego processes.

Consider for a moment the course of a typical day. We get up, eat breakfast, go to work, apply ourselves to the necessary tasks, take breaks, talk to our co-workers, eat lunch and perhaps read a book, go back to work, and so on. Trait theorists would be able to make certain predictions about this collection of behavior: Introverts are more likely to read at lunchtime and less likely to a spend a good deal of their day in social conversation; people high in neuroticism may wake up tired, get angry about the work expected of them, overeat at lunch; open people are more likely to spend their working hours on tasks like writing, teaching college, or doing research; closed people will more likely be attending to business and following strict routines.

But although information about traits can be extremely useful in predicting specifics of behavior, it cannot, by itself, account for the structured flow or temporal sequence of behavior. These are ego functions, as important in shaping the life course as in managing daily routines. In addition to schedules, Murray proposed the notion of *serials*, programs of action extended over time and intended to achieve long-range goals. Attending college and law school, working in a law firm, beginning one's own practice, and running for local office may all be steps toward a political career; only with planned and coordinated efforts, pursued diligently over a long period of time, could one achieve this end. Murray holds that the selection of realistic goals and their pursuit over extended portions of the life span are major tasks of the ego.

INDIVIDUAL DIFFERENCES IN EGO PROCESSES

Trait theory does not deal with the processes—instrumental learning, formal reasoning, creative planning, defensive distortion—by which behavior and experience are molded on a moment-to-moment basis. But although ego psychologists make these processes central to their theories, most are also concerned with characterizing individuals. People differ in the needs, values, and goals that must be organized and harmonized by the ego, but they also differ in the ways in which the ego goes about its task of coordination. It is not simply that people make plans for the future: Some plan wisely, some poorly, some hardly at all. Individual differences in ego processes are an important issue in personality theory.

Loevinger's theory of ego stages is a clear example. Men and women in the lower stages of development are subject to strong and primitive impulses and tend to express them immediately. Because their ego functioning is undeveloped, they cannot resolve conflicts effectively or set up efficient schedules. In the long run they are unable to satisfy many needs, at least without provoking guilt or reprisals from others. Persons with higher levels of ego development have far more sensitive and sophisticated ways of integrating their needs and values. On the other hand, the lives of individuals with high ego levels are correspondingly more complex, and they are troubled by abstract problems to which persons with low ego levels are oblivious. Thus, high ego development does not necessarily mean greater satisfaction or happiness (McCrae & Costa, 1983b).

Other theories of individual differences in ego functioning are more attentive to overall adjustment. *Ego strength* is a characteristic discussed by a number of psychoanalytic writers, who generally define it as the ability of the individual to manage successfully the competing forces of instinctual demands, internal prohibitions, and social reality. Murray uses the term to describe characteristics needed to lead a well-ordered life. People thought to be low in ego strength are less intelligent, more ethnocentric, and generally more prone to many kinds of psychopathology (Barron, 1980).

Block (1965) distinguished two dimensions of ego functioning. *Ego resiliency* is defined as the individual's ability to adapt to new demands. Individuals high in ego resiliency are resourceful and flexible; those who are low are touchy, moody, and uncomfortable in their world. *Ego control*, a second dimension, is seen in characteristic levels of impulse control. Overcontrolled individuals are overconforming, narrow in interests, and interpersonally distant; undercontrolled people are spontaneous, inclined toward immediate gratification of impulses, and willing to act in new and untried ways.

Traits and Metatraits?

Concepts such as ego level, ego strength, and ego control are intended to describe the functioning of the ego in different individuals, but as enduring characteristics, they resemble traits much more than ego processes. One way to distinguish them from more mundane traits is to grant them the status of superordinate traits or *metatraits*. These are the enduring dispositions that govern the expression and integration of other dispositions. Loevinger (1966) comes close to this formulation when she calls ego level the "master trait."

But as we begin to examine the idea of metatraits closely, their distinctiveness begins to evaporate. Block's description of ego resiliency makes it sound very much like low Neuroticism, and a measure of ego resiliency based on MMPI items showed a strong negative correlation with NEO-PI Neuroticism, $r = -.70$, $N = 274$, $p < .001$, in the BLSA. Similarly, ego control seems to represent low levels of Impulsiveness, Excitement Seeking, and Openness, and these hypotheses are also confirmed (r's $= -.27$, $-.54$, and $-.34$, $p < .001$). Barron's ego-strength scale is known to correlate with measures of maladjustment and Neuroticism. And Loevinger's master trait of ego level is strongly related to intelligence as well as to personality (McCrae & Costa, 1980). A study we conducted in Boston employed the sentence completions of 240 men to examine ego levels using Loevinger's own instrument. The scores we obtained were correlated with our measures of personality and intelligence. We found, as she has repeatedly, that there is a marked correlation with IQ (about .50), showing that higher ego levels are more often found in more intelligent people. But we also found that there was a significant correlation with Openness to experience, even when we controlled for intelligence. More open people are rated as being more mature in the Loevinger system.

One interpretation of these conceptual and empirical correspondences would suggest that traits and metatraits are not really distinct. The same traits that are organized by the ego are responsible for the individual differences in the way the ego organizes them. Intelligence is a trait, but it also modifies the ways other traits are expressed: Introverts read books; intelligent introverts read difficult books. Again, anxiety is a trait, but the disposition to experience anxiety may disrupt the efficient functioning of other traits. Test anxiety, for example, may lead to poor performance despite high intelligence.

If these speculations are correct, we do not need to introduce new traits to explain differences in ego organization or the resulting differences in the life structure. Instead, we must recognize that in order to describe fully the significance of a trait, we must not only specify the behaviors and feelings associated with it, but also identify the effects the trait has on the organization of other traits.

The other side of this interpretation is that in inferring traits we ought to look not simply at specific behaviors, but at the whole pattern of the individual's life. And this is precisely what we advocated in Chapter 2 as the best basis for inferring traits.

DEVELOPMENTAL CHANGES IN EGO PROCESSES

If the essence of personality is the organization and integration of experience and behavior, the most important question about age and personality would be what happens to the major ego functions with age. It is in this context, perhaps, that the issue of growth or decline in personality makes most sense. After all, what do we mean by growth in personality? It is easy to see that becoming taller or more intelligent is growth, but how does personality grow? Although we assumed in Chapter 4 that any change in the average level of a trait could be interpreted as either growth or decline, in fact it would have been difficult to interpret an increase in introversion or Openness to aesthetic experiences in these terms. Not all changes represent growth or decline.

But we could probably make a good case for the contention that there is a natural direction of growth in ego functioning. Loevinger suggests as much in her developmental stages, as does Erikson (1950) in his stages of psychosocial development. Many other writers have also proposed criteria of psychological maturity that could properly be seen as growth in personality and would generally be considered attributes of ego functioning. Bühler mentions formulation of a stable identity, willingness to assume responsibility, ability to form significant and lasting attachments to others, self-acceptance, emotional security, and commitment to life goals (Bühler, Keith-Spiegel, & Thomas, 1973).

Most of us would agree that these are signs of maturity, and we would probably suspect that adults possess more of them than do adolescents. But does maturity increase with age once we have become adults? Or do older individuals regress to more primitive ways of resolving conflicts, dealing with others, and organizing their activities?

If the argument we developed above is correct—if ego characteristics are determined by such traits as anxiety, depression, warmth, and openness to ideas—it would follow that there ought not to be major changes in the functioning of the ego across the adult life span, since the traits that determine it are themselves stable.

Consider the case of ego development. If individuals continue to mature in the period of adulthood, the ego levels of older individuals should be higher than those of younger individuals. But we know that ego level is related to the traits of intelligence and Openness and that both of these are generally stable in adulthood. We would predict, then, that there should be no changes in ego level. And cross-sectional data from the Boston sample clearly confirm that prediction (McCrae & Costa, 1980), as do other independent studies (Vaillant & McCullough, 1987). Longitudinal studies have shown that the predicted changes in ego development are seen as individuals move from childhood to adolescence, but there is no evidence of change after adulthood is reached. If ego level is indeed the master trait, this is one more evidence of stability at all levels of personality.

Conclusions on stability or change in ego processes are perhaps premature. It is much harder to describe the organization of elements than the elements themselves. Additionally, there is no consensus on what properties of the ego we should be measuring: Is control of impulses the key, or the arrangement of attitudes and beliefs? Should we be concerned with the normal daily functioning of individuals, with their responses to crisis situations, or with their long-range plans? Or must we develop a battery of tests to consider each of these separately?

And what kind of tests? It may be that individuals, although able to report adequately on emotional reactions or vocational preferences, are incapable of judging the more profound styles that tie together all these discrete elements. Perhaps an analysis of a deeper level of personality is needed. Projective tests are supposed to give a picture of the deeper layers of personality, and we will shortly review what they have to tell us about age and personality. But just as we were compelled to describe the rationale and evaluate the efficacy of self-report measures in Chapter 3, so now we must do the same to lay the groundwork for an evaluation of projectives.

PROJECTIVE ASSESSMENTS OF PERSONALITY

For reasons partly historical and partly theoretical, psychologists of the dynamic school have usually preferred evaluations of personality based on something other than self-reports. The first and most common argument offered against self-report assessments is that individuals may not be aware of important aspects of their personality and may in fact systematically distort their perceptions and reports of themselves. This is a perfectly reasonable point of view for Freudians, who locate the variables of real interest in the unconscious. We cannot expect individuals to report accurately the ways in which they deceive themselves and try to deceive others; yet, according to psychoanalysts, these defenses are among the most important aspects of personality.

As a result, clinicians and researchers have devised a number of methods of assessing personality indirectly. Most of these tests are called *projective*, from the belief that the individual projects his or her personality unwittingly into the task. Asked to describe a picture, individuals probably imagine that their responses tell about what they see. The psychologist, however, believes that the responses tell about the subject. A variety of techniques have been used to outsmart the subject in this way. The individuals being assessed may be asked to give associations to words, report what they see in inkblots, make up stories to accompany the cards of the Thematic Apperception Test (TAT), draw pictures, or write completions for unfinished sentences.

The scoring of these materials is, of course, very different from summing up the items on a scale. A judge (usually human, but occasionally a computer) must consider the subject's production in the light of some set of rules developed to judge the characteristic of interest. Sometimes the rules are quite specific; sometimes they require extensive intuition. The scoring system may be based on the empirical strategy of contrasting the responses of one group with those of another, or it may be derived from purely theoretical considerations. Psychoanalytically oriented researchers often propose scoring systems based on the presumed symbolic significance of responses. There is a strong tradition of assessing needs through the TAT on the assumption that the concerns of the story's hero are those of the story's creator (McClelland, 1980; Murray, 1938). A story about long struggles leading to a successful career, for instance, might be interpreted as evidence of a high need for achievement.

Some psychologists prefer unstructured, projective methods to self-report questionnaires for very different reasons. McClellend (1980) distinguished between what he called *operant* and *respondent* tests. The former consist of materials—a picture, a blank sheet of paper, a sentence fragment—that the subject can organize and interpret for him- or herself; the pictures on TAT cards are the primary example. Respondent tests are exemplified by questionnaire items, in which the subject must respond within a strictly limited number of alternative ways to a fixed set of items. McClelland objects that this regimentation, which makes scoring of respondent tests so convenient, introduces an artificiality. An older individual, for example, might find all the items in a test designed for college students irrelevant to her, though if urged she would still fill it out. What would the responses mean in that case? Operant tests are not subject to this criticism. The subject can always *make* a picture relevant by choosing what elements to respond to, or by creating a story that goes beyond the picture toward whatever concerns he or she has. Similarly, McGuire (1984) argued that psychologists should study the spontaneous self-concept, as revealed in free descriptions, to learn how individuals really see themselves.

Loevinger makes a different point in defending her choice of a sentence-completion test to measure ego development. What is of primary interest, she maintains, is not so much what the person decides as how he or she makes the decision. Asking the subject to complete stems (e.g., "What I like best about being a man is...") gives the researcher an opportunity to observe how the subject will structure and organize his responses, free from the promptings of the investigator. Since it is the processing of the ego that Loevinger wants to measure and since most situations in life present the same ambiguity as pictures or half-formed sentences, it can be argued that tests that simulate these conditions should give the best picture of the ego at work. In effect, such tests provide samples of ego functioning, rather than reports about how the individual thinks he or she is.

There are thus three major lines of argument about the superiority of projective tests over questionnaires. The first holds that the real personality is hidden from the subject and can only be inferred indirectly from signs and symbols that the trained psychologist must interpret. The second claims that structured questionnaires are often irrelevant, and only unstructured material can convey an accurate representation of the individual's nature. The third argument supposes that personality is best assessed by observation of its workings in an unstructured situation. All would concur in the belief that answers to personality inventories are largely irrelevant.

Problems in Projective Methods

Historically, these arguments have been very powerful. Projective methods continue to be among the most widely used of psychological tests in practice and in research (Lubin, Larsen, Matarazzo, & Seever, 1985). For many years, however, psychometricians and those who have reviewed the empirical literature have repeatedly pointed to serious problems in projective methods. Our examination of the issue has led us to side with the critics, but the reader should realize that this is a controversial, even unpopular position to take.

What kinds of problems do projective and other unstructured tests pose? They are highly inferential, ignore other factors that contribute to responses, are unreliable over time, and are inadequate as samples of behavior. The ultimate problem is that they frequently fail to show evidence of external validity; that is, they do not predict the kinds of outcomes they are supposed to.

Clinicians in the psychoanalytic tradition are trained to seek out the hidden meanings behind such seemingly innocuous or meaningless phenomena as dreams, slips of the tongue, or word associations. The Rorschach inkblots were designed to provide a standard ambiguous stimulus onto which the patient could project his or her inner conflicts and fixations, and clinicians were supposed to interpret these responses in terms of dynamic theories of symbolic expression. A skilled interpreter can often create a persuasive reading of inkblot responses, but it is usually impossible to tell if the interpretation is correct. We certainly would not want to trust peer or spouse ratings in such a case, since few friends or relatives are competent to judge degree of oral fixation or intrusion of the anima. The most promising test of the quality of an interpretation is its agreement with the interpretations of other qualified clinicians; yet extensive research has typically yielded little evidence of agreement on inferences about the so-called deep level of personality. Mischel (1968) put it this way:

> Statements about "deep-seated unconscious anxieties," "latent homosexual tendencies," "reaction formations," and other similar inferences about inferred covert dynamic processes or structures . . . may provide intriguing reading. No matter how fascinating personality descriptions may seem, however, they have little value when competent judges cannot agree about them. (p. 121)

Interpretation is difficult in part because so many things other than personality traits influence the responses. When we ask subjects to draw a picture or tell a story, their artistic abilities are likely to be much more in evidence than their intrapsychic dynamics. Under the naive assumption that the hero of the story represents the personality of the storyteller, we would have to infer that novelists, who are capable of describing a huge range of human characters, have multiple personalities. Perceptual problems (which are common in the elderly), verbal skill, and motivation all have a much greater impact on projective responses than they do on objective test results. Indeed, projective tests may be most valuable as samples of cognitive behavior—not personality.

Reliability has always been a thorny issue for projective tests. Personality is supposed to be consistent across time and situations; it is, almost by definition, that which endures as the momentary pressures of the environment and the body vary (Maddi, 1980). The specific behaviors may well change, but the psychologist should be able to infer the underlying unity throughout the changes. It seems reasonable to expect that the projective test results, which allegedly mirror personality, would show the same degree of consistency across different forms of the test, or at different times. This is the criterion of reliability, and it has always proven to be a sore spot in projective testing. TAT stories change from one time to another, and so do the scores derived from them (Winter & Stewart, 1977), perhaps because needs change as a result of their expression on the test (Atkinson, Bongort, & Price, 1977).

But if the expression of needs is subject to such marked fluctuations, we have no way of knowing whether the responses we obtain on the first test are characteristic of the individual or simply a reflection of the immediate situation. The TAT measures may be accurate reflections of the motivational *state* of the individual, but if they are not reliable over time, they are poor indicators of characteristic *traits* of the individual. The same argument, of course, also applies to projective tests of processes other than needs: defenses, complexes, attitudes, and cognitive styles. Demonstrable retest reliability is essential to the measurement of individual characteristics, and many projective tests fail to meet even minimal standards of reliability.

There are significant problems with the idea that unstructured tests can be used to obtain an interpretable sample of the operations of personality. A questionnaire item that asks "Are you often irritable and angry?" requires the subject to review his or her behavior over a period of months and to estimate the typical level of this state. To the extent that the person is able to weigh accurately his or her recollections, this item gives an average based on thousands of hours of living in a wide range of situations. By contrast, observing the responses of the individual to an inkblot or sentence fragment gives only a tiny sample of behaviors, all within the thoroughly artificial situation of a psychological testing session. One of the recent conclusions from the trait-consistency controversy is that any single instance of behavior is likely to be a very poor indicator of the average level (Epstein, 1979); if we really want samples of ego functioning, we must plan to spend a great deal more time and effort than we currently do.

Finally, and most compellingly, the results of careful research studies using projective tests to measure traits or predict outcomes have had almost uniformly disappointing results. In a detailed review of studies on projective tests conducted between 1950 and 1965, Suinn and Oskamp (1969) concluded, "There are only a few things which the clinician can predict from these personality tests with confidence that his judgments are being made on a scientific basis. The remainder of his predictive work is still based on faith or on theory rather than on evidence" (p. 117). A review based on only five studies (Parker, Hanson, & Hunsley, 1988) came to a more sanguine conclusion on the validity of Rorschach measures, but it is safe to say the weight of evidence is still against the scientific value of most projective measures.

Conscious versus Unconscious Elements

One of the most intriguing aspects of Suinn and Oskamp's review is the consistent finding that the most nearly valid tests were those that agreed most closely with self-report. Sentence-completion tests, for example, that come close to direct self-reports are among the better validated projective tests. Rotter and Rafferty (1950) constructed a sentence-completion test of maladjustment that was significantly correlated with both clinical judgments and self-reports of adjustment. In our study of ego level and Openness to experience (McCrae & Costa, 1980), we examined responses to Loevinger's sentence-completion stems for evidence of Openness (without knowledge of how subjects had rated themselves). We judged subjects as *open* when we found statements showing flexible views of rules, rejection of traditional sex roles, intrinsic interest in experience, or playfulness. When we compared our judgments with the self-reports of openness the same subjects had given us, we found agreement in 78% of the cases.

But projective assessments that make inferences about unconscious processes are more likely to fail to agree with self-reports. In these cases, there is usually also little agreement with any other external criterion of importance, such as suicide, sexual orientation, or improvement in therapy. Fascinating as the symbolic interpretations of the Freudians are, there is simply no good evidence that they are correct.

What all of this suggests to us is that the unconscious level of personality either cannot be measured by projectives or does not have much influence on human conduct. No one who has read Freud or Jung could fail to appreciate the marvelous insight that there are levels of the mind that operate by a logic different from that of our waking consciousness; that these are more characteristic of children than of adults; that they appear in dreams, in artistic productions, in psychotic delusions, and in culturally shared myths; and that the primitive ways of thinking we have inherited from our evolutionary ancestors often appear in them in undisguised form. The data collected over the past 50 years, however, have convinced us that these curious relics of our past have relatively little to do with our daily life or with such important outcomes as happiness, response to stress, or political beliefs.

PROJECTIVE TESTING AND THE STABILITY OF PERSONALITY

Let us summarize the argument so far and then proceed to a more specific consideration of the relationship between projectively assessed personality and aging. We have considered the reasons for preferring projective tests to self-reports and have rejected them. Some projective tests aim at a deeper level of personality, but that deeper level, if it is indeed tapped by such tests, does not appear to have much influence on important aspects of personality, at least in psychiatrically normal adults. Some unstructured tests aim to sample the ego, to judge it by its spontaneous functioning in an unstructured situation. But there is strong reason to believe that the samples obtained are generally inadequate and that when they approach adequacy they simply duplicate information that could more easily have been obtained by direct questioning.

We might, therefore, dismiss projective testing altogether and decline to review a literature based on such faulty instruments. We have noted that sentence-completion tests, the most reliable of projectives, show no cross-sectional relationship of ego development to age in adulthood

(McCrae & Costa, 1980). At the same time, it will be worthwhile to consider some examples of aging and personality research using projective techniques, if only as a way of illustrating the points already made.

Inkblot Tests

Cross-sectional studies of inkblot responses do in fact show a regular progression of age-related changes. Old people make fewer and more concrete descriptions of what they see and tend to give global responses instead of picking out minor details (Kahana, 1978). Both cross-sectional and longitudinal studies (Ames, 1965) have verified this tendency; but before concluding that here at last is evidence of personality change, we must bear in mind that the Rorschach is used to assess cognition and perception as well as personality. There is no doubt that there are age-related changes in learning, memory, perceptual closure, and visual acuity, and these, rather than personality change, may well account for the age differences. Caldwell made that argument as long ago as 1954, and Eisdorfer (1963) provided some strong evidence in favor of it. When he matched old and young subjects on cognitive abilities as measured by the Wechsler Adult Intelligence Scales or WAIS, he found no differences in Rorschach responses.

We (Costa & McCrae, 1986a) conducted a 2-year longitudinal study of age differences and changes on scales of the Holtzman Inkblot Technique or HIT (Holtzman, 1961). The HIT is intended to provide a psychometrically superior version of the better-known Rorschach test. Respondents are shown 45 blots and asked to tell what each looks like. Responses are scored for 22 variables, ranging from reaction time (how long it takes for the subject to offer an interpretation) to the content of the response (animal, human, anatomy) to the definiteness and appropriateness of the response for a given blot. These scales, alone and in combination, can be given psychodynamic interpretations (Hill, 1972).

We originally administered the HIT to 93 men and women in the BLSA aged 25 to 90. When correlated with age, only four of the 22 HIT variables showed significant associations, and all of these were small. Further, when the test was readministered to 44 of the subjects about 2 years later, only one of the four cross-sectional findings was replicated by longitudinal changes: Scores on the HIT Hostility scale were higher in older subjects and also increased over time, suggesting a possible maturational effect. However, this may well have been a chance finding, since Overall and Gorham (1972) did not replicate it in a much larger cross-sectional study.

We also examined stability coefficients for the 44 subjects with two administrations. These correlations ranged from .07 for Form Appropriateness to .73 for Form Definiteness; most of the HIT variables gave evidence of moderate to substantial stability over the 2-year interval. Finally, we correlated the HIT scales with measures of Neuroticism, Extraversion, and Openness, but we found no consistent pattern of associations. In particular, the HIT Hostility score was unrelated to Neuroticism. (Later analyses showed that none of the HIT scales was related to Agreeableness or Conscientiousness, either.)

Interpreting these results is difficult. Because they are not correlated with measures of the five factors, we cannot group the HIT scales into familiar domains of personality—in fact, we could conclude that the HIT does not measure personality at all. Perhaps it measures some form of perceptual or cognitive style, or perhaps merely idiosyncratic preferences: When looking at inkblots, some people tend to see animals, some to see people. Whatever it is that the HIT scales measure appears to be relatively stable over a 2-year period, and perhaps for much longer. We found little evidence of age-related change in HIT scores. If the HIT measures unconscious layers of personality, they do not appear to change with age.

TAT Studies

The Thematic Apperception Test (TAT) was introduced by Murray (1938) as a way of inferring motives or needs of which the individual might not be consciously aware. Veroff, Depner, Kulka, and Douvan (1980) used the TAT for this purpose in two national surveys, conducted in 1957 and 1976. They scored the stories for evidence of the needs for achievement, affiliation, and two forms of power: fear of weakness and hope of power. When controlled for time of testing and education, men showed higher hope of power in middle age, and women showed lower need for affiliation in old age. In each sex, the other three needs showed no significant cross-sectional differences.

The technique of eliciting stories from pictures as a basis for assessing needs, traits, and defenses has been particularly popular with gerontologists. Gutmann (1970) used TAT cards for his research on the concept of ego mastery. He scored TAT stories in terms of active, passive, and magical mastery. Cross-cultural longitudinal studies suggested that as men age they pass from a stage of active mastery (in which TAT heroes forcefully tackle the problems of their world) to a stage of passive mastery (in which they acquiesce in the demands of the environment) and then to a stage of magical mastery (in which problems are denied or wished away). Gutmann's description of ego mastery style as a measure of coping style or adaptational ability suggests that it should have some consequences for the ways in which older people adapt to stress.

The use of magical mastery in old age is consistent with some clinical views that hold that older people tend to use more primitive forms of defense, such as blatant denial of reality (Pfeiffer, 1977). These views may accurately reflect the behavior of older people with dementing disorders, but they are highly suspect when applied to cognitively intact older individuals. Once we move away from the patently bizarre delusions of psychotic or demented individuals, it is often difficult to know if behavior or attitudes are truly reflections of denial (Costa, Zonderman, & McCrae, in press). For example, older individuals, despite the proximity of death, generally do not show a heightened fear of death (Kastenbaum & Costa, 1977). To claim this as an instance of denial, we would have to assert that death really is a threat that should be feared—and we have no objective basis for such an assertion. Some people view death as a release or as a passage to a new and better life. Are they merely rationalizing? Who can say?

Stereotypes of old age have portrayed it as a dismal portion of the life span, and evidence that older men and women are generally as happy and satisfied with life as are younger individuals (Costa & McCrae, 1984) is taken by many as evidence of defensive distortion. But the appearance of happiness among older people is so common that we would have to assume that older people universally resorted to the use of primitive defenses, and this would be inconsistent with the fact that most cope relatively well and realistically with events such as retirement, death of spouse, and personal illness.

Objective studies of age and coping show no tendency for older people to use magical denial in solving real-life problems (McCrae, 1982a). In two studies, BLSA subjects were asked to describe how they had coped with recent stresses, chosen either by us or by the subjects themselves. Using a self-report checklist of ways of coping, we assigned them scores on 28 different coping mechanisms, including rational action, distraction, denial of affect, intellectual denial, and passivity. We found age differences in the kinds of stress older people faced—generally more threats to health and fewer occupational and family challenges—but when the responses had been corrected for these differences only two consistent findings emerged. Younger men and women were more likely than middle-aged and older ones to indulge in escapist fantasy and hostile reactions. There was no evidence whatsoever that magical solutions were chosen by the elderly.

Gutmann himself is careful to point out that the progression he posits occurs on the level of fantasy, not of reality. Among the Highland Druze of Israel, in particular, the old men are respected as leaders and decisions makers; they are anything but passive.

So it seems that neither self-reports nor direct observations of behavior show parallels to the developmental sequence inferred by Gutmann from TAT responses. Perhaps these changes result from cognitive or perceptual shifts, or perhaps they are changes in a deeper level of personality. In any case, they appear to have little impact on social or emotional functioning.

A few longitudinal studies have used the TAT to assess individual stability of projectively assessed dispositions. Skolnick (1966) reported 20-year stability coefficients ranging from .21 to .34 for the needs for power, affiliation, aggression, and achievement, although the findings were not consistently replicated across sexes. Britton and Britton (1972) also reported significant stability coefficients for TAT measures of personal and social adjustment over intervals of 3, 6, and 9 years in small samples of men and women aged 65 to 85 at first testing. The magnitude of these correlations is far smaller than the .60 to .80 that we are accustomed to seeing from self-reports, but that is to be expected. Given the limited reliability of projective tests, the long-term retest correlations from TAT studies can be seen as further evidence of stability.

Age and the Spontaneous Self-Concept

We have argued that unstructured methods that require little inference on the part of the researcher and thus approximate self-reports have generally been shown to be more valid than other projective methods. Measures of the spontaneous self-concept may combine the best of both worlds. In these techniques, individuals are simply asked to describe themselves, either in a few paragraphs or as a series of responses to the question, "Who am I?" (Kuhn & McPartland, 1954). These are certainly self-reports, but they are free of the usual constraints of questionnaires that ask a series of specific questions.

We studied the spontaneous self-concept of men and women in the BLSA (McCrae & Costa, 1988a). Subjects provided 20 different responses to the question, "Who am I?," and two raters categorized their responses. Recall that the self-concept is composed of many kinds of elements, of which personality dispositions are only one. Most people described themselves in terms of social roles ("a loving mother"; "a retired teacher"), physical characteristics such as health or attractiveness, and activities and attitudes ("I enjoy boating and camping"). Only about one-quarter of the responses specified personality traits ("I am hardworking and productive"). In addition to categorizing each separate response, our raters gave overall impressions of the individual's standing on each of the five personality factors and on general level of self-esteem.

There were several findings of note from this study. First, the impressions of personality that raters drew from the patterns of responses were fairly accurate: The two raters generally agreed with each other, and in most cases their combined ratings were significantly correlated with both self-reports and peer ratings on the NEO-PI. We apparently get much the same information when we ask specific questions of subjects or when we ask them for a general description of themselves and then evaluate the specific responses they make in terms of our basic dimensions.

Second, there was little evidence that personality expressed in the spontaneous self-concept was influenced much by age. Older subjects were somewhat less likely to describe themselves in terms of traits that reflected emotional instability or Neuroticism, but none of the other personality factors was significantly associated with age. Self-esteem was also unrelated to age; instead, it was associated with low levels of Neuroticism and high levels of Extraversion. Adjusted extraverts have high self-esteem at any age.

Third, age was only modestly related to the other scoring categories. Older subjects were somewhat less likely to describe themselves in terms of family relationships and somewhat more likely to mention daily activities and attitudes. Age itself was rarely mentioned as a salient part of the self-concept. Older people may think of themselves as citizens, parents, curious individuals, or gardening enthusiasts, but they apparently don't think much about being old. Perhaps they have learned that age itself is not very important for describing what they are like as persons.

* * *

This chapter set out to consider the criticisms of the stability position that might be offered by personologists with different theoretical and methodological preferences. We conceded that the processes by which behavior is integrated and organized, both moment by moment and over the sweep of a lifetime, are not explicitly addressed by trait models, as they should be in a complete theory of personality. But we also argued that individual differences in these processes, including differences between young and old people, were likely to have trait-like characteristics, and that, in fact, the traits we normally measure are as likely to influence the organization and integration of other traits as they are to influence specific behaviors. To the extent that this is true, we might argue that there are probably no age differences in ego processes.

But is that true? Or are there other organizing features of personality that have eluded the grasp of self-report trait measures? To answer this, we turned to the favored resort of theorists who concentrate on ego processes—projective methods. We found that, to the extent that they depart from the information that could be obtained from self-reports, these measures are generally unreliable and invalid, except perhaps as samples of cognitive behavior or as evidence of shadowy processes (like mastery style) that have little relevance to daily functioning or the course of life. To the extent that they mirror conscious concerns and tendencies, as in measures of the spontaneous self-concept, they tend to give evidence of stability in personality.

At this point the astute reader will have noticed that the issue has not really been resolved. We admitted that self-reports might not adequately assess the functioning of the ego and then suggested that we examine projectives. But our assessment of projective techniques hardly leaves us with confidence in any testimony they might offer. Is it not possible, you may ask, that there really are profound changes in the fundamental structure of personality, but that projective tests, with all their limitations, are simply inadequate to the task of finding and documenting them? And if we cannot trust self-reports or projective tests, is there another way to explore the deeper levels of personality? Is there a way to sample the ego at work without letting the ego do the sampling? Is there a way to look for age-related differences in the organization of behavior independent of the trait conceptions embedded in our measures? Perhaps an objective and trained observer, sensitized to issues of personality organization and allowed to collect whatever information seemed relevant, could accomplish the task. Perhaps what we need is an intensive clinical interview. Many people have thought so, and some of the most important theorizing on adult development has been generated by this method. We will examine it next.

·8·

ADULT DEVELOPMENT AS SEEN THROUGH THE PERSONAL INTERVIEW

The interview is a venerable psychological technique with many variants: The clinical interview is used to gain diagnostic information; the therapeutic interview to help the client think through his or her problems; Levinson's "biographical interview" to gain a sense of the individual's life; the research interview to gather information. Some interviews, such as those conducted by survey researchers and pollsters, are really questionnaires administered verbally rather than in writing; of these we have little to say, since they are essentially self-report instruments. But most interviews involve freer questioning at the discretion of the interviewer, and most require judgments by a rater (who may or may not be the interviewer) rather than simple tabulations of answers. It is these sorts of interviews that we need to consider next, since they have played an important role in theories of adult development.

As a technique for gathering information on personality, the interview has a privileged status. Clinicians, who have always dominated personality research and theory, are accustomed to talking directly to patients and to making diagnostic judgments about their condition; it is understandable that they would put particular faith in the results of interviews. The same principles and practices that are used in therapeutic interviews can be applied to normal subjects of pure research.

According to its proponents, the interview has all the advantages of self-report instruments and more. The same questions can be asked by either method, so that the unique experiences of the individuals and their wide knowledge of themselves can be exploited. But in the interview, these self-reports need not be taken at face value.

Perhaps the subject does not seem to understand the question—then it can be rephrased. Perhaps the answers are inconsistent—then the inconsistency can be pointed out or the issue probed more subtly. Perhaps the subject is squirming too much in his chair when certain topics are mentioned. The canny interviewer, who is normally a trained profes- sional, can use all these clues to qualify and evaluate the self-reported information. For many researchers the professional interview is the gold standard by which other personality assessments are judged. Farrell and Rosenberg (1981), for example, administered self-report questionnaires to 500 subjects drawn to represent the population in general. But most of the conclusions in the book they wrote on their studies are based on interviews with 20 of these men (and their families). The authors simply did not trust the self-reports to give them the complete and unvarnished truth. (As it turned out, the interviews upheld the major conclusions of the self-report study, although many more complexities were uncovered.)

Before deferring completely to the superiority of the interview, how- ever, we should weigh some of its limitations. The results of each interview depend on human judgment, and even expert judgment is fallible. Interviews are typically conducted in 1 or 2 hours; at best they may last 8 to 10. The interviewer or the rater who interprets the interview must formulate opinions about the person and his or her life on that rather slim basis. What if the subject is nervous and unused to talking about himself? What if he or she is having an off day? What if the interviewer simply misreads him, thinking that his jokes are intended seriously or that his serious comments are jokes? Is it really wise to try to second-guess the real meaning of an individual's statements?

Even more unsettling is the fact that interview methods are subject to certain kinds of error that are more serious because they are more systematic. If 100 40-year-old men are asked how they feel, some will certainly exaggerate how bad things are, and some will surely try to cover up their distress. Some will be having unusually bad days, some unusually good ones. None of the self-reports may be perfectly trustworthy—but *on the average* they are likely to be roughly correct. On the other hand, if one psychologist interviews 100 men, and if she happens to believe that there is a midlife crisis, she may well accept the stories of the distressed and dismiss the others as defensive distortion. Of course, if she has other biases, she may reach other conclusions equally inconsistent with the facts. The point is that interviewers are not usually impartial observers.

Clinicians are trained to see pathology, and see it they will, even in the best-adjusted subjects. Since theorists have a vested interest in finding evidence for the ideas they have advanced, the "data" they find in support of their own ideas must be taken with a certain degree of skepticism.

There are some precautions that can be taken to avoid the introduction of biases. For example, the interviews may be tape-recorded or videotaped, and two or more judges can then rate the subject on the variables of interest. Agreement between them would be evidence that there is some basis in the interview for the inferences that were made and would seem to be a minimum requirement for taking the study seriously. Even perfect agreement, however, would not necessarily mean much. A subject who was extremely nervous during the session might be characterized by both raters as anxious, although his behavior in the interview was unusual, the result of some temporary and extraordinary circumstance.

Further, an interview is an interpersonal encounter. The interviewer is not an uninvolved, dispassionate observer, but rather an active participant. As any courtroom lawyer will tell you, people can be led to say a great many things under the skillful questioning of an expert. In our courts of law, we try to compensate for this suggestibility by allowing a cross-examination in which a second lawyer, representing an opposite point of view, sees how far the testimony can be shifted in the other direction. In psychological research, this method is never employed (although it might be worth a try). When an adult developmentalist is looking for signs of a midlife crisis in a person, he must act as his own opposing counsel, cross-examining the subject to test all possibilities. Lawyers are not allowed to do this, since they are clearly motivated to help their clients. Researchers, on the other hand, are presumed to be motivated only by a desire for truth.

The pros and cons of the interview method reflect the larger issue that has always profoundly divided personality psychologists: the role of the unconscious. There are those who believe in the unconscious as the real heart of personality, the true source of action, meaning, and value; and there are those who relegate it to a minor role or dismiss it entirely. Communication between these two schools is like an exchange between a believer and an atheist: The fundamental premises are so different that neither can understand the other's point of view. Like religion, the unconscious must in part at least be taken on faith. Once its existence and importance are accepted, however, it seems to make sense of many phenomena.

Researchers who prefer interviews are generally believers in the unconscious; they prefer the interpretations of an outside observer because they are fundamentally skeptical of the utility of self-reports. They assume that people are not only unaware of what is really going on in the important parts of their being, but also that they are highly motivated to remain unaware, since conflicts, anxieties, and unwelcome impulses predominate in the unconscious. If survey after survey shows no marked increase in depression or anxiety at the midlife (Lacy & Hendricks, 1980; Tamir, 1982), this is taken as clear evidence that surveys don't measure the real state of mind.

Researchers who rely on consciousness as the focus of personality are equally skepticical about the claims of interpreters. They point out that hypotheses about the unconscious are often irrefutable: Nothing we can do would disprove a dynamic interpretation. If, after several hours of intense probing, an interviewer is unable to find any conflicts that might give evidence of a midlife crisis, he or she can always conclude that the turmoil and despair are repressed—in fact, this must be an extremely severe crisis, if it is necessary to repress it so thoroughly! Dire predictions of a future crisis are likely to be made, and if anything ever goes wrong in the person's life (as eventually something must), the prediction is trumpeted as proof of the theory.

By now, of course, it must be obvious to readers that our own biases favor conscious over unconscious processes and self-reports over outside interpretations of personality. Yet we are not prepared to dismiss entirely the contributions of a number of distinguished thinkers who have written extensively on the development of personality in adulthood. In reviewing their positions, we will certainly point out all the reasons we have for disputing many of their conclusions. But we will also try to point out the areas of agreement and the large areas in which their theories and research complement and enrich our own. As we will see, the substance of their findings can often be retained when it is modified or reinterpreted to make it consistent with the facts as we know them. The result, we hope, will be a contribution to the study of emerging lives as well as of enduring dispositions.

Form and Content in Psychological Interviews

As it happens, most of the major theories of adult development are based on interviews rather than on psychological test results. The formulations of Erikson and Gould originated in their clinical practices; the theories of Levinson and his colleagues are based on biographies reconstructed by subject and interviewer. If these researchers have discovered developmental courses standard measures cannot detect, the interview approach may be credited.

In our discussion of the interview method, we have so far been concerned only with the quality of the characterizations it produces. Is Jones an introvert? Do we believe it when he says he is? Or do we observe him during the interview and reach our own decision?

A review of theories of adult development shows, however, that theorists who rely on interviews do not have much to say about Extraversion. They are concerned with concepts such as the self and the sense of identity; they talk about relationships, roles, and life structure. This difference in substance between interviews and questionnaires is not coincidental. It seems to be a clear instance of form dictating content.

The typical questionnaire does not let you talk back. The questions must be phrased so that they can be meaningfully answered by all respondents with a choice from yes or no, true or false, or other fixed categories. If we are interested in job satisfaction, our questionnaire can ask, "Are you generally satisfied with your job?"; regardless of the kind of job one has, everyone who is employed can answer that question with a simple yes or no. It cannot ask, "What specifically do you like about your job, and what do you dislike?" since the answers to these questions would differ from one job to the next, and standard, precategorized answers would not suffice.

Again, if a questionnaire researcher wants to know how an individual gets along with others, that researcher is likely to write questions such as "Do you have many friends?" or "Are you usually dominant in relations to others?" or "Do you believe others are out to get you?" By contrast, an interviewer is likely to say something like "Tell me about your work. How do you get along with your bosses, co-workers, subordinates?" Or, "Describe your relationship with your wife and children."

In some respects, we would expect the two methods to yield comparable results. After all, if an individual is really dominant, it should show up in the way he or she deals with friends, co-workers, and family. On the other hand, there are also respects in which important differences may emerge. Questionnaire results are standardized and uniform, independent of the content of the individual's life. Interview results are permeated by the details of an individual's life: the politics at the office, the specific problems of raising a teenage daughter or of living in a declining neighborhood. Case studies with all these details seem to provide a much better feel for the individual's personality than do raw test scores. But what they in fact give is *a better feel for the individual's life structure*, which may or may not be an accurate guide to personality. One's life structure is determined by a thousand forces beyond one's control: economic realities, accidents and illnesses, the help or interference of relatives. These are important elements in understanding the individual's world, but a source of potential confusion when trying to understand the individual.

INTERVIEW-BASED THEORIES OF ADULT DEVLOPMENT

At least one of the major theorists we will discuss, Levinson, acknowledges this important difference. He says explicitly that by *adult development* he means the "evolution of the life structure"—although he believes that there is an inner, psychological side to that process that seems akin to personality development. We believe this distinction is crucial to an understanding of the field: Nothing we have said about the stability of personality should be interpreted to mean that the life structure does not evolve, and the theories of adult developmentalists need not contradict our position on enduring dispositions. Agreement in principle, however, is not necessarily agreement in practice, and it will be necessary to look at each case closely to see what portion we are willing to believe. We will find, in addition to the distinction between life structure and personality, a second, related, distinction between self and personality that will also be useful in reconciling differences. That distinction will be explored in the next chapter.

Levinson's Seasons

One of the most influential works on adult development had its major impact before it was published. While still working on his book, *The Seasons of a Man's Life* (1978), Daniel Levinson discussed his ideas with Gail Sheehy, who went on to write the best-selling *Passages* (1976). Levinson's research was based on 10 to 20 hours of interviews with each of 40 men in the age range from 35 to 45. Four occupational groups—executives, workers, biologists, and novelists—were selected to provide some variation, since occupation has a decisive effect on shaping the life course. The subjects were normals; that is, they were not recruited from hospitals or psychiatric clinics, although several had been in psychotherapy at some time in the past.

In the course of the interviews, Levinson and his co-workers began to see a pattern. Instead of finding that the life course was shaped by external events like marriage, job promotions, or illness, they believed they had found evidence of a universal, age-linked series of stages, organized into broader eras. Childhood, Early Adulthood, Middle Adulthood, and Late Adulthood (and possibly Late-Late Adulthood) were the major eras, each lasting about 20 years, and each was broken further into alternating stages of transition and stabilization. The major transitions, including the Midlife Transition at age 40 to 45, overlapped both the preceding and following eras.

The names given to the different stages summarize their developmental meaning. The Early Adult Transition (17 to 22) involves breaking away from home and facing adulthood. This stage has already been heavily researched (e.g., Constantinople, 1969), since for many individuals it occurs at college, where most subjects for psychological studies are recruited. Entering the Adult World comes next, as the man begins to function as an adult, usually starting a career and family. These initial attempts at acting like a grown-up are likely to be clumsy, because they begin without the benefit of experience and often with a premature haste to settle down and prove one's adulthood; so between ages 28 and 33 the Age Thirty Transition occurs, in which the early occupational and marital choices are reexamined and either rejected, modified, or reaffirmed.

Having made these adjustments, the man enters the period of Settling Down, in which he begins to take life seriously and sets foot on the ladder of success towards his Dream, the ambition he harbors deep down. He is likely in this period to come under the protection, guidance, or sponsorship of a mentor, a somewhat older man whom he admires and who encourges him in his Dream. His wife, also, must do her part to encourage him if he is to be successful. The mentor, who acts somewhat as an older brother, helps the man go from junior adult to senior, but in the latter years of the thirties Becoming One's Own Man becomes crucial, and achievement of occupational aspirations is often accompanied by alienation of the mentor.

Just when life seems to have peaked (at least for those who made it up the ladder), the Midlife Transition enters, and everything has to be reevaluated. If men have been successful in striving for their goals, they question whether the goals were meaningful. If they have not been successful, they must reconcile themselves to their failures. In addition, Levinson says, a number of other issues that emerge here must also be dealt with. Men must face the fact that they are getting older, a realization brought about by the beginnings of physical decline and perhaps by the death or disability of their parents. They must also resolve conflicts about masculinity/femininity, creation/destruction, and attachment/separation. In some men these conflicts are expressed as conscious introspection and philosophizing or in artistic creations; in most the conflicts are recognizable only as a sense of turmoil, stagnation, alienation, and confusion.

After age 45 the individual enters the Midlife period with a new basis for living and interpreting life. In the best of cases, concern over personal advancement and proving one's worth has been replaced by a more altruistic concern for the welfare of others and posterity (Erikson's *generativity*); and the single-mindedness of the 30s is replaced by a new perspective in which previously neglected aspects of the self are given expression.

Although he has not yet made a systematic study of men over age 50, Levinson assumes that similar stages will continue throughout life. The process of *life review* (Butler, 1963), once thought to be a characteristic of old age, may in fact simply be the last in a series of life reviews, undertaken at each transition point throughout life.

Levinson's theory, as he promised, is directly concerned with the life structure and only secondarily with personality. Yet there are two points with important implications for the student of personality. First, to the extent that personality can be identified with values, concerns, and interests, it appears that major changes in personality are postulated to be the result of aging. Second, the turbulent nature of the life course as described by Levinson suggests that something like cyclical change in Neuroticism is involved. If individuals go through 5-year periods of anguish, conflict, and alienation every few years, measures of psychological distress ought to show it.

This theory is certainly more interesting than the bland assertion that personality is stable in adulthood; the question is, is it true? A careful and critical review of available evidence casts more than a little doubt on the entire scheme. These are among the problems:

Is It Universal?   Levinson claims that the sequences he found are universal, at least in his sample. But reading the cases even as he presents them leaves doubts. Some people had ostensibly smooth transition periods; some tried to break out of their life structure when they should have been settling down (of course, they paid the penalty later for that transgression). Among the workers in particular, the success-ladder model did not seem to make much sense: in America there is not much hope for advancement for a 35-year-old factory worker.

Even if the scheme were descriptive for all Americans, the claim for universality seems premature. In support of his claim, Levinson offers the stage theories of Solon, Confucius, and the ancient Hebrews, which he believes show parallels to his theory. But none of these three incorporates periods of crisis—surely the cardinal feature of Levinson's scheme—and one is on a 10-year cycle, another on a 7-year cycle. Confucius, for example, says that at age 40 he "no longer suffered from perplexities." Does that sound like the beginning of a midlife transition?

What these timetables seem to indicate is a universal recognition that there are growth and activity in the first half of life, and reflection and decline in the second. They also illustrate the universal appeal of dividing up the "seamless web" of adult life into convenient, although essentially arbitrary, stages. The remarkable variety of "natural" divisions of the lifecycle is clearly shown in an essay on Shakespeare's "seven ages of man" (Chew, 1947).

Is It Intrinsically Age-related?   One of the most controversial features of Levinson's theory is his use of chronological age as the basis for his stages. Most other adult developmentalists prefer to break up the life cycle with marker events such as marriage, birth of the first child, and retirement. Sociologically, they argue, the newlywed 18-year-old is more like the newlywed 28-year-old than like his bachelor age peers. Levinson counters by noting that the marriage of teenagers is likely to be as immature as they are; the event is colored by the period in which it occurs, not vice versa. On the other hand, the teenage father may be immature because he has not had the work and family experience of the 28-year-old. Experience, not age per se, may be the crucial variable.

Is It Discontinuous?   The notion of stages implies qualitative differences between one period and another. Even if the changes that Levinson suggests actually come about, is there evidence that they do so in quantum leaps? Take, for example, the realization that one is growing older. Levinson is probably quite correct in pointing out that the fact of aging requires readjustment. Time goes by continuously, but our conception of ourselves does not change at the same rate. We tend to think we are as we have always been until something confronts us with our age and forces us to acknowledge the change. But it seems unlikely that this occurs in discrete, age-related stages. A thousand incidents may contribute to this insight: a first gray hair, a 20th anniversary or 40th birthday, the death of a friend or parent, a newsreel from one's childhood with grotesquely dated fashions and expressions, the observation that college students get younger and more immature each year. Each of these small realizations may be something of a jolt, but is there any evidence that they all occur together, at precisely timed intervals? A man who still thought of himself as a teenager at age 39 probably *would* be in line for a midlife crisis, but are there many men like that?

Is It Personality Change?   When Levinson is confronted with evidence of stability in basic personality traits (Rubin, 1981), he tends to dismiss it. Dispositions such as anxiety, gregariousness, or aesthetic sensitivity are trivial in his view, superficial aspects of temperament that do not address the real, deep level of personality. For him, the fact that a 50-year-old man views himself as middle-aged when once he viewed himself as young is a startling change in personality; *young* and *old* are not merely age categories, and calling oneself middle-aged does not mean simply that one is concerned about retirement plans and grandchildren. Young and old are symbols, Jungian archetypes carrying profound connotations of vitality, immortality, and springtime in contrast with death, decay, and winter. Acknowledgment of middle age is thus a change in the deepest symbolic significance of the self.

Certainly, with age and experience come changes in some aspects of how we view ourselves, and the idea of aging is obviously related at some level to the metaphor of life and death. Perhaps poets are moved by these metaphors to change the style of their poetry as they age. But does the change in the self-concept bring about important changes in the behavior or experience of most individuals? Does it lead them to depression and suicide or to altruistic self-sacrifice? The answer, we think, is "No." When children leave home, when aged parents require care, when one retires from a lifelong occupation, there are profound changes in the daily routines that constitute the bulk of behavior, but these changes do not amount to changes in personality, and they come about in reponse to external necessity rather than internal development. Men do not give up playing tennis because they start to feel old; they are more likely to feel old because they have been forced to give up tennis. Nor is there much evidence, as we will soon see, that people feel different during or after one of the hypothesized transition periods.

Is It Developmental?   The field of gerontology has always been fundamentally ambiguous about the *value* of the changes it studies. University departments in this area are typically called "Aging and Human Development," as if the negative connotations of the first word had to be offset by more positive ones. Levinson usually writes as if what he is describing were *development*, a positive change, growth, the attainment of higher unity and deeper wisdom. As he progresses through life, the young man learns more about himself and his world and, in the best of cases, is able to rise above the conflicts and illusions of youth to a greater maturity. He can accept the feminine side of his nature and can acknowledge the individuality of his wife; his judgment is improved, marked by realistic compassion rather than by idealism or egocentrism. The older man sees the universal rather than the particular and is no longer bound by short-sighted or parochial views. With the abatement of instinctual drives, the older man can grow in rationality and ego strength. (Of course, Levinson would add, not every man succeeds in development: Some despair, some die too young. And the goal is never finally reached: Late life, like middle age, is marked by conflict, reassessment, and growth.)

On the other hand, in a discussion of this topic near the end of his book, Levinson expressly denies that his scheme is hierarchical, that later stages are better than earlier. Each has its strengths and weaknesses. But whereas no one stage is intrinsically better than another, the traversing of stages is itself the mark of growth. Individuals who do not change—who experience no periods of crisis—are arrested in development; they are, as a leading theorist of adult development, Orville Brim, says, "stuck" (Rubin, 1981). This view, however appealing and humanistic it seems, has as yet no basis in evidence. Change *per se* is not necessarily good, nor is stability necessarily the same as stagnation.

Gould's Transformations

If Levinson is fundamentally a Jungian theorist, Gould is clearly a Freudian. He sees adult development as the dismantling of illusions of safety developed in childhood and maintained in a quasiunconscious fashion through the first half of adulthood. His ideas were also borrowed by Sheehy, and he too wrote a book in 1978 expounding his more fully formed theory.

Externally, there are both similarities and differences between Gould's and Levinson's work. Gould divides adulthood into five periods: from 16 to 22, when the adolescent is breaking ties with parents; from 22 to 28, when a new, adult life is started; from 28 to 34, when life is reassessed in view of conflicting internal needs and values; from 35 to 45, when the problems of evil, death, and destruction are faced; and post-midlife, when the individual is finally in control of his or her own destiny. Whereas Levinson calls for alternating periods of stability and transition, Gould sees a continually deepening—and progressively liberating—struggle. Gould expects no futher development after 50, whereas Levinson does (note that neither of them has studied individuals in this age period). The time frames show some overlap, especially if Levinson's stable periods are ignored, but whereas Levinson views the timetable as inherent in human nature, Gould believes it is a function of life events and social forces (marriage, birth of children, corporate schedules of advancement). Gould also acknowledges the profound differences of social class. Perhaps the most distinctive feature of Gould's book is his effort to report on women as well as men and his particular attention to couples.

But the more fundamental differences are to be found in the theoretical underpinnings of *Transformations*. Gould sees the basis for adult development in the unfinished business of childhood. As children we are fundamentally helpless in the face of both outer danger and inner passions of lust, rage, and greed. We depend wholly on our parents to control both of these threats, and we internalize a series of false assumptions, illusions that allow us to believe that we are perfectly safe. Maintaining these beliefs has the benefit of preserving our sense of security, but it also has a cost: We are confined by the rules that bound us as children. We cannot get free of these confining inhibitions without facing the illusory nature of some of our most fundamental beliefs and without giving up the security they provide. But when we do get free, we come to see reality more clearly and thus stop the rude and unexpected shocks that must repeatedly occur when our illusions collide with life. And, says Gould, we also gain from this process real freedom to be our own persons, in touch with our inner needs and passions, living vital and meaningful lives.

Now, these ideas are by no means novel. Most versions of depth psychology claim that neurotic hangups stem from defenses we adopted in childhood to deal with a reality that no longer exists. Even cognitively based theories of psychotherapy, like Ellis's (1962) Rational-Emotive Therapy, recognize the entrapping and self-perpetuating role of irrational beliefs. Gould's unique contribution is to insist that there is an *age-ordering* of these irrational beliefs. Teenagers entering adulthood confront the assumption that they will always belong to their parents and believe in their world. Achieving independence from parents and their values, taking charge of one's life and one's body, means giving up the comforting assurance that parents will always be there to help and guide.

The young adult who is building a family and beginning a career has joined the establishment—and, says Gould, has done so with a vengeance. The roles of adult, parent, husband, woman, breadwinner are adopted wholesale, in part because the inexperienced adult has no other basis for guidance and in part because he believes that following all the rules, working hard, and persevering will guarantee happiness. To be sure, these kinds of activity may well be the best bet for creating a satisfying life, but no behavior can *guarantee* happiness, love, or success, and that is the lesson that must be learned, on an emotional as well as an intellectual level.

By age 28 a new phase starts. The difficulties of building a life tend to have been mastered well enough, and the internal side now clamors for attention. Wishes, values, and feelings that were ignored during the early pragmatic years of getting started suddenly take on a new importance. Career and marriage choices are reevaluated, and we come to the painful conclusion that life is not the simple, controllable affair we imagined. The illusions that we knew ourselves and that we were rational, consistent, and independent people are challenged.

Finally, in the midlife decade, an even harder pill must be swallowed: We must admit to ourselves that evil, death, and destruction are a real part of the world and even a real part of us. We have an evil side that may be controlled, but cannot be eliminated; and we face a certain death, with time the only question. The decline of our parents at this time plays a part in shaking the belief that they can save us from ourselves or from external danger. Facing these facts may lead to a period of intense struggle and distress, a midlife crisis. But once the challenge has been confronted, once we have come face to face with our existential aloneness, we achieve the freedom that comes from what Gould called "owning ourselves."

How do we evaluate this theory? As a theory of psychotherapy, its first test would be in its effectiveness in helping clients to resolve their problems. In the hands of a skilled clinician such as Gould, the theory seems to be effective—but the history of psychotherapy teaches us that, in the hands of a skilled clinician, almost any theory can be effective. More convincingly, research Gould (1972) conducted on a large sample of adults who were not patients confirmed that there is a change in the "march of concerns" over the early adult life span: Young adults are concerned with getting along with (or away from) their parents; men and women in their 20s are concerned with starting family and career; those in their 30s complain more of stagnation; and for those at midlife, facing death and decline are relatively more frequent problems.

This is important information, although hardly surprising. And a shift in the focus of concerns is something quite different from the evolution of adult consciousness. We might argue, for example, that irrational beliefs would be a dominant feature of the consciousness of only a small minority of individuals—those who require psychiatric treatment. We might grant that all individuals show some of the insights outlined by Gould, but maintain that these changes are trivial readjustments in thinking and not the stuff on which life decisions are made. We might contend that the order of the stages is essentially arbitrary, a result of the most frequent course of events encountered by Americans. A 20-year-old diagnosed as having cancer may deal with issues of destruction and death before taking on other illusions. If this is the case, then *development* seems to be an inappropriate word. Instead, we might view the whole process as one of adaptation to the challenges of living as an adult.

Because Gould's theory is more elastic than Levinson's, it is harder to test. But one of the deductions that can be made from it is that there ought to be notable differences between young and old in basic adjustment and also in Openness to feelings. As Chapter 4 showed, there is little support for that hypothesis. A second deduction would be that there are specific periods in adulthood when the stuggle with irrational beliefs is particularly strong and overt crisis is likely. For Gould, this is most likely to be in the midlife period, from 35 to 45. We consider that possibility next.

IN SEARCH OF THE MIDLIFE CRISIS

Of all the features of adult development, the most celebrated is the midlife crisis. Jaques (1965) studied the lives of artists and determined that they all went through a period of crisis precipitated by the recognition of their own mortality. "Time since birth" was replaced by "time left to live" in the mind of the middle-aged man. Peter Chew (1976) wrote a popular account of the crisis, suggesting that marriage stales and the quest for a lost youth leads men to intensified sexual yearnings. Among women, menopause and the loss of children from home were viewed as likely causes of a period of depression and crisis. Levinson et al. (1978) wrote that "for the great majority of men . . . this period evokes tumultuous struggles within the self and the external world" (p. 199) that may appear like neurosis to an outside observer.

These ideas have become so prevalent in both the popular and the scientific press that most people take it for granted that around age 40 there is a marked increase in such events as divorce and separation, suicide, job change, and admission to psychiatric hospitals. But epidemiologists who have scrutinized the figures on this issue find very little support for a period of crisis (Kramer & Rednick, 1976). Divorce is most common in the 20s, suicide among the young and the old. Admissions to psychiatric hospitals show no peak at age 40. Still, these are all very rough markers of crisis; perhaps the midlife transition leads to more subtle manifestations.

When Levinson, Gould, and others were first presenting their views on adult development in the early and middle 1970s, the case for stability in personality had not yet been made. The midlife crisis had been pointed out so often that we, as did most other psychologists, assumed that it occurred. The major question, we thought, was to determine its exact timing. Was it between 37 and 40, 40 and 45? Was the time different for working-class and middle-class men? We used our usual questionniare methods to try to find an answer. Drawing on the literature describing the characteristics and concerns of men at midlife and the items that Gould (1972) had reported to differentiate patients of different ages, we created a Midlife Crisis Scale and administered it to about 350 men aged 30 to 60 (Cooper, 1977). The scale had items covering sense of meaninglessness, dissatisfaction with job and family, inner turmoil and confusion, and sense of impending physical decline and death.

When we contrasted midlife groups with pre- and postmidlife groups, using various age cut-offs to define the mid-life, we were surprised to find no evidence at all of a peaking of midlife concerns at any age in our range. We had also asked our men to describe in their own words how their lives were going just then. Only seven men (about 2%) seemed to fit the category of crisis, and these ranged in age from 34 to 56, distributed randomly over the age range we studied. Our conclusion: at any given time, only a small percentage of men are in a crisis, and they are not likely to cluster at any particular age.

Since this conclusion flew in the face of the rest of the literature, our first concern was to replicate it. With a different group of about 300 men, we used a shortened version of the Midlife Crisis Scale. The results were an exact reconfirmation: There was not the slightest evidence of a peaking of distress or midlife characteristics anywhere in the age range we studied (Costa & McCrae, 1978).

Again, the most persuasive data may come from the NHANES survey (Costa et al., 1986). Short scales measuring Neuroticism, Extraversion, and Openness were administered to nearly 10,000 men and women; about half of the respondents were in the age range from 34 to 54. With so many subjects, we were able to plot personality scores year by year. A crisis or temporary alteration in personality should be apparent as a spike in the graph, yet Figure 6 shows that neither men nor women showed any pronounced peaking at any point during the period. It is particularly noteworthy that there is no increase in Neuroticism around age 40, when the theories call for a period of emotional upset and psychological crisis.

Our disenchantment with stages of adult development can be traced to such results, but we are not alone in our reappraisal of the crisis. Farrell and Rosenberg (1981), who had once been proponents of the theory, undertook a major study of the midlife period. They commissioned a probability sample of about 500 men in the age ranges 25 to 30 and 38 to 48, a sample from which generalizations about American men could be made with confidence. They put together a battery of measures of alienation, distress, depression, and crisis, including a midlife crisis scale much like ours in content. They also had measures of what they called *authoritarian denial*, which might be construed as Openness versus closedness to experience.

Their analyses, dividing subjects by age and by social class, showed almost exactly what we had: Midlife men were slightly higher in authoritarian denial, but they were actually a bit *lower* in alienation. There was no difference at all on the midlife crisis scale.

But perhaps all these studies make the mistake of tying the crisis to age when stage of life is more important. Among 40-year-old men, some are only recently fathers, many have young children in the home, many

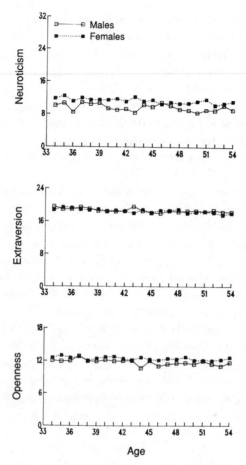

FIGURE 6. Mean levels of Neuroticism, Extraversion, and Openness to Experience for 1-year age groups of men and women aged from 34 to 54 years. Adapted from Costa et al. (1986).

others have teenagers, and some have seen all their children grow up and leave home. Perhaps the crisis occurs during one of these stages instead of at a particular chronological age. Indeed, there is evidence from large-scale epidemiological studies (Tamir, 1982) that men with teenage children are a bit less happy than other men (hardly a surprising finding for those acquainted with teenagers). But most theorists had supposed that the real crisis would come when the children left home, leaving parents to face each other again, the stark silence reminding them that they were growing old. Some parents do react badly to the departure of their sons and daughters, but in one of the few systematic studies of this stage in the family Lowenthal and Chiriboga (1972) reported that, if anything, parents were somewhat happier in the empty nest.

"But this proves nothing!" say the critics; "these studies all employed paper-and-pencil tests. What is needed is the insight, probing, and sensitivity of a trained interviewer. He would cut through the facade of well-being and see the crisis brewing just beneath the surface, ready to explode at any time into depression, suicide, divorce, alcoholism, dramatic career shifts."

Perhaps. Levinson's interviewers seem to have seen these things. But Farrell and Rosenberg (1981) also conducted interviews with 20 of the men they had surveyed, and they came to quite different conclusions. Many men had difficulties in life, but there was no evidence that problems were concentrated at certain periods. Further, the life histories they compiled from several hours of talking with the subjects and their wives and children convinced them that, for the minority who appeared to have a crisis, "the difficulties they experience have their roots in conflicts and problems of earlier origin" and are likely to lead to a "more general process of depressive decline" (p. 215). By contrast, they said of one man who showed Openness and positive adaptation in the middle years that "the sense of self he experiences at midlife is not a marked change from that of early adulthood." In search of a midlife crisis, these researchers emerged from intensive interviews with an impression of stability in the life course.

*   *   *

The interview, it seems, provides more ambiguous accounts of the period of adulthood than do standard personality tests. Some interviewers come to the conclusion that development proceeds in stages; some see no stages at all. There is even greater disparity when the stability of objective test results is contrasted with the "growth and development" described by interviewers. In part, this result from the flexibility of the interview as a method of gathering data: if it is more sensitive to the subtle thoughts and feelings of the subject, it is also more sensitive to the biases and preconceptions of the interviewer. In part, however, it also results from the fact that interviews are typically filled with concrete details from the individual's life, not generalizations about dispositions. Lives surely change, perhaps in stages; personality, we maintain, does not.

We see little reason to adopt the model of development proposed by Levinson and his colleagues, or the more widely held theory of a midlife crisis, and we are skeptical that the processes described by Gould are univeral developmental changes in personality or consciousness. But we must admit that the simple statement that personality is stable does not begin to do justice to the full complexity of adult life. The five-factor model of personality traits cannot explain the life course, but it may provide some illumination of it. In the next chapter we will try to examine both internal changes of consciousness and external modifications of the life structure in terms of an *interaction* of age and personality. Enduring dispositions may form the scaffolding on which emerging lives are erected.

·9·

THE INFLUENCES OF
PERSONALITY ON THE LIFE
COURSE

We have argued throughout this book that personality does not change much after age 30. Our conclusion is based not on theories of development or idealizations of aging but on a hard look at such facts as we could find. But when we consider with equal objectivity the work of theorists such as Levinson and Gould, we cannot escape the conclusion that there is a great deal of change in people's lives. As Gould (1978) wrote, "Adulthood is not a plateau." Most people do not begin a career as soon as they leave school and continue in it uneventfully until retirement. Circumstances change, and people change. Part of the resistance to our message of stability comes from the older adult's recognition that life is often unpredictable and the younger adult's profound hope that there is yet some variety, adventure, and surprise in store. There is.

For some reason, the notion of change without growth seems hard to grasp. Perhaps an analogy would help. By the end of high school, or certainly college, most individuals have reached their peak of intellectual development. They are, in a number of demonstrable ways, not only more knowledgeable, but actually more intelligent than they were a few years before. They can think more abstractly, reason more cogently, learn new ideas more quickly, grasp more intricate patterns. At the same time there are enormous differences among 20-year-olds in intelligence.

Over the course of the life span, we know pretty well what happens to intelligence. Aside from a slow growth in knowledge (as shown by vocabulary test scores) and a progressive decline in reasoning and perceptual ability, particularly late in life, there is very little change. The average 50-year-old is about as bright as the average 20-year-old, and the above-average 50-year-old is almost certain to have been an above-average 20-year-old.

But this certainly does not mean that the mind is sunk in stagnation for the greater part of life. Novelists use their intelligence to write books, teachers to educate students, business executives to improve management and expand sales. The work of a lifetime does not lead to *development* of intelligence: Nobel Prize winners would score no higher on IQ tests after years of research than they would have in college. But surely their minds have not been wasted. Personality, we submit, is similar in its influence on the adult life. Life does not lead to change or growth in personality, but it allows a fascinating variety of situations in which personal dispositions, for good or ill, play a part.

Some Implications for Personality Theory

We have been concerned throughout this book with the implications of personality research for life-span development, and we continue this theme throughout this chapter. But it is also worthwhile to pause to consider the implications of our developmental findings for personality theory. We have mentioned in passing that the stability of personality traits is important testimony to their reality. If traits were mere fictions or passing fancies, the fleeting reflections of the social pressures of the moment, it would be hard to explain why and how such enduring descriptions of personality could be found.

However, our findings speak to the nature of traits as well as to their existence. The widely held belief that personality is the product of childhood experiences, and particularly of styles of child rearing, does not square well with the repeated finding that there are relatively few and small generational differences in such traits as anxiety, impulsiveness, and openness to feelings. As we discussed in Chapter 4, there have been profound changes in the nature of child-rearing practices in the past 50 years, but their impact on adult personality has been slight. Recent studies have called into question the importance of child-rearing practices and parent–child relationships for the formation of adult personality (McCrae & Costa, 1988b; Plomin & Daniels, 1987).

One interpretation of this finding would be that traits are determined genetically. There is in fact a growing body of evidence that many traits are in part inherited (Buss, 1983; Rowe, 1987; Young, Eaves, & Eysenck, 1980). In view of the utility to the species of consistent individual differences, an evolutionary explanation of traits would make sense. Further, genetic theories of personality would certainly be consistent with the stability of personality. But many other theoretical positions could also account for stability, and the evidence to date suggests that a substantial portion of most personality traits *cannot* be explained by genetics.

One of the intriguing problems for personality psychologists is the identification of mechanisms that promote stability. Swann and Hill (1982) have shown experimentally that individuals will actively resist feedback about themselves that is discrepant with their self-conceptions, and self-consistency theorists (Lecky, 1945) have hypothesized that individuals are strongly motivated to maintain a consistent view of themselves. One's associates have the same vested interest in keeping one predictable, so social pressure may also act to preserve the status quo in personality.

Millon (1981) described self-perpetuating features in personality disorders. For example, avoidant personalities are so fearful of social interaction that they shun the situations that would give them an opportunity to learn social skills and thus gain more confidence. It was once thought that such vicious circles distinguished abnormal personality characteristics; now it appears that many or most personality traits have self-sustaining features. The extravert's extensive experience with other people makes social interaction easier and encourages an extraverted lifestyle.

Caspi, Elder, and Bem (1987) have described two processes they call *cumulative* and *interactional continuity* that help to perpetuate some personality characteristics. Cumulative continuity occurs when the consequences of a trait reinforce it:

> The ill-tempered boy who drops out of school may thereby limit his future career opportunities and select himself into frustrating life circumstances that further evoke a pattern of of striking out explosively against the world. His maladaptive behaviors increasingly channel him into environments that perpetuate those behaviors. (p. 308)

Interactional continuity refers to the fact that the interpersonal styles of individuals elicit reciprocal responses in others that sustain the trait. Hostile people make enemies, and enemies make them hostile.

It seems likely that all these processes and more will be needed to explain the remarkable stability of personality despite changes in social roles, health, and life experiences. Very little else in our world is so dependable.

WHAT CHANGES?

Let us step back and review for a moment the changes that do occur across the adult portion of the life span. Physically, aging brings with it changes in mobility, sensory capacity, strength, and vigor. Certain cognitive functions, particularly perceptual abilities and memory, show declines, gradually at first, but at an increasing rate as we enter old age. The world also changes as we age (with all the headaches that brings for researchers, as we saw in Chapter 4). Our children grow up and move out; our parents grow old and die. Nor are we simply passive victims of the crush of time: We make plans and decisions, change jobs and occasionally spouses. Some of us often and all of us at times think our life is stale and stagnant, but most of us are too busy living to worry about the fact that our personality is not growing.

Leaving aside external influences, we must certainly acknowledge that there are extensive changes in a number of psychological processes. Here are a few.

Behaviors and Habits

Behaviorally oriented psychologists sometimes attempt to define personality as the sum total of all behaviors. Personality psychologists usually laugh at such a definition (if they don't cry) because it represents an incredibly naive attempt to maintain the notion that personality encompasses the whole individual while at the same time it reduces that personality to observable facts. In many circumstances behaviors *reflect* personality, although they also, and probably more often, reflect situational demands and constraints and what we have learned by dealing with similar situations. In any case the behavior is not the same thing as the entity it expresses.

Consequently, there is no contradiction at all in saying that personality remains stable whereas behavior changes. All this means is that the situation we face in young adulthood, at a certain point in the history of the world, is usually quite different from the situation we face in old age. An active, conventionally masculine individual, for example, is likely to be interested in sports all his life. He will probably participate in team and individual sports in high school and college, but once he takes on a family and career his opportunities for active participation in athletics may be cut drastically, since he no longer has the time or the institutional support. As he moves into middle age, physical limitations may pose yet another obstacle to participation. Professional athletes at this point are normally forced to retire or to become coaches or managers instead of players. Amateurs may change their preferred sport, replacing basketball with tennis, or tennis with golf. Physical limitations continue with age, and medical conditions may completely rule out vigorous activity. But an interest in sports and vicarious participation generally continue undiminished: The spirit remains willing, even if the flesh is weakened. And the pace of activity (although not perhaps its vigor) also continues. People who like to keep busy manage to do so in old age by choosing activities that they can handle and perhaps by becoming more efficient in their motions. The range of individual differences even in physical vigor is enormous, and some 80-year-olds keep up a pace that few 20-year-olds can match.

Or consider another example. Physicians trained in the 1940s learned to practice a form of medicine that has since been revolutionized several times. Although many of these men and women are still active today, they certainly do not continue to prescribe the same drugs, use the same diagnostic procedures, or perform surgery in the same way. Their interest in medicine and in dealing with patients has continued unabated over the years, but their behavior has changed dramatically. In fact, it is precisely because of their stable commitment to medicine that they have bothered to learn newer developments.

Attitudes and Opinions

The same considerations hold true for ideas, beliefs, and attitudes. Social psychologists devote much of their time to studying the complex and mysterious processes by which attitudes are changed, but we know without doubt that they do change. New developments—such as nuclear power and genetic engineering—call for new opinions, and at least some people change their minds on old issues as they continue to think about them. None of this, however, means a change in personality.

Adolescents and young adults are probably more willing than older adults to adopt new value and attitudes or revise old ones (although it is not clear that there is much difference between 30- and 80-year-olds in this regard). There are two major reasons for this. One is that, as a person ages genuinely new ideas become increasingly infrequent, and, as White (1952) remarks, "accumulated experience . . . more and more outweighs the impact of new events" (p. 333). Another is that, once settled into a life structure, we have much more to lose by changing basic values. The executive rising on the corporate ladder has little incentive to embrace communism; the lawyer who has invested years in learning her profession is understandably reluctant to question it. Our values, like our personality, help to shape our life structure and are themselves perpetuated by it.

But people do change their minds, just as they sometimes change religions, political parties, and occupations. In fact, the enduring personality disposition of Openness to experience is in part characterized by the ability to keep an open mind, to consider new opinions, and, at least occasionally, to change attitudes and values. We would expect open people to revise their ideas and values repeatedly, whereas closed people would cling tenaciously to the opinions of their parents and other respected authorities.

Note, however, that change is not necessarily growth. Openness to experience does not guarantee that new opinions and attitudes will always be better, wiser, more differentiated, more in keeping with contemporary reality. Many open people are simply flighty, moving from one world view to another with an amazing regularity. When he or she combines Openness with critical capacity, however, the open person certainly appears to be in a better position to adapt to a changing world. The point is that change in opinions is not only consistent with stability of personality: It is itself an enduring quality of some individuals.

Social Roles

Few ideas in the social sciences can match the scope or power of the concept of *role*. Social-psychological jargon is full of qualifications of the basic metaphor: role expectation, role performance, public role, deviant role, roleless role. Role theorists (Goffman, 1959; Mead, 1934), who tend to be sociologists rather than psychologists, have spent considerable time and effort in proposing and debating various definitions of that eminently useful concept, but for our purposes most of them are equally good. Allport (1961), for example, defined a role as "a structured mode of participation in social life. More simply, it is what society expects of an individual occupying a given position in the group" (p. 181).

Roles are so peculiarly useful because they bridge two of the most crucial of gaps: that between the individual and the society and that between the self and behavior. Roles are functional units of social systems, and without even mentioning individual persons, a sociologist can describe a society by specifying the nature and interaction of roles. A nuclear family, for example, consists of a father and mother (in the complementary roles of husband and wife) and one or more children, who, in addition to being sons and daughters to their parents, are also sisters and brothers to each other. Everyone in this system has a pre-defined part to play: Parents are supposed to take care of the children, but also to control and guide them; children are supposed to love and obey their parents. (The fact that this model family is so seldom seen in reality is a cause for distress to all concerned, but a sophisticated role theorist would point out that the role of teenager in modern America is defined as much by defiance as by obedience.) Other social systems are also understandable in terms of roles: A business consists of bosses, workers, and customers; a city has officials and citizens.

Roles serve an equally important function for individuals, forming the basis for both social definitions and self-definitions. As we saw in the study of the spontaneous self-concept, when people are asked to respond to the question, "Who am I?" they frequently describe themselves by reference to what is called their *social identity*: I am a doctor, a Republican, a mother, a Lutheran. Each person occupies, simultaneously and succes-sively, a dazzling variety of roles, and one of the chief functions of the ego described in Chapter 7 is keeping all of these straight. Much of the individual's sense of identity is tied to the set of roles to which he or she is more or less permanently committed. Nowhere else is the fusion of self and society seen so clearly as in the centrality of role in the definition of both.

For this reason, some psychologists take the view that personality is, or is largely, the collection of roles one plays. To one who maintains such a conception, the contention that personality is stable must seem some-what silly. Don't people become parents and then grandparents? Don't they retire or make midcareer shifts? Doesn't age increase the probability that one will adopt the sick role? Of course. If one insists on a role theory of personality, the whole issue of stability becomes trivial.

Other psychologists, also influenced by social-role theories, distinguish between roles and underlying personality, but expect that acting out certain roles will lead to changes in personality. The man who takes a job as a policeman may become authoritarian, so the theory goes, because everyone thinks he is and treats him accordingly (Mead, 1934). In laboratory settings, this kind of manipulation can induce changes in people's reports of what they are like, and social psychologists have sometimes asserted that age-related "role transitions . . . must continuously redefine our personalities" (Veroff, 1983, p. 341), especially in old age (Baltes & Schmid, 1987).

Our findings of stability present a problem for this theory. Assuming that our measures are taken seriously (and we have spent a good deal of time arguing why they should be), two possibilities emerge as likely explanations. The first is that because role changes are not as pronounced as we might have thought, they leave personality basically unaltered. Perhaps the change from mother to grandmother is not very significant in comparison with differences between fathers and mothers. Again, retirement from an occupation may not be a radical change if, as Havighurst and others have shown (1979), many people continue their professional activities after formal retirement. Age does not seem to be a major influence on social identity as seen in the spontaneous self-concept (McCrae & Costa, 1988a).

A second interpretation is that the role-based theory of personality is simply wrong. Perhaps people do not internalize the perceptions others have of them, laboratory studies notwithstanding. Swann and Hill (1982) showed that subjects given feedback inconsistent with their own conceptions of their personality changed their images of themselves—but only until they were given a chance to reassert themselves.

Interpersonal Relationships

Some aspects of interpersonal relationships are based on roles, and as roles change, so do relationships. Soldiers who fought on opposite sides can be friends when the war is over; students become the colleagues of their professors when they graduate; retired executives can no longer dominate others as they used to. These changes in relationships are perhaps the most significant feature of changes in roles.

Other aspects of interpersonal behavior are expressions of traits that cut across many different roles and impart a personal flavor to their interpretation. As far as role requirements allow, the friendly person is likely to respond with warmth to employers, neighbors, and relatives. The shy person will be self-conscious among strangers, but also with friends when he or she is too much the center of attention. Because these dispositions cut across roles, the changes in roles that come with age do not affect their expression, and they tend to remain stable across the adult years.

But there are some relationships that are shaped by more than social-role requirements or personal dispositions. Farrell and Rosenberg (1981) for example, in their discussion of husbands and wives at midlife acknowledge that the adage that opposites attract has rarely been supported by research, but point out that couples seem to develop a pattern of complementary behavior. Two assertive individuals may make a couple in which one is clearly dominant, or they may carve out separate domains in which to exercise their dominance: Traditionally, the wife ran the house and the husband made decisions about the car. Whenever two individuals share a significant and lasting relationship, its characteristics are likely to be the result of the particular ecology of both of the persons and of the situation, a series of compromises and adaptations evolved over a period of time.

We might describe a relationship as the patterns of power and dependency, the emotional support given or received, the depth and nature of the bond of love or hatred. Little is known about the stability of these features of relationships. Do newlyweds quickly set up a pattern that will endure throughout married life, or are the terms constantly renegotiated as new problems and opportunities—the birth of a child, a career for the wife, an older parent moving in—emerge? Is it possible that there are regular developmental changes that characterize relationships, not individuals? Do wives take over the decision-making roles in the family after middle age, even though they do not otherwise become more assertive or masculine?

One set of relationships does show change closely related to age. As we age, we become independent of our parents and our children become independent of us. Interview studies seem unanimously to suggest that the intrapsychic rate of change by no means keeps pace with the behavioral. Years after moving away from home and taking financial responsibility for themselves, adults sometimes seem curiously tied to the approval and opinions of their parents. Some writers argue that it is only the shock of a parent's death or chronic disability that convinces middle-aged men or women that they are really as big and strong as their parents once were. The struggles of the adolescent to break away from parental domination sometimes result in periods of many years in which there seems to be no feeling at all left for parents. Levinson's interviews suggest that at middle age the feelings, positive and negative, may reawaken and lead to a new, perhaps more mature relationship. An ongoing longitudinal study of young adults and their parents (White et al., 1983) may give clearer answers to these questions. Preliminary cross-sectional analyses suggest that there may be a developmental progression from individuation, in which young adults emphasize their separateness from their parents, through a period of increasingly better perspective on the parents as individuals, to full peer-like mutuality between adult children and their parents.

It is of some interest to note that studies of the external trappings of family life show great continuity between generations (Troll, Miller, & Atchley, 1979). The majority of adult children see their parents at least once a week, and considerable mutual support is offered in the form of money, favors, and so on. These family ties generally continue until death; the notion that most old people are abandoned by their children is largely myth.

Identity and the Self

Having considered separately values, roles, and relationships, we are in a position to talk about the self and its development in adulthood. But we are immediately faced with another of the problems in terminology that plague psychology: There are no generally agreed on definitions of the self; we will offer some distinctions that can at least be useful here.

We use the term *self* to refer to the entire person from a psychological perspective. Correspondingly, the *self-concept* is the individual's view of his or her self. Every assertion one might agree to in the form of "I am . . ." describes an aspect of the self. As Rosenberg (1979) explains, the contents of the self-concept include social roles, intimate relationships, body image, and self-ideal, as well as abilities and dispositions. What we have been calling *personality*—enduring dispositions in the domains of Neuroticism, Extraversion, Openness, Agreeableness, and Conscientiousness—thus forms only one part of the self, although certainly a major part. Our finding of stability in this part of the self does not imply that other parts of the self do not change.

Our use of the words *self* and *personality* is almost the opposite of that adopted by a noted developmentalist, Douglas Kimmel (1974). Kimmel used the term *personality* to represent the entire psycho-social system and restricted the *self* to its central core. He concurred in our finding that personality traits are generally stable, whereas social behavior and roles (which he considered less central) change with age. He expressed this, however, by saying that some aspects of personality are more stable, some less stable. We agree in substance, but would rephrase his formulation to say that personality is one aspect of the self that is stable in adulthood.

Kimmel's usage does draw attention to the fact that some parts of the self seem to be more meaningful and consequential than others. We would recommend the word *identity* to refer to those aspects of the self that are essential to one's self-definition. Personality traits may be a salient part of one's identity, but so may social definitions or body image. Whether and in what ways identity changes in adulthood are only beginning to be explored. Whitbourne and Waterman (1979) have traced the development of identity from college age (by which time Erikson suggested it should be formed) through the 30s, and they report an increase in commitment over this period—a conclusion that echoes White's (1952) finding of "stabilization of ego identity" in his case studies covering a similar period of development. Does identity continue to stabilize, or are the identity crises of adolescence revived at middle age? Our studies (McCrae & Costa, 1988a) and some others (Whitbourne, 1986a) point to stabilization in the self-concept and perhaps also in those central elements that constitute one's identity.

One aspect of the self has been studied extensively: self-evaluations. *Self-esteem* is measured as often as any other personality variable, in part because it has commanded the attention of sociologists and in part because it has seemed to be central to many self-based theories of personality and psychopathology. Our research suggests that poor self-esteem is heavily influenced by Neuroticism, especially depression and vulnerability, and that positive self-esteem, or self-confidence, is related to Extraversion. We would thus expect stability in measures of self-esteem, and the literature to date sustains our conclusions (Bengtson, Reedy, & Gordon, 1985; Mortimer et al., 1981). Age may bring changes in social roles, and perhaps in aspects of the self-concept, but regardless of how they see themselves or how that view changes, extraverts are likely to be pleased, neurotics unhappy, with what they see.

STUDYING LIFE STRUCTURE AND LIFE COURSE

In view of the evidence of stability in adulthood, there would seem to be two directions in which the study of adult development might proceed: It might be restricted to samples where change might be expected, including individuals undergoing psychotherapy or those under age 30; or it might redefine the field as the psychology of adulthood, in which enduring dispositions would be viewed as a foundation for adaptation to the changing demands of life.

We believe both of these approaches are useful: Researchers should study change where it occurs, and stability where it does not. Psychotherapy, in particular, remains an area in which much remains to be done. Longitudinal studies are observational, not experimental; they tell us what happens to a sample of people during the normal course of events. The fact that most people do not change much does not necessarily mean that they could not change given the right set of circumstances. The recently renewed interest in psychotherapy research (VandenBos, 1986) may provide an incentive for long-term, large-scale studies of the effects of different forms of therapy on personality.

Equally exciting to us is the research agenda that flows from a reversal of the conventional approach to adult development. Students of age and personality have traditionally asked, "How does aging affect personality?" The complementary question—"How does personality affect the aging process?"—is still new. As recently as the first edition of this book (McCrae & Costa, 1984), we lamented the scarcity of research on this topic. In the past few years, things have begun to change (Costa & McCrae, 1989b). There is even a Life History Research Society which considers such topics as "Straight and Devious Pathways from Childhood to Adulthood" and "Pathways to Adult Competence."

Much remains to be done in charting the influence of each of the five domains of personality on people's careers, familial relationships, and adaptation to stress and disease, but enough has already been done to show the powerful effect personality can have.

For example, Conley (1985) traced the couples who had participated in E. Lowell Kelly's pioneering longitudinal study—a study that had provided some of the first strong evidence of personality stability (Kelly, 1955). Conley used self-reports and ratings gathered in 1935 and 1955 to predict aspects of life in 1980 and found evidence of pervasive influences of personality. Men and women rated by peers in 1935 as being high in Neuroticism were more likely to have had an emotional disorder in the succeeding years; men rated as poor in impulse control (or Conscientiousness) were more likely to have become alcoholics.

Conley sampled a number of variables that give a flavor of daily life in 1980 for these men and women. What he called intuitive types, whom we would describe as open to experience, had artistic hobbies and preferred to watch public television. His sensing types, closed to experience, listed gardening, sewing, and cooking as hobbies and preferred to watch game shows. Dispositions tapped early in life can make sense of the activities of older individuals.

The most fundamental influence of personality stability on life is the fact of stability itself. As we noted in Chapter 6, in order to make a life for oneself at all one must have some firm foundations, some predictable regularities. Some sources of continuity are external to us, including our cultural background and social class and socialization into particular professions or groups. We remain much the same in our talents and abilities, and, although we face uniform declines in health and vigor, the changes tend to be gradual.

The same considerations apply to personality dispositions. Choosing a major in college, deciding whom to marry, accepting a job transfer, planning for retirement—all depend on the knowledge that our basic motives and styles will endure. Bandura (1982) argued that part of the reason for stability in personality may be that we choose and create environments that will reinforce our dispositions; regardless of the reasons, stability is a fact we must and do count on.

Psychological Adjustment Across the Life Span

One of the saddest truths that has emerged from the experience of psychologists in the last century is that individuals with difficulties in living generally continue to have problems, even after extensive treatment. Tsuang, Woolson, Winokur and Crowe (1981) have shown that 92% of individuals once diagnosed as schizophrenic are still judged schizophrenic 30 years later. Twenty-five years after World War II,

Keehn, Goldberg, & Beebe (1974) found that soldiers given psychiatric discharges were more likely to have died from suicide, homicide, accidents, or alcohol-related illnesses than normal soldiers with the same war experiences. Robins (1966) showed that deviant children are much more likely than others to become adult criminals, and recidivism rates from police records show that an adult criminal generally leads an entire lifetime of crime. But schizophrenia is an illness, and the social system may trap some individuals into a pattern of crime. Do enduring personality traits in normal individuals affect long-term adjustment to life?

Certainly. Neuroticism is the aspect of personality most relevant to adjustment, and those high on this dimension are likely to show evidence of maladjustment at all ages. They are, for example, likely to be dissatisfied with life and exhibit low morale (Costa & McCrae, 1980a). Maas and Kuypers (1974) found in a 40-year follow-up study of a group of men that "old age does not usher in or introduce decremental psychological processes. Rather, old age may demonstrate, in perhaps exacerbated form, problems that have long-term antecedents" (p. 203). There is evidence that, regardless of age, individuals high in Neuroticism are more likely to use ineffective coping mechanisms such as hostile reactions, passivity, wishful thinking, and self-blame in dealing with stress (McCrae & Costa, 1986). Vaillant (1977) has documented the pervasive influence of neurotic coping styles on the lives of an elite group, Harvard graduates.

The antecedents of Neuroticism can be seen in childhood, and its lifelong consequences have begun to be traced. For example, children with a history of temper tantrums (who were perhaps low in Agreeableness as well as high in Neuroticism) later showed disturbances in career and marriage, with a higher probability of downward occupational mobility and divorce (Caspi et al., 1987). Those veterans who were characterized by higher levels of inadequacy and anxiety during adolescence were more likely to have had stress reactions after World War II than were other combat veterans (Elder & Clipp, 1988).

In a sense, this is nothing new; it is merely a restatement of the fact that Neuroticism is an enduring and consequential disposition. It is in interaction with age and life circumstances that the influence of Neuroticism becomes most intriguing. Consider, for example, individuals who experience a so-called midlife crisis. Everyone acknowledges that there are such people, although there is dispute as to how many. The problems and concerns of this syndrome are distinct: They revolve around the themes of lost youth, abandoned dreams, meaningless relationships. When Farrell and Rosenberg (1981) interviewed five subjects who seemed to be in this state, they concluded from detailed life histories that this was not simply a "developmental emergent" without precedent in the life of the individual. Even if the individual had led a relatively solid and satisfying life up to that point, these researchers believed that the seeds of crisis had already been laid by defects in his character and the resulting poor choices he had made.

We found evidence of another sort for the same phenomenon. In our questionnaire studies of the midlife crisis (described in Chapter 8), we found that only a minority of men of any age felt themselves to be in a crisis. When, however, we examined the scores these few had received on personality measures taken 10 years earlier, we found that even then they had been significantly higher in Neuroticism. If we spoke to these men today, we might find them blaming all their troubles on recent events or on their age or health. But they had had more than their share of complaints many years earlier, and it begins to seem that they carried their troubles with them. It may be that the *form* of the trouble varies with the period of life in which they happen to be. Gould (1972) found that the nature of the concerns that brought patients to therapy differed by age: Adolescents had problems with their parents, young adults with career choices. Well-adjusted individuals who go through the same situations regard them as challenges rather than insoluble problems.

A somewhat different interaction is seen in recent work by Liker and Elder (1983). They set out to explore the joint impact of an environmental event (downward economic mobility caused by the Great Depression) and the disposition of Neuroticism on a significant life outcome: the quality of marital relations. They made a number of interesting findings in a design that included several measurements over a period of years. The emotional stability of both partners had a continuing impact on the quality of their marriage, although the quality of their marriage had no influence on their personality. Economic depression seemed to have a psychologically depressing effect on some individuals, since the general level of adjustment declined a bit.

Most interesting to us, however, was the *differential* effect of financial loss. Initially well-adjusted men tended to bounce back, whereas those who were neurotic to begin with became more so under stress: "Depression losses affected the temperament of irritable men more than three times as much as the temperament of relatively calm men . . . Economic pressure accentuated personality tendencies harmful to marriage."

Such studies as these point the way to whole new lines of research, since they show that neither our dispositions in themselves nor the circumstances that age and history confront us with are sufficient to explain the forms (or failures) of our adjustment. Instead of being content to ask, "How do older people adjust to retirement or bereavement or relocation?" we may find that we have to ask "How do older neurotic people . . . ?" or "How do older open extraverts . . . ?" We need to develop a contextual psychology of aging that integrates personality traits with changing life situations and social roles.

Personal Projects, Life Narratives, and Psychobiography

Much of the conduct of life is routine: going to work, doing errands, cleaning the house, watching television. However humdrum they may seem, these routines are generally the result of an elaborate evolution intended to allow us to gratify most of our needs most of the time as well as we can in our circumstances. What seems unremarkable from its familiarity is in fact an intricate construction, a life structure. As we continue to age a succession of life structures forms a life course, our own personal history.

As a technique for studying the structure of life at the day-to-day level, Little (1983) has proposed a new unit of analysis, the *personal project*. Personal projects are sets of acts intended to achieve a goal; they range from "getting a better job" to "overcoming my shyness" to "going to the ballet" (p. 293). Individuals appear to be able to list the projects that concern them at any given time quite easily and can then rate them on such dimensions as importance, difficulty, control, and absorption (the degrees to which they are involved in and preoccupied with them). One advantage of personal projects as units of analysis is that they provide a detailed specification of the life structure at a single time, one that is phenomenologically real to the individual. An occupational history that includes only type of work and dates of hiring, promotion, and firing misses the richness that can be drawn from an analysis of personal projects: Are job concerns central to life, or simply an economic necessity? Are tasks part of an ongoing career plan or a series of unrelated activities? Is the work pleasant or unpleasant, absorbing or dull, imposed or chosen?

Personal projects are also intriguing because the dimensions on which they are rated can be related to dimensions of personality. We may find that highly conscientious people feel their projects are under their control, that open people become deeply absorbed in their projects, and that those high in Neuroticism are dissatisfied with their progress on various projects. These kinds of analyses help to spell out the implications of personality traits and their influence on life at a molecular level.

On a larger scale, Helson, Mitchell, and Moane (1984) examined effects of personality on *social clock projects*. Some life goals, such as marrying, raising a family, and having a successful career, are shared by nearly everyone in the culture and have a prescribed time course: There is a social clock by which we can tell if our life is progressing at the rate it should. Helson and her colleagues examined personality scores gathered at the time of college graduation (between 1958 and 1960) for a group of women they subsequently followed. Nearly all the women of this group professed a desire to marry and start a family. They found that "women who started their families on time may be characterized as having been confident and assertive in college in addition to having the motivations and skills to adjust in conventional ways" (p. 1083). We would probably describe them as conscientious extraverts. A minority of women in this sample aspired to a career in addition to marriage. Those who succeeded by age 42 had been assertive, forceful, self-confident, and ambitious in college; they appeared to be more open and extraverted than the women whose career plans failed.

Although society may dictate the major directions of life, individuals in modern societies have considerable latitude for personal choices, some of which reshape the life course. These critical choices, and the reasons behind them, form the substance of biographies (Herold, 1963): Napoleon decides to restore order to the French Revolution, in part because of his conservative social views; he has himself crowned Emperor to satisfy his quest for personal aggrandizement; he divorces Josephine and marries Maria Louisa to ensure the rights of his progeny; he invades Russia because he believes he can bully Alexander into submission; he returns from Elba because he has become convinced that, despite all odds, it is his destiny. Biographers generally feel that the best way to understand the individual's personality is to record the subject's life, to analyze the circumstances that helped shape the life course (in part to separate external influences from the inner characteristics), and then to interpret the action in terms of the inner drives, talents, or weaknesses of the person (Runyan, 1981). Erikson (1962) has devoted much of his career to such psychobiographies, and most clinicians rely heavily on the life history as a means of understanding their clients.

This type of research has recently witnessed a resurgence of interest (Birren & Hedlund, 1987; McAdams & Ochberg, 1988). Some personality psychologists have turned their attention to *life narratives* or *stories*—the stories people tell about their lives (Bertaux, 1981). These researchers are not concerned with the historical accuracy of the accounts, but with their psychological significance. Life stories may reveal inner dreams or fears that help individuals make sense of their own lives. In this sense, they are akin to TAT stories: Subjects may project their inner needs into the story of their lives. Life narrative data might be analyzed in terms of enduring dispositions, for surely the individual's perception of his or her life as revealed in a life story will be colored by prevailing emotions and experiential styles. One of Conley's (1985) subjects who scored as intuitive (or high in Openness) in 1935 assessed his life in 1980 as follows: "As long as I can do new things, see new places, and see new faces, living is fine. When I cannot do this for any reason, it will be enough and time to go." For this person, the meaning of life, and even its desired extent, were determined by lifelong Openness.

Other psychologists (Runyan, 1980) are concerned with psychobiography, the psychological study of particular lives. Life narrative may form part of the raw material of psychobiography (for instance, when autobiographies are analyzed), but other sources, such as historical documents and other informants, can also be used. In some respects psychobiography is a variation on retrospective research, except that the focus is on understanding the individual rather than the process of aging *per se.*

In Chapter 8 we argued that life histories should not be used as the basis of a psychology of personality development; rather, we think that knowledge about personality and its continuity in adulthood can form a basis for understanding lives. The psychodynamic approaches of Freud and Erikson have had a tremendous influence on the thinking of historians and literary critics as well as psychologists, because psychoanalytic formulations can be used to make sense of historical and literary figures. The same benefit can be offered by trait psychology; in fact, the stronger empirical basis of trait psychology makes it, in our view, a much better candidate for this role. Historians, of course, generally cannot administer standardized personality questionnaires to their cases, but they can use the behavior patterns of a lifetime to estimate standing on dimensions of personality and then use these as a framework for interpreting the significant events in the lives of their subjects (cf. Winter & Carlson, 1988). (It would also be possible to gather personality ratings on historical or literary characters from panels of experts, using standard question-naires such as the NEO-PI. This would provide a more objective alter-native to the subjective interpretations usually offered by historians and literary critics.)

Empirically oriented psychologists have usually felt uncomfortable with psychobiographies, and with good reason: Various explanations can usually be offered for the same facts, and there is no conclusive way to choose among them. Different historians have vastly different views of the character of Napoleon and make widely different hypotheses about what he would have done if Wellington had left him any choice. But we cannot conduct an experiment, cannot go back in time and manipulate history so as to test these theories. And, according to most philosophers of science, what is untestable is beyond the bounds of science.

However, as Birren and Hedlund (1987) pointed out, it is perfectly reasonable to examine autobiographies as a source of testable hypotheses. If we are interested in people in general, rather than in some particular historical figure, we can move from speculative biography to testable psychology. We can also abandon the post hoc method of looking for traits that underlie life choices and begin a systematic study of the effects of specified traits on individual lives. We are not all Napoleons, but we all make choices: if and when and whom to marry; whether to have children and how many; what career to pursue, when to change it, when to persist despite adversity; whether to move to another city and reestablish friends and routines. Curiously, the two most significant and most thoroughly researched life choices—marriage and career—show quite different patterns.

Marriage and Divorce

Theories of marital choice have generally looked for a basis in either similarity or complementarity. There is good evidence that people do marry others of similar social, ethnic, and religious backgrounds, and that physical attractiveness is a powerful determinant–the rich and beautiful tend to marry the rich and beautiful. There is also clinical evidence, of the kind reported by Farrell and Rosenberg, that marital relationships often evolve complementary functions. But when personality measures are used, they frequently fail to predict marital choice. Extraverts are just as likely to marry extraverts as introverts; adjusted people choose neu-rotic spouses as often as adjusted ones. There seems to be a small influence of similarity in the domain of Openness—open people tend a bit toward marrying open people—but that may be an artifact of similarities in social class, education, and so on. When two college graduates marry, both of them are likely to be more open than high school dropouts.

This might seem to be a defeat for trait psychologies: The major dimensions of individual difference seem to have little influence on one of the most significant decisions of our life. Indeed, it is a healthy reminder that traits cannot explain *everything*. But it leads to a series of fascinating and thus far almost completely unexplored questions. Why would a well-adjusted person take on the difficult task of trying to live with an anxious, hostile, and depressed mate? Why would an open person consent to live with one who was closed? And, more than why, *how* do they manage together? When an introvert marries an extravert, does it lead to conflicts in their joint social life, do they arrange to live separate lives, or does the extravert "bring out" the extraverted side of his or her spouse? Does it matter whether the husband or the wife is the introvert: Will the husband's preferred style of socializing prevail regardless of what it is? Psychologists have spent a great deal of time studying how one individual adapts to an environment; but how do two individuals adapt to the environment they create for each other?

Buss and Barnes (1986) have begun to study some of these issues by looking at mate preferences. Individuals seek spouses with different characteristics: kindness, intelligence, attractiveness, wealth, and so on. In Buss and Barnes' study these preferences tended to reflect personality characteristics—although there appeared to be frequent sex differences. For example, kind and considerate spouses were preferred by men high in Extraversion and by women high in Neuroticism. Preferences, in turn, were related to the actual personalities of spouses: Women who preferred kind husbands tended to marry men who scored high on measures of Agreeableness. It appears that personality is related to marital choice, but not in a straightforward fashion.

There is considerably more information on divorce. Not surprisingly, marital dissatisfaction and divorce are chiefly related to Neuroticism, as a number of prospective longitudinal studies have shown. Between 1935 and 1938 E. Lowell Kelly began a study of 300 engaged couples. He obtained personality ratings on both partners from five acquaintences; 45 years later he assessed marital status and satisfaction (Kelly & Conley, 1987). Neuroticism in both husband and wife and low Conscientiousness in the husband predicted divorce. An analysis of the causes of divorce suggested an explanation:

> A wide variety of reasons for divorce were reported, but a number of these (in particular, emotional instability, arguments, emotional overreactions, and sexual problems) are probable manifestations of neuroticism, and others (particularly infidelity, alcohol abuse, and irresponsible social behavior) are probable manifestations of low impulse control [or Conscientiousness]. (p. 32)

Kelly and Conley also considered the case of individuals who remained unhappily married. These men and women had been rated as being higher in Neuroticism, but the men were also seen as introverted and disagreeable. Perhaps aloof and antagonistic men saw little prospect of a better second marriage and settled for what they had.

Interestingly, Kelly and Conley also had measures of many other variables thought to be important to marital adjustment: early home environment of the partners, including their parents' marital adjustment; attitudes towards marriage during the engagement period; sexual histories; and stressful life events during the marriage. All these variables were far less important than personality in predicting marital adjustment.

Careers

On the second issue, career choice, the influence of personality is both better understood and more obvious. Given a choice, people tend toward occupations that allow the expression of their personality. This is most clearly seen in inventories of vocational interest, such as the Holland (1985) Self-Directed Search, which provides scores for six categories of interests. Individuals with enterprising and social vocational interests tend to be extraverts; those with artistic interests tend to be open. Investigative interests are found among intelligent introverts, realistic interests among masculine men and women, and conventional interests among those closed to experience. Not surprisingly, open people report interest in a wider variety of occupations of all sorts (Costa et al., 1984).

Similar relationships are found when other vocational interest inventories, with different categorizations of interests, are used. And after age 25 vocational interests are known to be extremely stable. Some of the best early evidence for stability in personality was provided by Strong's (1955) 25-year retest of vocational interests.

When we move from vocational interests to actual occupation, the data become less clear. Open people may be interested in the occupation of poet or concert pianist, but how many of them have the talent or the financial resources to make a career of these interests? At this point in history at least, one's gender and educational level are the primary determinants of occupational choice, and economics is the major incentive. By and large, people take the highest-paying job they are qualified for, regardless of their preferences. Given a choice, they will gravitate toward the positions best fitted to their temperament—but most of us are not really given a choice. Nevertheless, studies do show that salespeople are more likely to be extraverts than introverts, and that cooks are less open to experience than are creative writers (Cattell et al., 1970). Data from the Myers–Briggs Type Indicator suggest that most psychologists are high in Intuition or what we would call Openness; those who are also high in Agreeableness are more likely to be clinicians, whereas those low in Agreeableness gravitate toward experimental psychology (Myers & McCaulley, 1985).

Once one has taken a job, for whatever reason, personality is likely to manifest itself in the way the job is performed. The extraverted bank clerk will spend more time than others chatting with customers; the librarian who is closed to experience may make more efforts to maintain quiet than to encourage reading. And if the gap between the occupational demands and personal disposition is too large, the individual is likely to quit and find a different line of work.

We know from studies in Boston (Costa & McCrae, 1978) and in Baltimore (McCrae & Costa, 1985) that individuals who have started a new career or switched to a different line of work are much more likely to be open than closed to experience. This is as true for women as it is for men. Longitudinal studies have also allowed us to separate cause from effect: People are not open *because* they were broadened by a new vocational experience; instead, they were open to experience years before they made the change, and so it seems likely that Openness contributed to the decision to start a new career.

Like most researchers, we have been concerned primarily with changes that overtake the individual, and failed to consider the changes that come as the individual overtakes his or her own life. One of the chief merits of the studies of Levinson, Gould, and others is that they remind us that problems can result when life fails to change. We strive to succeed in our careers and must cope with failure, but we must also deal with success. What motivation remains for the Nobel laureate who has won the prize that inspired her life's work? What happens to the couple whose dream of a house in the suburbs is finally realized? People soon come to take for granted the achievements that once dominated their lives. What happens then—depression, new dreams, rededication to the same cause? And what is the role of personality in this process?

PERSONALITY INFLUENCES ON THE DEVELOPMENT OF IDENTITY

We have tried to distinguish among personality traits, the self, and identity, noting that personality forms one unchanging aspect of the self, whereas identity consists of the most central aspects of the self (self-definitions in terms of roles, relationships, and values, as well as personal characteristics) and may or may not change. Since traits and identity elements are usually mixed indiscriminately under the label *personality* or *self-concept*, few researchers have thought to ask whether traits influence the development of identity. The question, however, is intriguing.

It is useful to begin by recalling that there is no one-to-one correspondence between the roles one plays in society and the definitions one has of oneself. The fact that one works from 9:00 to 5:00 as a secretary does not mean that being a secretary is part of one's self-definition. In fact, many secretaries probably see themselves as home-makers, novelists, or doctors who are merely taking a job as a secretary; their dreams and aspirations are elsewhere. Conversely, even when we fill a role that we have always hoped to fill, we may not really believe we fit in. In the eyes of the law, we may be fully adult at age 18 or 21; in our own eyes it may take many more years. In the meantime we act as adult as possible and hope that others will believe our bluff. Symbols are often important in establishing our sense of identification with a role. Stethoscopes may be more important than licenses in making men and women feel like doctors; military and religious uniforms are indispensable in creating the sense of commitment and identification that is required by these institutions.

A number of clinicians have remarked on the discrepancies between the face we present to the world—our persona or mask, as Jung called it—and our real sense of self. Alienation and a sense of meaninglessness may result from acting out roles with which we cannot identify. Conversely, we may identify too closely with superficial roles at the risk of being at best shallow, at worst seriously out of touch with our own inner needs.

It seems likely that Openness to experience would figure importantly in the correspondence between inner and outer versions of the self. Those who are open to their own feelings, willing to think out and try out new ways of living, should develop a better fit in the long run and should be better able to differentiate assigned roles from inner needs and values. There is a bit of empirical support for this hypothesis in a study of organizational behavior conducted by Kahn, Wolfe, Quinn, Snoek and Rosenthal (1964). They employed the California Psychological Inventory to measure a trait called *flexibility-rigidity*, apparently a close cousin of Openness. Said Kahn et al., "The strong identification with his superiors and with the official goals of the organization, together with the heavy emphasis on authority relations, leads the rigid person to a rather complete internalization of his roles. His role tends to become his identity. While the flexible person may be in the course of the work day a manager, friend, personal confidant, sports fan, and explorer, the rigid person is *manager*" (p. 294). What becomes of such a person when he retires? Is he now *retired*, content to be nothing more productive? Or does he face a crisis in the loss of an identity in which he was too heavily invested? Is the departure of children from the home more stressful for the closed woman who has always regarded herself as nothing but *mother*? Surely these transitions must have different impacts on open and closed people.

Theorists have often noted the importance of fantasy in the acquisition of new roles. Imagining oneself as a Senator, making speeches and debating foreign policy, may be important as a first step in running for election—even to a much lesser office. The housewife's ability to see herself with an independent career probably smoothes the way for her when she begins looking for a job or returns to school. A certain flexibility in the self-concept as well as a degree of Openness would thus appear to contribute to change (Whitbourne, 1986b).

The same considerations may apply to relationships as to roles. We know that closed persons espouse traditional family ideologies (Costa & McCrae, 1978); they may also be the kinds of people who preserve a single style of relating to significant others throughout their lives. For them, perhaps, Father and Mother remain the only real adults, to be loved or feared but never recognized as people with their own limitations.

For them, perhaps, wives remain homemakers and husbands breadwinners, and woe to a spouse who fails to live up to these expectations or tries to exceed them! For them, perhaps, children never grow up and are always to be advised or scolded or praised according to how well they live up to parental standards.

Gould's work on adult development is concerned with the achievement of adult consciousness: The profound realization that we control our own lives and must take responsibility for them; that life is not necessarily fair and railing against injustice will not make it so; that we ourselves are not innocents, but have a darker side; that death will come to us as to our parents. Gould sees these insights emerging over the first half of life in a regular sequence. But are they universal? Or is it perhaps only the open individual who sees and feels enough of life to make these discoveries and reach the real freedom that freedom from illusion allows?

*   *   *

The last few years have been extraordinarily productive ones for the field of personality and aging. Longitudinal studies begun years ago by farsighted researchers have offered clear and consistent evidence of what happens to personality dispositions with age. In the same period, personality psychology itself has revived from a period of skepticism and stagnation, bringing new vitality to an area that has proved itself indispensable in helping us to understand human beings and their lives. We have made conceptual advances and have come to see that much of what we were quarreling about was words instead of facts. A good deal has now been established, and a completely new direction for research on personality and aging can now be envisioned.

Personality has often been identified with the organizing force in human behavior, and more systematic studies of the processes of organization are still necessary. But personality can also be viewed as the product of organization, the sum of recurring regularities that mark the style of each person and distinguish him or her from others. We call these individual consistencies *traits*.

The five-factor model of personality has brought order to the competing systems of personality structure by showing that most traits can be understood in terms of the basic dimensions of Neuroticism, Extraversion, Openness, Agreeableness, and Conscientiousness. We know that we can measure these traits with an acceptable degree of accuracy by either self-reports or ratings from knowledgeable sources.

We have learned all the pitfalls of assuming that cross-sectional comparisons show age changes, and have considered the evidence from longitudinal and sequential designs as well. And study after study has shown that over the adult portion of the life course there is little change in the average level of most commonly measured personality traits. In general, there is neither growth nor decline in adult personality. A psychology whose purpose was to explain how personality changes with age would have nothing to say. Indeed, it becomes more pertinent to explain how personality remains stable.

For stable it is, not only in groups, but in individuals. Longitudinal studies using a variety of instruments, and using raters as well as individuals' own reports, find great continuity in the level of traits in individuals. These same findings are confirmed by retrospective accounts that show the same traits active in youth and in old age.

But the stability of traits does not imply that life itself must be repetitious and stagnant. Lives change, history moves on, and all of us must work to adapt to change, or actively reshape our lives. Internally, our sense of self, our fundamental identity, may change as the social roles, values, physical attributes, and personal relationships that are central to it shift.

It is in the study of these changes that the future of personality and aging lies. Ask not how life's experiences change personality; ask instead how personality shapes lives and gives order, continuity, and predictability to the life course, as well as creating or accommodating change. For the psychologist as well as the aging individual, enduring dispositions form a basis for understanding and guiding emerging lives.

REFERENCES

Adler, A. (1964). *Social interest: A challenge to mankind.* New York: Capricorn Books. (Original work published 1938)

Allport, G.W. (1937). *Personality: A psychological interpretation.* New York: Holt.

Allport, G.W. (1955). *Becoming: Basic considerations for a psychology of personality.* New Haven: Yale University Press.

Allport, G.W. (1961). *Pattern and growth in personality.* New York: Holt, Rinehart & Winston.

Allport, G.W. (1966). Traits revisited. *American Psychologist, 21,* 1–10.

Allport, G.W., & Odbert, H.S. (1936). Trait names: A psycho-lexical study. *Psychological Monographs, 47* (Whole No. 211).

Ames, L. B. (1965). Changes in the experience balance scores on the Rorschach at different ages in the life span. *Journal of Genetic Psychology, 106,* 279–286.

Arenberg, D., & Robertson-Tchabo, E. A. (1977). Learning and memory. In J. E. Birren & K. W. Schaie (Eds.), *Handbook of the psychology of aging,* 1st ed. (pp. 421–449). New York: Van Nostrand Reinhold.

Atkinson, J. W., Bongort, K., & Price, L. H. (1977). Explorations using computer simulation to comprehend thematic apperceptive measurement of motivation. *Motivation and Emotion, 1,* 1–27.

Bachman, J. G., O'Malley, P. M., & Johnston, J. (1978). *Adolescence to adulthood: Change and stability in the lives of young men.* Ann Arbor, MI: Institute for Social Research.

Baltes, M. M., & Schmid, U. (1987). Psychological gerontology. *German Journal of Psychology, 11,* 87–123.

Baltes, P. B., & Nesselroade, J. R. (1972). Cultural change and adolescent personality development. *Developmental Psychology, 7,* 244–256.

Baltes, P. B., Reese, H. W., & Nesselroade, J. R. (1977). *Life-span developmental psychology: Introduction to research methods.* Monterey, CA: Brooks/Cole.

Bandura, A. (1977). *Social learning theory.* Englewood Cliffs, NJ: Prentice-Hall.

Bandura, A. (1982). The psychology of chance encounters and life paths. *American Psychologist, 37,* 747–755.

Barron, F. (1980). The ego-strength scale and its correlates. In W. G. Dahlstrom & L. Dahlstrom (Eds.), *Basic readings on the MMPI: A new selection on personality measurement.* Minneapolis: University of Minnesota Press.

Bengtson, V. L., Reedy, M. N., & Gordon, C. (1985). Aging and self-conceptions: Personality processes and social contexts. In J. E. Birren & K. W. Schaie (Eds.), *Handbook of the psychology of aging,* 2nd ed. (pp. 544–593). New York: Van Nostrand Reinhold.

Berg, I. A. (1959). The unimportance of test item content. In B. M. Bass & I. A. Berg (Eds.), *Objective approaches to personality assessment* (pp. 83–99). New York: Van Nostrand.

Bertaux, D. (1981). *Biography and society.* Beverly Hills, CA: Sage.

Birren, J. E., & Hedlund, B. (1987). Contribution of autobiography to developmental psychology. In N. Eisenberg (Ed.), *Contemporary topics in developmental psychology* (pp. 394–415). New York: Wiley.

Block, J. (1961). *The Q-sort method in personality assessment and psychiatric research.* Springfield, IL: Charles C Thomas.

Block, J. (1965). *The challenge of response sets.* New York: Appleton-Century-Crofts.

Block, J. (1971). *Lives through time.* Berkeley, CA: Bancroft Books.

Block, J. (1977). Advancing the psychology of personality: Paradigmatic shift or improving the quality of research? In D. Magnusson & N. S. Endler (Eds.), *Personality at the cross-roads: Current issues in interactional psychology* (pp. 37–64). Hillsdale, NJ: Lawrence Erlbaum Associates.

Block, J. (1981). Some enduring and consequential structures of personality. In A. I. Rabin (Ed.), *Further explorations in personality.* New York: Wiley-Interscience.

Block, J. H., & Block, J. (1980). The role of ego control and ego resiliency in the organization of behavior. In W. A. Collins (Ed.), *Development of cognition, affect, and social relations: The Minnesota symposium on child psychology* (Vol. 13). Hillsdale, NJ: Lawrence Erlbaum Associates.

Borkenau, P. (1988). The multiple classification of acts and the Big Five factors of personality. *Journal of Research in Personality, 22,* 337–352.

Britton, J. H., & Britton, J. O. (1972). *Personality changes in aging: A longitudinal study of community residents.* New York: Springer.

Bühler, C. (1935). The curve of life as studies in biographies. *Journal of Applied Psychology, 19,* 405–409.

Bühler, C., Keith-Spiegel, P., & Thomas, K. (1973). Developmental psychology. In B. B. Wolman (Ed.), *Handbook of general psychology* (pp. 861–917). Englewood Cliffs, NJ: Prentice-Hall.

Buss, D. M. (1983). Evolutionary biology and personality psychology: Implications of genetic variability. *Personality and Individual Differences, 4,* 51–63.

Buss, D. M., & Barnes, M. (1986). Preferences in human mate selection. *Journal of Personality and Social Psychology, 50,* 559–570.

Butler, R. N. (1963). The life review: An interpretation of reminiscence in the aged. *Psychiatry, 26,* 65–76.

Caldwell, B. McD. (1954). The use of the Rorschach in personality research with the aged. *Journal of Gerontology, 9,* 316–323.

Campbell, D. T., & Fiske, D. W. (1959). Convergent and discriminant validation by the multitrait–multimethod matrix. *Psychological Bulletin, 56,* 81–105.

Caspi, A., Elder, G. H., Jr., & Bem, D. J. (1987). Moving against the world: Life-course patterns of explosive children. *Developmental Psychology, 23,* 308–313.

Cattel, R. B. (1946). *The description and measurement of personality.* Yonkers, NY: World Book.

Cattel, R. B., Eber, H. W., & Tatsuoka, M. M. (1970). *The handbook for the Sixteen Personality Factor Questionnaire.* Champaign, IL: Institute for Personality and Ability Testing.

Chew, P. (1976). *The inner world of the middle-aged man.* New York: Macmillan.

Chew, S. C. (1947, April). *This strange eventful history.* Paper presented at the Folger Shakespeare Library, Washington, DC.

Coan, R. W. (1972). Measurable components of openness to experience. *Journal of Consulting and Clinical Psychology, 39,* 346.

Cohen, J. (1969). *Statistical power analysis for the behavioral sciences.* New York: Academic Press.

Conley, J. J. (1985). A personality theory of adulthood and aging. In R. Hogan & W. H. Jones (Eds.), *Perspectives in personality,* Vol. 1 (pp. 81–115). Greenwich, CT: JAI Press.

Constantinople, A. (1969). An Eriksonian measure of personality development in college students. *Developmental Psychology, 1,* 357–372.

Cooper, M. W. (1977). *An empirical investigation of the male midlife period: A descriptive, cohort study.* Unpublished undergraduate honors thesis, University of Massachusetts at Boston.

Cornoni-Huntley, J., Barbano, H. E., Brody, J. A., Cohen, B., Feldman, J. J., Kleinman, J. C., & Madans, J. (1983). National Health and Nutrition Examination I—Epidemiologic Followup Survey. *Public Health Reports, 98,* 245–251.

Costa, P. T., Jr. (1986, August). *The scope of individuality.* Invited address, Division 8, presented at the Annual Convention of the American Psychological Association, Los Angeles, CA.

Costa, P. T., Jr., & McCrae, R. R. (1976). Age differences in personality structure: A cluster analytic approach. *Journal of Gerontology, 31,* 564–570.

Costa, P. T., Jr., & McCrae, R.R. (1977). Age differences in personality structure revisited: Studies in validity, stability, and change. *International Journal of Aging and Human Development, 8,* 261–275.

Costa, P. T., Jr., & McCrae, R. R. (1978). Objective personality assessment. In M. Storandt, I. C. Siegler, & M. F. Elias (Eds.), *The clinical psychology of aging* (pp. 119–143). New York: Plenum Press.

Costa, P. T., Jr., & McCrae, R. R. (1980a). Influence of extraversion and neuroticism on subjective well-being: Happy and unhappy people. *Journal of Personality and Social Psychology, 38,* 668–678.

Costa, P. T., Jr., & McCrae, R. R. (1980b). Somatic complaints in males as a function of age and neuroticism: A longitudinal analysis. *Journal of Behavioral Medicine, 3,* 245–257.

Costa, P. T., Jr., & McCrae, R. R. (1980c). Still stable after all these years: Personality as a key to some issues in adulthood and old age. In P.B. Baltes & O. G. Brim, Jr. (Eds.), *Life-span development and behavior,* Vol. 3 (pp. 65–102). New York: Academic Press.

Costa, P. T., Jr., & McCrae, R. R. (1982). An approach to the attribution of age, period, and cohort effects. *Psychological Bulletin, 92,* 238–250.

Costa, P. T., Jr., & McCrae, R. R. (1984). Personality as a lifelong determinant of well-being. In C. Malatesta & C. Izard (Eds.), *Affective processes in adult development and aging* (pp. 141–157). Beverly Hills, CA: Sage.

Costa, P. T., Jr., & McCrae, R. R. (1985). *The NEO Personality Inventory manual.* Odessa, FL: Psychological Assessment Resources.

Costa, P. T., Jr., & McCrae, R. R. (1986a). Age, personality, and the Holtzman Inkblot Technique. *International Journal of Aging and Human Development, 23,* 115–125.

Costa, P. T., Jr., & McCrae, R. R. (1986b). Cross-sectional studies of personality in a national sample: 1. Development and validation of survey measures. *Psychology and Aging, 1,* 140–143.

Costa, P. T., Jr., & McCrae, R. R. (1986c). Personality stability and its implications for clinical psychology. *Clinical Psychology Review, 6,* 407–423.

Costa, P. T., Jr., & McCrae, R. R. (1988a). From catalog to classification: Murray's needs and the five-factor model. *Journal of Personality and Social Psychology, 55,* 258–265.

Costa, P. T., Jr., & McCrae, R. R. (1988b). Personality in adulthood: A six-year longitudinal study of self-reports and spouse ratings on the NEO Personality Inventory. *Journal of Personality and Social Psychology, 54,* 853–863.

Costa, P. T., Jr., & McCrae, R. R. (1989a). *The NEO-PI/NEO-FFI manual supplement.* Odessa, FL: Psychological Assessment Resources.

Costa, P. T., Jr., & McCrae, R. R. (1989b). Personality continuity and the changes of adult life. In M. Storandt & G. R. VandenBos (Eds.), *The adult years: Continuity and change* (pp. 45–77). Washington, DC: American Psychological Association.

Costa, P. T., Jr., McCrae, R. R., & Arenberg, D. (1980). Enduring dispositions in adult males. *Journal of Personality and Social Psychology, 38,* 793–800.

Costa, P. T., Jr., McCrae, R. R., & Arenberg, D. (1983). Recent longitudinal research on personality and aging. In K. W. Schaie (Ed.), *Longitudinal studies of adult psychological development* (pp. 222–265). New York: Guilford Press.

Costa, P. T., Jr., McCrae, R. R., & Dembroski, T. M. (1989). Agreeableness vs. antagonism: Explication of a potential risk factor for CHD. In A. Siegman & T. M. Dembroski (Eds.), *In search of coronary-prone behavior: Beyond Type A* (pp. 41–63). Hillsdale, NJ: Lawrence Erlbaum Associates.

Costa, P. T., Jr., McCrae, R. R., & Holland, J. L. (1984). Personality and vocational interests in an adult sample. *Journal of Applied Psychology, 69,* 390–400.

Costa, P. T., Jr., McCrae, R. R., Zonderman, A. B., Barbano, H. E., Lebowitz, B., & Larson, D. M. (1986). Cross-sectional studies of personality in a national sample: 2. Stability in neuroticism, extraversion, and openness. *Psychology and Aging, 1,* 144–149.

Costa, P. T., Jr., Zonderman, A. B., & McCrae, R. R. (in press). Personality, stress, and coping in older adulthood. In A. L. Greene, E. M. Cummings, & K. H. Karraker (Eds.), *Life-span developmental psychology, Vol. 11: Perspectives on stress and coping.* Hillsdale, NJ: Lawrence Erlbaum Associates.

Crandall, J. E. (1975). A scale for social interest. *Journal of Individual Psychology, 31,* 187–195.

Crowne, D., & Marlowe, D. (1964). *The approval motive.* New York: Wiley.

Cumming, E., & Henry, W. (1961). *Growing old.* New York: Basic Books.

Dicken, C. (1963). Good impression, social desirability, and acquiescence as suppressor variables. *Educational and Psychological Measurement, 23,* 699–720.

Digman, J. M., & Inouye, J. (1986). Further specification of the five robust factors of personality. *Journal of Personality and Social Psychology, 50,* 116–123.

Dollard, J., & Miller, N. E. (1950). *Personality and psychotherapy: An analysis in terms of learning, thinking, and culture.* New York: McGraw-Hill.

Douglas, K., & Arenberg, D. (1978). Age changes, cohort differences, and cultural change on the Guilford–Zimmerman Temperament Survey. *Journal of Gerontology, 33,* 737–747.

Edwards, A. L. (1954). *Statistical methods for the behavioral sciences.* New York: Holt, Rinehart, & Winston.

Edwards, A. L. (1957). *The social desirability variable in personality assessment and research.* New York: Dryden.

Eisdorfer, C. (1963). Rorschach performance and intellectual functioning in the aged. *Journal of Gerontology, 18,* 358–363.

Elder, G. H., Jr., & Clipp, E. C. (1988). Combat experience, comradeship, and psychological health. In J. Wilson, Z. Harel, & B. Kahana (Eds.), *Human adaptations to extreme stress: From the Holocaust to Vietnam.* New York: Plenum.

Ellis, A. (1962). *Reason and emotion in psychotherapy.* New York: Lyle Stuart.

Epstein, S. (1973). The self-concept revisited: Or a theory of a theory. *American Psychologist, 28,* 404–416.

Epstein, S. (1977). Traits are alive and well. In D. Magnusson & N. S. Endler (Eds.), *Personality at the crossroads: Current issues in interactional psychology* (pp. 83–98). Hillsdale, NJ: Lawrence Erlbaum Associates.

Epstein, S. (1979). The stability of behavior: I. On predicting most of the people much of the time. *Journal of Personality and Social Psychology, 37,* 1097–1126.

Erikson, E. H. (1962). *Young man Luther: A study in psychoanalysis and history.* New York: Norton.

Eysenck, H. J., & Eysenck, S. B. G. (1975). *Manual of the Eysenck Personality Questionnaire.* San Diego: EdITS.

Farrell, M. P., & Rosenberg, S. D. (1981). *Men at midlife.* Boston: Auburn House.

Finn, S. E. (1986). Stability of personality self-ratings over 30 years: Evidence for an age/cohort interaction. *Journal of Personality and Social Psychology, 50,* 813–818.

Fiske, D. W. (1974). The limits for the conventional science of personality. *Journal of Personality, 42,* 1–11.

Fiske, D. W. (1978). *Strategies for personality research.* San Francisco: Jossey-Bass.

Freud, A. (1936). *The ego and the mechanisms of defense.* New York: International Universities Press.

Freud, S. (1933). *New introductory lectures in psychoanalysis* (W. J. H. Sprott, Trans.). New York: Norton.

Freud, S. (1938). The interpretation of dreams. In *The basic writings of Sigmund Freud.* New York: Random House.

Friedlander, J. S., Costa, P. T., Jr., Bossé, R., Ellis, E., Rhodes, J. G., & Stoudt, H. (1977). Longitudinal physique changes among healthy white veterans at Boston. *Human Biology, 49,* 541–558.

Goffman, E. (1959). *The presentation of self in everyday life.* New York: Doubleday Anchor.

Gold D., Andres, D., & Schwartzman, A. (1987). Self-perception of personality at midlife in elderly people: Continuity and change. *Experimental Aging Research, 13,* 197–202.

Goldberg, L. R. (1981). Language and individual differences: The search for universals in personality lexicons. In L. Wheeler (Ed.), *Review of personality and social psychology* (Vol. 2, pp. 141–165). Beverly Hills, CA: Sage.

Goldberg, L. R. (1982). From ace to zombie: Some explorations in the language of personality. In C. D. Spielberger & J. N. Butcher (Eds.), *Advances in personality assessment* (Vol. 1, pp. 203–234). Hillsdale, NJ: Lawrence Erlbaum Associates.

Gould, R. L. (1972). The phases of adult life: A study in developmental psychology. *American Journal of Psychiatry, 29,* 521–531.

Gould, R. L. (1978). *Transformations.* New York: Simon and Schuster.

Guilford, J. P. (1959). *Personality.* New York: McGraw-Hill.

Guilford, J. P., & Guilford, R. B. (1934). An analysis of the factors in a typical test of introversion–extroversion. *Journal of Abnormal and Social Psychology, 28,* 377–399.

Guilford, J. S., Zimmerman, W. S., & Guilford, J. P. (1976). *The Guilford–Zimmerman Temperament Survey handbook: Twenty-five years of research and application.* San Diego, CA: EdITS.

Gullette, M. M. (1989, January 29). Midlife exhiliration. *The New York Times Magazine,* pp. 18, 20.

Gutmann, D. L. (1964). An exploration of ego configurations in middle and later life. In B. L. Neugarten (Ed.), *Personality in middle and later life* (pp. 114–148). New York: Atherton.

Gutmann, D. L. (1970). Female ego styles and generational conflict. In J. M. Bardwich, E. Douvan, M. S. Horner, & D. L. Gutmann (Eds.), *Feminine personality and conflict* (pp. 77–96). Belmont, CA: Brooks/Cole.

Gutmann, D. L. (1974). Alternatives to disengagement: The old men of highland Druze. In R. LeVine (Ed.), *Culture and personality: Contemporary readings.* Chicago: Aldine.

Haan, N., Millsap, R., & Hartka, E. (1986). As time goes by: Change and stability in personality over fifty years. *Psychology and Aging, 1,* 220–232.

Hale, E. (1981, June 8). Your personality—you're stuck with it. *The Idaho Statesman,* Boise, ID.

Halverson, C. F., Jr. (1988). Remembering your parents: Reflections on the retrospective method. *Journal of Personality, 56,* 435–443.

Havighurst, R. J., McDonald, W. J., Maculen, L., & Mazel, J. (1979). Male social scientists: Lives after sixty. *The Gerontologist, 19,* 55–60.

Helson, R., Mitchell, V., & Moane, G. (1984). Personality and patterns of adherence and nonadherence to the social clock. *Journal of Personality and Social Psychology, 46,* 1079–1096.

Helson, R., & Moane, G. (1987). Personality change in women from college to midlife. *Journal of Personality and Social Psychology, 53,* 176–186.

Herold, J. C. (1963). *The age of Napoleon.* New York: American Heritage.

Hill, E. F. (1972). *The Holtzman Inkblot Technique*. San Francisco: Jossey-Bass.

Hogan, R. T. (1979). Of rituals, roles, cheaters, and spoilsports. *The John Hopkins Magazine, 30,* 46–53.

Hogan, R. T. (1983). Socioanalytic theory of personality. In M. M. Page (Ed.), *1982 Nebraska Symposium on Motivation: Personality—current theory and research* (pp. 55–89). Lincoln, NE: University of Nebraska Press.

Holland, J. L. (1985). *Self-Directed Search—1985 edition*. Odessa, FL: Psychological Assessment Resources.

Holtzman, W. H. (1961). *Guide to administration and scoring: Holtzman Inkblot Technique*. New York: Psychological Corporation.

Howard, A., & Bray, D. W. (1988). *Managerial lives in transition: Advancing age and changing times*. New York: Guilford Press.

Jackson, D. N. (1984). *Personality Research Form manual* (3rd ed.). Port Huron, MI: Research Psychologists Press.

Jackson, D. N., & Messick, S. (1961). Acquiescence and desirability as response determinants on the MMPI. *Educational and Psychological Measurement, 21,* 771–790.

James, W. (1890). *Principles of psychology*. New York: Henry Holt.

Jaques, E. (1965). Death and the mid-life crisis. *International Journal of Psychoanalysis, 46,* 502–513.

Jessor, R. (1983). The stability of change: Psychosocial development from adolescence to young adulthood. In D. Magnusson & V. L. Allen (Eds.), *Human development: An interactional perspective* (pp. 321–341). New York: Academic Press.

John, O. P., Angleitner, A., & Ostendorf, F. (1988). The lexical approach to personality: A historical review of trait taxonomic research. *European Journal of Personality, 2,* 171–203.

Jung, C. G. (1971). *Psychological types* (H. G. Baynes, Trans., revised by R. F. C. Hull). Princeton, NJ: Princeton University Press. (Original work published 1923)

Jung, C. G. (1933). *Modern man in search of a soul* (W. S. Dell & C. F. Baynes, Trans.). New York: Harcourt.

Kagan, J. (1971). *Change and continuity in infancy*. New York: Wiley.

Kagan, J., & Moss, H. A. (1962). *From birth to maturity*. New York: Wiley.

Kahana, B. (1978). The use of projective techniques in personality assessment of the aged. In I. C. Siegler, M. Storandt, & M. F. Elias (Eds.), *The clinical psychology of aging* (pp. 145–180). New York: Plenum.

Kahn, R. L., Wolfe, D. M., Quinn, R. P., Snoek, J. D., & Rosenthal, R. A. (1964). *Organizational stress: Studies in role conflict and ambiguity*. New York: Wiley.

Kastenbaum, R. & Costa, P. T., Jr. (1977). Psychological perspectives on death.

Annual Review of Psychology, 28, 225–249.

Kausler, D. H. (1982). Experimental psychology and human aging. New York: Wiley.

Keehn, R. J., Goldberg, I. D., & Beebe, G. W. (1974). Twenty-four year mortality follow-up of army veterans with disability separations for psychoneurosis in 1944. Psychosomatic Medicine, 36, 27–46.

Kelly, E. L. (1955). Consistency of the adult personality. American Psychologist, 10, 659–681.

Kelly, E. L., & Conley, J. J. (1987). Personality and compatibility: A prospective analysis of marital stability and marital satisfaction. Journal of Personality and Social Psychology, 52, 27–40.

Kimmel, D. C. (1974). Adulthood and aging. New York: Wiley.

Kohlberg, L. (1971). From is to ought: How to commit the naturalistic fallacy and get away with it in the study of moral development. In T. Mischel (Ed.), Cognitive development and epistomology. New York: Academic Press.

Kramer, M., & Rednick, R. W. (1976). Epidemiological indices in the middle years. Unpublished paper cited in O. G. Brim, Jr., Theories of the males midlife crisis. The Counseling Psychologist, 6, 2–9.

Kuhn, M. H., & McPartland, T. S. (1954). An empirical investigation of self-attitudes. American Sociological Review, 19, 68–76.

Lacy, W. B., & Hendricks, J. (1980). Developmental model of adult life: Myth or reality? International Journal of Aging and Human Development, 11, 89–110.

Leary, T. (1957). Interpersonal diagnosis of personality. New York: Ronald Press.

Lecky, P. (1945). Self consistency: A theory of personality. New York: Island Press.

Leon, G. R., Gillum, B., Gillum, R., & Gouze, M. (1979). Personality stability and change over a 30-year period—middle age to old age. Journal of Consulting and Clinical Psychology, 47, 517–524.

Levinson, D. J., Darrow, C. N., Klein, E. B., Levinson, M. L., & McKee, B. (1978). The seasons of a man's life. New York: Knopf.

Liker, J. K., & Elder, G. H. (1983). Economic hardship and marital relations in the 1930s. American Sociological Review, 48, 343–359.

Little, B. R. (1983). Personal projects: A rationale and method for investigation. Environment and Behavior, 15, 273–309.

Livson, N. (1973). Developmental dimensions of personality: A life-span formulation. In P. B. Baltes & K. W. Schaie (Eds.), Life-span developmental psychology: Personality and socialization (pp. 98–123). New York: Academic Press.

Loevinger, J. (1966). The meaning and measurement of ego development. American Psychologist, 21, 195–206.

Lowenthal, M. F., & Chiriboga, D. (1972). Transition to the empty nest: Crisis, challenge, or relief. Archives of General Psychiatry, 6, 8–14.

Lowenthal, M. F., Thurner, M., & Chiriboga, D. (1975). Four stages of life. San

Francisco: Jossey-Bass.

Lubin, B., Larsen, R. M., Matarazzo, J. D., & Seever, M. (1985). Psychological test usage patterns in five professional settings. *American Psychologist, 40,* 857–861.

Maas, H. S., & Kuypers, J. A. (1974). *From thirty to seventy.* San Francisco: Jossey-Bass.

Maddi, S. R. (1976). *Personality theories: A comparative analysis* (3rd ed.). Homewood, IL: Dorsey Press.

Maddi, S. R. (1980). *Personality theories: A comparative analysis* (4th ed.). Homewood, IL: Dorsey Press.

Maddi, S. R., & Costa, P. T., Jr. (1972). *Humanism in personology: Allport, Maslow and Murray.* Chicago: Aldine.

Maddox, G. L. (1968). Persistence of life style among the elderly: A longitudinal study of patterns of social activity in relation to life satisfaction. In B. L. Neugarten (Ed.), *Middle age and aging: A reader in social psychology* (pp. 181–183). Chicago: University of Chicago Press.

Maslow, A. H. (1954). *Motivation and personality.* New York: Harper & Row.

McAdams, D. P., & Ochberg, R. L. (Eds.). (1988). Psychobiography and life narratives. *Journal of Personality, 56(1)* (Special issue).

McClelland, D. C. (1980). Motive dispositions: The merits of operant and respondent measures. In L. Wheeler (Ed.), *Review of personality and social psychology,* Vol. 1 (pp. 10–41). Beverly Hills, CA: Sage.

McCrae, R. R. (1982a). Age differences in the use of coping mechanisms. *Journal of Gerontology, 37,* 454–460.

McCrae, R. R. (1982b). Consensual validation of personality traits: Evidence from self-reports and ratings. *Journal of Personality and Social Psychology, 43,* 293–303.

McCrae, R. R. (1989). Why I advocate the five-factor model: Joint analyses of the NEO-PI and other instruments. In D. M. Buss & N. Cantor (Eds.), *Personality psychology: Recent trends and emerging directions.* (pp. 237–245). New York: Springer-Verlag.

McCrae, R. R., & Costa, P. T., Jr. (1980). Openness to experience and ego level in Loevinger's sentence completion test: Dispositional contributions to developmental models of personality. *Journal of Personality and Social Psychology, 39,* 1179–1190.

McCrae, R. R., & Costa, P. T. Jr. (1982). Self-concept and the stability of personality: Cross-sectional comparisons of self-reports and ratings. *Journal of Personality and Social Psychology, 43,* 1282–1292.

McCrae, R. R., & Costa, P. T., Jr. (1983a). Joint factors in self-reports and ratings: Neuroticism, extraversion, and openness to experience. *Personality and Individual Differences, 4,* 245–255.

McCrae, R. R., & Costa, P. T., Jr. (1983b). Psychological maturity and subjective well-being: Toward a new synthesis. *Developmental Psychology*, 19, 243–248.

McCrae, R. R., & Costa, P. T., Jr. (1983c). Social desirability scales: More substance than style. *Journal of Consulting and Clinical Psychology*, 51, 882–888.

McCrae, R. R., & Costa, P. T., Jr. (1984). *Emerging lives, enduring dispositions: Personality in adulthood*. Boston: Little, Brown.

McCrae, R. R., & Costa, P. T., Jr. (1985). Openness to experience. In R. Hogan & W. H. Jones (Eds.), *Perspectives in personality*, Vol. 1 (pp. 145–172). Greenwich, CT: JAI Press.

McCrae, R. R., & Costa, P. T., Jr. (1986). Personality, coping, and coping effectiveness in an adult sample. *Journal of Personality*, 54, 385–405.

McCrae, R. R., & Costa, P. T., Jr. (1987). Validation of the five-factor model of personality across instruments and observers. *Journal of Personality and Social Psychology*, 52, 81–90.

McCrae, R. R., & Costa, P. T., Jr. (1988a). Age, personality, and the spontaneous self-concept. *Journal of Gerontology: Social Sciences*, 43, S177–S185.

McCrae, R. R., & Costa, P. T., Jr. (1988b). Recalled parent–child relations and adult personality. *Journal of Personality*, 56, 417–434.

McCrae, R. R., & Costa, P. T., Jr. (1988c, August). Different points of view: Self-reports and ratings in the assessment of personality. In M. Amelang & W. Wittmann (Chairs), *The predictability of human behavior: 20 years after*. Symposium conducted at the XXIVth International Congress of Psychology, Sydney, Australia.

McCrae, R. R. & Costa, P. T., Jr. (1989a). Reinterpreting the Myers–Briggs Type Indicator from the perspective of the five-factor model of personality. *Journal of Personality*, 57, 17–40.

McCrae, R. R., & Costa, P. T., Jr. (1989b). Rotation to maximize the construct validity of factors in the NEO Personality Inventory. *Multivariate Behavioral Research*, 24, 107–124.

McCrae, R. R., & Costa, P. T., Jr. (1989c). The structure of interpersonal traits: Wiggins's circumplex and the five-factor model. *Journal of Personality and Social Psychology*, 56, 586–595.

McCrae, R. R., Costa, P. T., Jr., & Busch, C. M. (1986). Evaluating comprehensiveness in personality systems: The California Q-Set and the five-factor model. *Journal of Personality*, 54, 430–446.

McCrae, R. R., Costa, P. T., Jr., Dahlstrom, W. G., Barefoot, J. C., Siegler, I. C., & Williams, R. B., Jr. (1989). A caution on the use of the MMPI K-correction in research on psychosomatic medicine. *Psychosomatic Medicine*, 51, 58–65.

McGowan, J., & Gormly, J. (1976). Validation of personality traits: A multicriteria approach. *Journal of Personality and Social Psychology, 34,* 791–795.

McGuire, W. J. (1984). Search for the self: Going beyond self-esteem and the reactive self. In R. A. Zucker, J. Aronoff, & A. I. Rabin (Eds.), *Personality and the prediction of behavior* (pp. 73–120). New York: Academic Press.

McKinley, J. C., Hathaway, S. R., & Meehl, P. E. (1948). The MMPI: VI. The K scale. *Journal of Consulting Psychology, 12,* 20–31.

Mead, G. H. (1934). *Mind, self and society.* Chicago: University of Chicago Press.

Millon, T. (1981). *Disorders of personality: DSM III: Axis II.* New York: Wiley.

Mischel, W. (1968). *Personality and assessment.* New York: Wiley.

Mortimer, J. T., Finch, M. D., & Kumka, D. (1981). Persistence and change in development: The multidimensional self-concept. In P. B. Baltes & O. G. Brim, Jr. (Eds.), *Life-span development and behavior,* Vol. 4 (pp. 264–315). New York: Academic Press.

Moskowitz, D. S. (1988). Cross-situational generality in the laboratory: Dominance and friendliness. *Journal of Personality and Social Psychology, 54,* 829–839.

Murray, H. A. (1938). *Explorations in personality.* New York: Oxford University Press.

Murray, H. A., & Kluckhohn, C. (1953). Outline of a conception of personality. In C. Kluckhohn & H. A. Murray (Eds.), *Personality in nature, society, and culture,* 2nd ed. (pp. 3–52). New York: Knopf.

Mussen, P., Eichhorn, D. H., Honzik, M. P., Bieber, S. L., & Meredith, W. M. (1980). Continuity and change in women's characteristics over four decades. *International Journal of Behavioral Development, 3,* 333–347.

Myerhoff, B. G., & Simić, A. (Eds.). (1978). *Life's career—aging: Cultural variations on growing old.* Beverly Hills, CA: Sage.

Myers, I. B., & McCaulley, M. H. (1985). *Manual: A guide to the development and use of the Myers–Briggs Type Indicator.* Palo Alto: Consulting Psychologists Press.

Neill, A. S. (1977). *Summerhill: A radical approach to child-rearing.* New York: Pocket Books.

Neugarten, B. L. (1964). *Personality in middle and late life.* New York: Atherton Press.

Neugarten, B. L. (1968). Adult personality: Toward a psychology of the life cycle. In B. L. Neugarten (Ed.), *Middle age and aging: A reader in social psychology* (pp. 137–147). Chicago: University of Chicago Press.

Neugarten, B. L. (1977). Personality and aging. In J. E. Birren & K. W. Schaie (Eds.), *Handbook of the psychology of aging,* 1st ed. (pp. 626–649). New York: Van Nostrand Reinhold.

Neugarten, B. (Ed.). (1982). *Age or Need?* Beverly Hills, CA: Sage.

Norman, W. T. (1963). Toward an adequate taxonomy of personality attributes: Replicated factor structure in peer nomination personality ratings. *Journal of Abnormal and Social Psychology, 66,* 574–583.

Overall, J. E., & Gorman, D. R. (1972). Organicity versus old age in objective and projective test performance. *Journal of Consulting and Clinical Psychology, 39,* 98–105.

Ozer, D. J. (1985). Correlation and the coefficient of determination. *Psychological Bulletin, 97,* 307–315.

Parker, K. C. H., Hanson, R. K., & Hunsley, J. (1988). MMPI, Rorschach, and WAIS: A meta-analytic comparison of reliability, stability, and validity. *Psychological Bulletin, 103,* 367–373.

Peatman, J. G. (1947). *Descriptive and sampling statistics.* New York: Harper.

Pfeiffer, E. (1977). Psychopathology and social pathology. In J. E. Birren & K. W. Schaie (Eds.), *Handbook of the psychology of aging,* 1st ed. (pp. 650–671). New York: Van Nostrand Reinhold.

Plomin, R., & Daniels, D. (1987). Why are children in the same family so different from one another? *Behavioral and Brain Sciences, 10,* 1–16.

Reichard, S., Livson, F., & Peterson, P. G. (1962). *Aging and personality.* New York: Wiley.

Robins, L. N. (1966). *Deviant children grown up.* Baltimore: Williams & Wilkins.

Rogers, C. R. (1961). *On becoming a person: A therapist's view of psychotherapy.* Boston: Houghton Mifflin.

Rogers, C. R., & Dymond, R. F. (Eds.). (1954). *Psychotherapy and personality change.* Chicago: University of Chicago Press.

Rokeach, M. (1960). *The open and closed mind.* New York: Basic Books.

Rosenberg, M. (1979). *Conceiving the self.* New York: Basic Books.

Rotter, J. B., & Rafferty, J. E. (1950). *Manual: The Rotter Incomplete Sentences Blank.* New York: The Psychological Corporation.

Rowe, D. C. (1987). Resolving the person–situation debate: Invitation to an interdisciplinary dialogue. *American Psychologist, 42,* 218–227.

Rubin, Z. (1981). Does personality really change after 20? *Psychology Today, 15,* 18–27.

Runyan, W. McK. (1980). A stage-state analysis of the life course. *Journal of Personality and Social Psychology, 38,* 951–962.

Runyan, W. McK. (1981). Why did Van Gogh cut off his ear? The problem of alternative explanations in psychobiography. *Journal of Personality and Social Psychology, 40,* 1070–1077.

Salthouse, T. A. (1989). Age-related changes in basic cognitive processes. In M. Storandt & G. R. VandenBos (Eds.), *The adult years: Continuity and change* (pp. 9–40). Washington, DC: American Psychological Association.

Schaie, K. W. (1977). Quasi-experimental research designs in the psychology of aging. In J. E. Birren & K. W. Schaie (Eds.), *Handbook of the psychology of aging*, 1st ed. (pp. 36–69). New York: Van Nostrand Reinhold.

Schaie, K. W., & Labouvie-Vief, G. (1974). Generational vs. ontogenetic components of change in adult cognitive behavior: A fourteen-year cross-sequential study. *Developmental Psychology*, 10, 305–320.

Sheehy, G. (1976). *Passages: Predictable crises of adult life*. New York: Dutton.

Shweder, R. A. (1975). How relevant is an individual difference theory of personality? *Journal of Personality*, 43, 455–484.

Siegler, I. C., George, L. K., & Okun, M. A. (1979). Cross-sequential analysis of adult personality. *Developmental Psychology*, 15, 350–351.

Skinner, B. F. (1983). Intellectual self-management in old age. *American Psychologist*, 38, 239–244.

Skolnick, A. (1966). Stability and interrelationships of thematic test imagery over twenty years. *Child Development*, 37, 389–396.

Small, S. A., Zeldin, R. S., & Savin-Williams, R. C. (1983). In search of personality traits: A multimethod analysis of naturally occurring prosocial and dominance behavior. *Journal of Personality*, 51, 1–16.

Spock, B. (1946). *Baby and child care*. New York: Pocket Books.

Strong, E. K., Jr. (1955). *Vocational interests 18 years after college*. Minneapolis, MN: University of Minnesota.

Stuart, R. B. (Ed.). (1977). *Behavioral self-management*. New York: Brunner/Mazel.

Suinn, R. M., & Oscamp, S. (1969). *The predictive validity of projective measures: A fifteen year evaluative review of research*. Springfield, IL: Charles C. Thomas.

Swann, W. B., Jr. (1983). Self-verification: Bringing social reality into harmony with the self. In J. Suls & A. G. Greenwald (Eds.), *Psychological perspectives on the self* (Vol. 2, pp. 33–66). Hillsdale, NJ: Lawrence Erlbaum Associates.

Swann, W. B., Jr., & Hill, C. A. (1982). When our identities are mistaken: Reaffirming self-conceptions through social interactions. *Journal of Personality and Social Psychology*, 43, 59–66.

Tamir, L. M. (1982). *Men in their forties: The transition to middle age*. New York: Springer.

Tellegen, A., & Atkinson, G. (1974). Openness to absorbing and self-altering experiences ("absorption"), a trait related to hypnotic susceptibility. *Journal of Abnormal Psychology*, 83, 268–277.

Tesch, S. A., & Cameron, K. A. (1987). Openness to experience and development of adult identity. *Journal of Personality*, 55, 615–630.

Thomas, A., Chess, S., & Birch, H. G. (1968). *Temperament and behavior disorders in children*. New York: New York University Press.

Troll, L. E., Miller, S. J., & Atchley, R. C. (1979). *Families in later life*. Belmont,

CA: Wadsworth.

Tsuang, M. T., Woolson, R. F., Winokur, G., & Crowe, R. R. (1981). Stability of psychiatric diagnosis: Schizophrenia and affection disorders followed up over a 30- to 40-year period. *Archives of General Psychiatry, 38,* 535–539.

Tupes, E. C., & Christal, R. E. (1961). *Recurrent personality factors based on trait ratings* (USAF ASD Technical Report No. 61-97). Lackland Air Force Base, TX: U. S. Air Force.

Vaillant, G. E. (1977). *Adaption to life.* Boston: Little, Brown.

Vaillant, G. E., & McCullough, L. (1987). The Washington University Sentence Completion Test compared with other measures of adult ego development. *American Journal of Psychiatry, 144,* 1189–1194.

VandenBos, G. R. (Ed.). (1986). Psychotherapy research. *American Psychologist, 41(2)* (Special issue).

Veroff, J. (1983). Contextual determinants of personality. *Personality and Social Psychology Bulletin, 9,* 331–343.

Veroff, J., Depner, C., Kulka, R., & Douvan, E. (1980). Comparison of American motives: 1957 versus 1976. *Journal of Personality and Social Psychology, 39,* 1249–1262.

Vestre, N. D. (1984). Irrational beliefs and self-reported depressed mood. *Journal of Abnormal Psychology, 93,* 239–241.

Werner, H. (1948). *Comparative psychology of mental development.* New York: Science Editions.

Whitbourne, S. K. (1986a). *The me I know: A study of adult identity.* New York: Springer.

Whitbourne, S. K. (1986b). Openness to experience, identity flexibility, and life change in adults. *Journal of Personality and Social Psychology, 50,* 163–168.

Whitbourne, S. K., & Waterman, A. S. (1979). Psychosocial development during the adult years: Age and cohort comparisons. *Developmental Psychology, 15,* 373–378.

White, K. M., Spiesman, J. C., & Costos, D. (1983). Young adults and their parents: Individuation to mutuality. *New Directions for Child Development, 22,* 61–76.

White, R. W. (1952). *Lives in progress: A study of the natural growth of personality.* New York: Holt, Rinehart and Winston.

Widiger, T. A., & Frances, A. (1985). The *DSM-III* personality disorders: Perspectives from psychology. *Archives of General Psychiatry, 42,* 615–623.

Wiggins, J. S. (1968). Personality structure. *Annual Review of Psychology, 19,* 293–350.

Wiggins, J. S. (1979). A psychological taxonomy of trait-descriptive terms: The interpersonal domain. *Journal of Personality and Social Psychology, 37,* 395–412.

Wiggins, J. S., & Pincus, A. L. (in press). Conceptions of personality disorders and dimensions of personality. *Psychological Assessment: A Journal of Consulting and Clinical Psychology.*

Wiggins, J. S., Trapnell, P., & Phillips, N. (1988). Psychometric and geometric characteristics of the Revised Interpersonal Adjective Scales (IAS-R). *Multivariate Behavioral Research, 23,* 119–134.

Winter, D. G., & Carlson, L. A. (1988). Using motive scores in the psychobiographical study of an individual: The case of Richard Nixon. *Journal of Personality, 56,* 75–104.

Winter, D. G., & Stewart, A. (1977). Power motive reliability as a function of retest instructions. *Journal of Consulting and Clinical Psychology, 45,* 436–440.

Woodruff, D. (1983). The role of memory in personality continuity: A 25 year follow-up. *Experimental Aging Research, 9,* 31–34.

Woodruff, D. S., & Birren, J. E. (1972). Age changes and cohort differences in personality. *Developmental Psychology, 6,* 252–259.

Wright, J. C., & Mischel, W. (1988). Conditional hedges and the intuitive psychology of traits. *Journal of Personality and Social Psychology, 3,* 454–469.

Young, P. A., Eaves, L. J., & Eysenck, H. J. (1980). Intergenerational stability and change in the causes of variation in personality. *Personality and Individual Differences, 1,* 35–56.

Zuckerman, M. (1979). *Sensation seeking: Beyond the optimal level of arousal.* Hillsdale, NJ: Lawrence Erlbaum Associates.

Index